THE MISTRESS

THE MISTRESS

HISTORIES, MYTHS AND
INTERPRETATIONS OF THE
'OTHER WOMAN'

VICTORIA GRIFFIN

BLOOMSBURY

First published 1999
Copyright © 1999 by Victoria Griffin

All rights reserved. No part of this book may
be used or reproduced in any manner whatsoever without
written permission except in the case of brief quotations
embodied in critical articles or reviews. For information address
Bloomsbury Publishing, 175 Fifth Avenue, New York, N.Y. 10010.

Published by Bloomsbury Publishing, New York and London.
Distributed to the trade by St. Martin's Press.

A CIP catalogue record for this book
is available from the Library of Congress

ISBN 1-58234-053-6

10 9 8 7 6 5 4 3 2 1

Typeset by Hewer Text Ltd, Edinburgh
Printed in Great Britain by Clays Ltd, St Ives Plc

ACKNOWLEDGEMENTS

For permission to reproduce copyright extracts, the following copyright holders are gratefully acknowledged: for *The Golden Ass: or Metamorphoses* by Apuleius, translated by E.J. Kenney, to Penguin Books Ltd; for *The Gospel According to Woman* by Karen Armstrong, to The Peters, Fraser & Dunlop Group Ltd; for *The Brontes: Their Lives, Friendships & Correspondence*, edited by T.J. Wise & J.A. Symington, to Blackwell Publishers; for *The Medieval Idea of Marriage* by Christopher Brooke, to Oxford University Press; for *Royal Mistresses* by Charles Carlton, to Routledge & Kegan Paul; for *Passions & Ancient Days: 21 New Poems*, by C.P. Cavafy, translated by Edmund Keeley & George Savidis, to the estate of C.P. Cavafy; for *Rose Macaulay* by Jane Emery, to the author; for *Rodin: A Biography* by F.V. Grunfeld, to Hutchinson; for *Augustus John: The New Biography* by Michael Holroyd, to Secker & Warburg; for *A Radical Life: The Biography of Megan Lloyd George, 1906–66* by Mervyn Jones, to the author; for *Ford Madox Ford* by Alan Judd, to David Higham Associates Ltd; for *Collected Works* of C.G. Jung, translated by R.F.C. Hull, to Routledge & Kegan Paul; for *George Eliot: A Biography* by F. Karl, to HarperCollins*Publishers* Ltd; for Rosamond Lehmann's *The Echoing Grove*, to The Society of Authors; for *Letters to a Friend, 1950–1958* by Rose Macaulay, to Constance Babington Smith; for *The Towers of Trebizond* by Rose Macaulay, to HarperCollins*Publishers* Ltd; for an extract from a letter by Rose Macaulay, to the Peters Fraser & Dunlop Group Ltd on behalf of the Estate of Rose Macaulay; for *Cupid & the King* by HRH Princess Michael of Kent, to HarperCollins*Publishers*

Ltd; for *Madame de Pompadour* by Nancy Mitford, to Peters, Fraser & Dunlop; for *The Art of Courtly Love*, translated by John Jay Parry, to Columbia University Press; for *The Letters of Aberlard and Heloise*, translated by Betty Radice, to Penguin Books Ltd; for *The Story of O* by Pauline Réage, to Editions Jean-Jacques Pauvert; for *Parallel Lives* by Phyllis Rose, to Alfred A. Knopf Inc.; for *Reflected Glory: The Life of Pamela Churchill Harriman* by Sally Bedell Smith, to Prentice Hall; for *Lloyd George: A Diary by Frances Stevenson*, edited by A.J.P. Taylor, to Hutchinson; for *H.G. Wells in Love: Postscript to an Experiment in Autobiography*, edited by G.P. Wells, to Faber & Faber Ltd; for *H.G. Wells: Aspects of a Life* by Anthony West, to Hutchinson.

Every effort has been made to trace or contact all rights' holders. The publishers will be glad to make good any omissions brought to their attention.

There are various people I could thank for encouragement and conversations in the preparation of this book, but I think they would prefer not to be named, in case they are mistakenly assumed to be mistresses or lovers. So the only person to whom I will record my thanks here is my meticulous, modest and ever-helpful editor at Bloomsbury, Rosemary Davidson.

Victoria Griffin

Dedicated to the Abbess of the Paraclete

Heaven is my witness, I had rather be Abelard's mistress, than lawful wife to the emperor of the whole world.★

★ *The Lives, Loves & Misfortunes of Abelard & Heloise*, F. Lewis, Leigh-on-Sea, 1947, p.21

CONTENTS

INTRODUCTION:
A PERSONAL STATEMENT

I am a mistress.

In making that statement I mean not only that I am currently involved with a married man, but that there has been a consistent pattern in my life of playing the part of the 'other woman'. The men I attract to myself are invariably already attached – legally or otherwise – to someone else.

So my primary reason for writing this book is self-examination. I have reached a stage in my life where it is impossible to view repeating patterns as accident.

I am not setting out either to justify or to condemn my way of life. I don't intend to denigrate the roles of either wife or mistress, but I do intend to demonstrate how these are both separate and can be complementary. Trouble generally arises, in my view and to some extent in my experience, when these roles are confused – particularly when the mistress decides she wants to become the wife. She very rarely succeeds in this aim, and usually ends up wrecking the relationship she could have gone on enjoying.

There are plenty who will say one should never become involved with married men in the first place. Maybe so. And if it has never happened to you, I am certainly not suggesting you should go out and look for an 'affair'. But I'm sure there are also women who know, along with me, that once you've started on this particular path, stopping is virtually impossible. The men just seem to present themselves – you don't have to be looking for them; sometimes women of the mistress-type find they're involved with a man before they even 'knew' he was married. Conscious 'knowing' doesn't necessarily come into it.

Recognising how clearly in myself the role of mistress was to the fore led me to want to examine mistress figures from the past – in history, and also in literature and mythology: to find examples of those who played their roles to perfection, as well as those who destroyed themselves and the people around them. The characters I have chosen to investigate have selected themselves in the course of my reading because they illustrate a particular aspect of the mistress, or because they show how the same situation can be handled either negatively or positively. This does not set out to be an exhaustive study or an encyclopedia of who went to bed with whom; one could go on discovering mistress figures for ever. There seems a particular concentration of them around the end of the last century and the beginning of this – perhaps partly because of the easing of the Victorian moral straitjacket, perhaps partly as a reaction against its continued stranglehold and a result of the limitations still imposed on women and their place in society. Experimental relationships seem to have gone hand in hand with experiments in art and literature. Or maybe it was just that people started to talk about themselves more.

I don't for a minute deny that the mistress role is a dangerous part to play. If I get through life without major wreckage around me, in the form of heartbroken wives (and husbands) and damaged children, I will have been lucky. I have been lucky so far, but my main hope for the future happiness of those with whom I become involved – and of myself – is less in luck than in consciousness of what I'm doing. Knowing that my role is actually *not* to set myself up in opposition to the wife, *not* to become dependent on a particular relationship, to know how to love and let go and, most importantly perhaps, *when* to let go. And sometimes when to send away. To do this, I think, the vital thing is to understand and to practise the fundamental difference be-tween *loving* and *possessing*.

Nothing offered in this book is intended as a prescription for how to live. Rather, I am interested in ways of looking. I think everything I say can be qualified by: 'Well, that's one way of looking at it . . . there are no doubt others . . .' I am interested in exploring ways of living more imaginatively than we often manage, and it is my contention that the mistress need not be a threat to the wife. Nor need the mistress be heartbroken that she doesn't 'have' her man full-time or that he 'puts his wife first'. We needn't impose these clichés on ourselves.

Phyllis Rose in her book *Parallel Lives* underlines how so frequently and thoughtlessly we live clichéd lives: 'The plots we choose to impose on our own lives are limited and limiting. And in no area are they so banal and sterile as in this of love and marriage. Nothing else being available to our imaginations, we will filter our experience through the romantic clichés with which popular culture bombards us.'[1] She goes on to say: 'Easy stories drive out hard ones. Simple paradigms prevail over complicated ones.'[2] In attempting to go beyond the 'simple paradigm', I recognise how easy it is to slip back into the cliché. To live successfully as a mistress, I have constantly to remind myself not to fall back into conventional attitudes: not to mope on parting from my lover, not to imagine I need him beside me all the time, not to imagine jealousy of the wife's role where really none – or at least very little – exists.

Well-meaning friends do not always help. In their desire to extend sympathy, they may offer consolation for a sadness which wasn't there until they put it in one's head. 'It must be very difficult for you when X is out with his wife' or 'Don't you wish he'd leave her?' invite a conventional response which is not appropriate to the true mistress-type. After a conversation of this sort, I may for a time feel gloomy and hard-done-by, but will eventually (and sooner rather than later the more I come to understand myself and my role)

1 Phyllis Rose, *Parallel Lives: Five Victorian Marriages*, Vintage, New York, 1984, p.8
2 Ibid., p.9

'wake up' and say to myself: 'No, I feel fine that he's out with his wife because I'm enjoying doing something on my own, and anyway I fully accept the fact he's married and I've no desire for the marriage to break up.' But I have to admit such an attitude can be easier said than lived, particularly after one of those interludes of time spent away with the lover, when the relationship has been focused on and enjoyed with an intensity which is generally denied to legal spouses, with all their social and domestic ramifications. And I also know that there is a part of me that *does* want the marriage to break up. It's the devilish part that loves drama and intrigue and being at the centre of it, as well as the selfish part that wants my man all to myself. But I know that's only a part of me and that it's not the part to be listened to (for one thing it would be completely wrong to assume a marriage break-up would lead to me 'getting' my man – far more likely that that way I'd lose him altogether).

It is worth noting at this point that I am working from two basic premises: *not all women want to marry* and *not all women want to have children.* When I started working on this book it seemed unnecessary to me to make such self-evident remarks; but in the last couple of years the dominance of fictional characters like Ally McBeal and Bridget Jones in the popular conception of 'what women want' makes it important to keep on repeating that women don't have to behave like characters out of American sitcoms and that the value of a woman's life need not be determined by whether, or how soon, she adopts the roles of wife and mother.

I approach the writing of this book as a mistress and as a poet, and by the latter designation I mean that I am committed to letting my imagination make connections between people and ideas, connections that might not occur to the strictly scholarly, reasoning mind. Hence George Eliot may find herself allied with Dido, the President of the United States may turn up on Mount Olympus, or Pauline Réage's O be engaged in conversation with the heroines of Rosamond Lehmann and Zhivago's Lara.

The psychologist James Hillman has said: '[Myths] are no longer stories in an illustrated book. *We* are those stories, and we illustrate them with our lives.'[3] This certainly seems to me a good way of playing with myths, using them to gain fresh perspectives on our lives, freeing ourselves from clichés. By allowing ourselves to view life events from a variety of perspectives, we can begin to reject oppressive formulae (if we want to). One formula runs: 'If I discover my spouse is having an affair, it inevitably means our marriage is over. I feel hurt and betrayed and must either retreat or take my revenge.' A more imaginative response might include such questions as: 'How can we re-negotiate the terms of our marriage? Do I really feel betrayed? Perhaps I might even feel relieved that some of the pressure is off. Do we really want to throw away all the good aspects of our relationship because of this change? How can the change be incorporated to enrich all the parties involved? Do I now have more freedom than previously and how might I use it? What do I really feel, as opposed to what current conventions and the tabloid press tell me I'm supposed to feel?' A study of figures in myth, history and literature may help us to pose such questions and maybe find some interesting and unexpected answers. I have nevertheless increasingly realised throughout the course of my researches how difficult – if not impossible – it is to view anything without the distortions of one's own perspective. For a start, as a self-confessed mistress, my understanding of the wife's point of view is necessarily limited, and may be completely misguided. I would further contend that we *none of us* can see the issue of relations between the sexes with absolute clarity precisely because we are in the thick of it. We can never get outside of where we are in order to look in and say, 'Now I see it all.' All our viewing, all our commenting, is by nature partial, dim and out of focus. This is a truism – but it bears repetition, because it is too often forgotten.

There is nothing new under the sun. 'Whereas we think in

3 James Hillman, *Re-visioning Psychology*, Harper & Row, New York, 1977, p.102

periods of years, the unconscious thinks and lives in terms of millennia. So when something happens that seems to us an unexampled novelty, it is generally a very old story indeed.'[4] In the affairs and relationships of human beings, the old stories go on repeating themselves; it is worth reflecting on those old stories, to see where the choices lie and where there may be no choices.

Sexual Arrangements, by social scientists Janet Reibstein and Martin Richards, examines the prevalence and impact of affairs in a way which is both imaginative and sensible. Even a committed mistress like myself finds the statistics they give fairly startling: 'judging from the admittedly flawed studies which have been done, we estimate that between 50 per cent and 75 per cent of men and an only slightly smaller proportion of women have had or are having affairs while married'.[5] In discussing why so many married people have affairs – despite a continuing and indeed growing belief in the ideal of mono-gamy – they divide people into three categories: those who believe 'marriage is for everything', those who have a 'seg-mented marriage' in which the marriage partner may fulfil many roles and expectations but not necessarily all of them, and those who profess 'open marriage'.

According to the model a couple either consciously or unconsciously adopts, affairs – and the impact of affairs (or more particularly of the revelation of them) on the marriage – will also vary. For those following the 'marriage is for everything' model, an affair is a complete betrayal and the attempt to understand why it happened will focus on the assumption that something must have been missing from the marriage. If the affair is to be survived, then what the straying partner found in the affair needs to be identified and incorporated into the marriage. It goes without saying that

4 C.G. Jung, *Collected Works Vol. 9i: The Archetypes and the Collective Unconscious*, Routledge, London, 1969, p.280
5 Janet Reibstein & Martin Richards, *Sexual Arrangements: Monogamy, Marriage & Affairs*, Mandarin, London, 1993, p.4

the affair must end and there must be an agreement to have no more.

In the case of the 'segmented marriage' model, the partner having the affair may feel that it doesn't affect the marriage at all, being quite separate from it and the 'affair partner' playing a different – but often complementary – role from that of the spouse. It may even be seen by the person having the affair as enhancing the marriage, by making him or her more content, more accepting of what he or she perceives as the spouse's limitations. The trouble with this model is that one marriage partner may adopt it on his (usually) or her own initiative without consulting the other partner – frequently because they know it is unlikely to be accepted – while the other partner remains with the 'marriage is for everything' model. I realise that this 'segmented' version is the marriage model from which I am generally working in my consideration of the role of the mistress.

In both the 'marriage is for everything' and the 'segmented' models it is often the secrecy and deceit which have necessarily been part of the affair which are the most difficult aspects for the 'betrayed' partner to come to terms with, if and when the affair becomes known. 'Open marriage' may sound from its name as though anything goes and that it is free from these problems of secrecy, but in fact marriage partners who have negotiated some degree of openness may find themselves as bound by 'rules' – albeit self-imposed – as those who have taken a more ready-made marriage off the traditional shelf. Frequently part of the agreement is that affairs must not 'matter' too much, that sex may be acceptable but falling in love isn't – and again, secrecy, felt to be necessary if these rules are inadvertently transgressed, is the great crime.

The 'affair partner', particularly the unmarried one – that is, the mistress or lover – is largely, though not entirely, a silent presence in the case histories discussed by Reibstein and Richards, acted upon rather than acting in these marital dramas.

Zelda West-Meads in *To Love, Honour & Betray: Why affairs*

happen & how to survive them seems almost unconsciously to operate on the 'marriage is for everything' model. Though she explicitly sets out to be non-judgemental and not take a moral line, the underlying assumption of this former spokeswoman for Relate is that an affair indicates there is something missing in a marriage: 'I believe that by far the most common reason why people have affairs is because of unresolved problems in their marriage, such as lack of communication, constant rows and arguments, or a marriage where each of you is under-mining the other, where put-downs and criticism are the order of the day, rather than support and affirmation.'[6] And in her short section on 'Mistresses and Lovers' the implication is that most mistresses really want to be wives. She talks about the 'security' of marriage (as opposed to the less secure enjoyment of an affair) and yet the subject matter of her whole book demonstrates, if nothing else, that marriage is not 'secure' at all, that the only security to be found by anyone is interior. She also makes the assumption that the words 'infidelity', 'betrayal' and – the most enormous of all – 'love', mean one thing to all readers: that 'infidelity' always refers to a sexual act, that the partner of an 'unfaithful' spouse is always 'betrayed', and that a phrase like 'he does/doesn't love his wife' can be taken at face value as an adequate way of describing an infinitely complex relationship. I would suggest that the use of cliché in language leads to clichéd living, that the way we talk not only reflects but also informs the way we think and live. We don't have to impose other people's meanings on our lives.

An earlier book on the mistress, by Wendy James and Susan Jane Kedgley, is based on the replies to a questionnaire completed by thirty-five women who did not all define themselves by the word 'mistress' but who nevertheless fitted the definition used by the authors. They describe the purpose of their book as being 'to look at the everyday reality involved in being a modern mistress. By doing so we become the

6 Zelda West-Meads, *To Love, Honour & Betray: Why affairs happen & how to survive them*, Coronet, London, 1997, p.69

apologists for the mistress, past and present. She is an integral part of our society yet must not be considered so. People may despise her existence but we feel that her role is very necessary.'[7] James and Kedgley take the view that society considers mistresses to be sinful but that it is wrong to do so, that the structure of society itself gives rise to mistresses and that mistresses are therefore victims of society and a mono-gamous culture: 'The mistress is inescapably affected by society's interpretation of her as a woman committing a crime.'[8] And (this is their concluding sentence), 'The modern mistress is a scapegoat for the failings of monogamy, but she is too conditioned to stand up and declare her right to love.'[9] This approach is altogether too simplistic. Whereas it is true that the licit always gives rise to the illicit, that the existence of laws is part of the reason for the existence of those who break them (you can't break a law if there isn't a law to break), and that in this sense monogamous matrimony gives rise to the extra-marital, it doesn't follow that the individual is thereby relieved of the responsibility for his or her own actions. Maybe mistresses have taken too much blame in the past; but it doesn't redress the balance for a mistress to refuse to take any blame at all. Human behaviour is infinitely complex, motives are always mixed, selfless love coexists with self-seeking, nothing can ever be reduced to a simple formula. Mistresses, like everybody else, are only victims if they choose to be; and, again like everybody else, if they are ever 'saints' it is only for very brief unexpected moments. Moreover, no one is questioning anyone's 'right to love': love is only the starting point; it's what you do with the love that counts – it's in action where the issues arise. To put it plainly: you may have a 'right to love' but you probably don't have a 'right' to move in and seduce another woman's husband. If you decide that's nevertheless what you're going to do, then you have to put up

7 Wendy James & Susan Jane Kedgley, *The mistress*, Abelard-Schuman, London, 1973, p.8
8 Ibid., p.9
9 Ibid., p.142

with 'society' not exactly leaping around in delight and congratulating you. And if you care very much about what 'society' thinks, then you're probably better off not becoming a mistress in the first place. I would, however, wholeheartedly endorse one thing James and Kedgley say: 'What a mistress expects of the relationship considerably affects her chances of happiness within it. If she is pursuing marriage and permanency, she is likely to be disappointed.'[10]

I have dedicated this book to someone who, at first glance, may not appear to have much to do with my topic, as she lived most of her life in a convent and was renowned for her wisdom and piety. The figure of Heloise will be investigated in depth later on, but I have chosen her as my dedicatee partly because she revelled in the title of Abelard's mistress – or she would have, if he hadn't bullied her into marriage – and because she understood and lived to perfection the non-possessive love which, I would suggest, needs to be the love practised by the mistress. Heloise can also be viewed as an 'other' woman, a mistress, in the sense that Abelard's true 'wife' could be taken to be the Church or, alternatively, the Lady Philosophy.

I use Heloise as my inspiration in a way suggested by Hillman: 'The figures of history taken psychologically are the progenitors, the cultural ancestors, of the ideas in our minds . . . We search for the myths within the facts, the archetypal patterns that can broaden and deepen connections in ourselves, offering our painfully raw experiences a bed of culture.'[11] Of course Heloise my inspirer is the Heloise of my imagination, but what other way is there to conceive of anyone or anything? She inspires me to remain true to my love wherever it may lead me, and to seek the truth, however damaging it may be to my conception of myself. I am inspired by her courage to allow myself to think anything, to question myself and my motives, to consider whether the opposite of

10 Ibid., p.26
11 James Hillman, *Re-visioning Psychology*, p.xv

everything I say can also be said, to be honest to a point which may be to invite opprobrium, not to fear the 'fires of hell', or any other possible consequence of being true to myself.

It is likely that some people will be shocked by this book, especially perhaps those of my friends who thought they knew me, but may now conclude they knew only certain aspects, and those not the most 'real' ones. I hope other mistress-types may be encouraged by it, and maybe given some insights into how to play their role. I hope some wives may find their anxieties lessened. It occurs to me I haven't yet said anything about my lovers. I hope they too, past, present and to come, will find what I have to say enlightening. Men who love more than one woman at a time are in plentiful supply, and no doubt merit investigation. But I will leave it to them to carry out their own self-examination, and attend to my subject which is 'The Mistress'.

WHAT IS A MISTRESS?

We have mistresses for our enjoyment,
concubines to serve our person, and wives for
the bearing of legitimate offspring.[1]

Perhaps the first thing to notice about this famous dictum by the orator Demosthenes from the fourth century BC is the obvious one – it's written by a man, and it's written in the language of power: 'We have'. Not 'There are' or 'Women are', but 'We have'. This, it can be inferred, is what men have done to women, classifying them into particular roles. There is no mention of women outside these roles, of women who exist for some other purpose than that of relating to men. Mistresses are to be enjoyed, concubines are to serve, wives are to bear legitimate offspring. Whether women enjoy any or all of these roles is not mentioned; women's feelings are irrelevant.

The second thing to notice is, of course, the actual division or 'splitting'. Several twentieth-century writers[2] have commented on this tendency of the image of woman to 'split', to become divided into, for instance, virgin and whore, or 'angel in the house' (as most notably portrayed by the Victorian poet Coventry Patmore) and 'fallen woman'. In this case the split is threefold: mistresses are not wives, wives are not for enjoyment, mistresses and concubines do not provide legitimate offspring, and so on. Perhaps mistresses have a better time than concubines as they are there to do more than 'serve'. And

1 Quoted in Sarah B. Pomeroy, *Goddesses, Whores, Wives, & Slaves: Women in Classical Antiquity*, Schocken, New York, 1976, p.8
2 E.g. Eva Figes in *Patriarchal Attitudes: Women in Society*, Macmillan, London, 1986, Anne Baring & Jules Cashford in *The Myth of the Goddess*, Penguin/Arkana, London, 1991 and Elaine Hoffman Baruch in *Women, Love, & Power: Literacy & Psychoanalytic Perspectives*, New York University Press, New York & London, 1991

perhaps wives have a degree of respect – but only as the bearers of legitimate offspring.

So one question is: do women fall naturally into these categories, or have they been placed there solely by men? I imagine it's a bit of both: men created the categories, and women slotted themselves into them. It's always hard when considering attitudes in patriarchal society to work out which came first – attitudes or patriarchy – they have a symbiotic relationship, feeding back and forth. And one can only view life and one's role from within the prevailing system. That system is one where men are in control and have been for centuries, millennia, and it has been argued that one way they have maintained that control is by this 'splitting' of women, so that the female becomes less than whole and therefore never equal to the male. Eva Figes is not alone in ascribing this strategy to the fear of women by men, the fear of the oppressed by the oppressors: '. . . because man has refused to abandon an inch of ground more than necessary, having so much to lose, he has been afraid of the dormant power he has subdued, and recognized woman as profoundly dangerous.'[3]

The *Oxford English Dictionary* definition of 'mistress' is: 'A woman who illicitly occupies the place of wife'. A search under 'mistress' in the British Library's computerised catalogues yields interesting results. Interspersed with books about the mistresses of famous men, or novels about mistresses, are memoirs of a rather raunchier sort (*Mistress of the Lash*, for instance), alongside instruction manuals written by 'mistresses' to their maidservants, and textbooks by biology mistresses. The consequences of ordering some of these books range from having to sit at a special table reserved for readers of pornography, with strict instructions not to leave the book unattended, in order to consult *How to find and fascinate a mistress, and survive in spite of it all* by Will Harvey (1972), which tells of the importance of simultaneous orgasms and

3 Eva Figes, *Patriarchal Attitudes*, p.26

categorises mistresses as Ladybugs or Honeybees, to the discovery that *The Cardinal's Mistress* is the title of a novel written by one Benito Mussolini, published in 1929. An Internet search yields thousands of entries, nearly all of which seem to be the electronic equivalent of cards placed in phone booths by dominatrixes.

The word 'mistress', it was suggested on a radio programme recently, carries risqué connotations in a way that the more modern, neutral word 'partner' doesn't. 'Partner' tends in any case to refer to the other half of a couple, and not usually to the extra third of a threesome. Likewise 'lover' or 'girlfriend', though they could denote the possibility of an extant wife, do not necessarily do so. 'Mistress', on the other hand, always sounds illicit, as well as rather luxurious. There are those who think of the word as old-fashioned, though I don't see why it should be considered to be any more out of date than 'wife' or 'husband'. In all three cases, the roles may have been modified in recent years, while the names remain the same. It has also been pointed out that there is no male equivalent of 'mistress'.

Penelope Orth, in her book published in the early 1970s about contemporary American mistresses, draws up the following definition: 'A mistress is a single woman, divorced, widowed, or never married, who is having an enduring affair with a married man who may support her but who today more frequently subsidises her or merely improves her standard of living. The three essential ingredients of a lover–mistress relationship are that it lasts, that marriage is not realistically expected, and that the man assumes some financial responsibility.'[4] It is rather surprising that there should be this expectation of a financial element as recently as 1972; it certainly does not enter into my expectations as a mistress. (It was, however, a significant factor in a recent memoir by an ex-mistress, Dani Shapiro's *Slow Motion*.[5] Orth, in what is a fairly perceptive and at times amusing book, draws up several

4 Penelope Orth, *An Enviable Position: The American Mistress from Slightly Kept to Practically Married*, D. McKay Co., New York, 1972, p.3
5 Bloomsbury, London, 1998

categories of mistress, such as the Career Woman (who has no time for marriage so takes a married lover), the Assistant (who works for her lover), the One-Man Call Girl (which doesn't need explaining), and the Masochistic Mistress (who desperately wants to marry but has to set up scenarios to ensure she does not get what she wants). Such categories may be rather more fluid than Orth makes them out to be; possibly most mistresses have a bit of the masochist in them.

Wendy James and Susan Jane Kedgley use slightly different criteria: 'A mistress by our definition is a woman with whom a married man has a parallel relationship, or a woman who, outside her own marriage, has a relationship with another man. All these illicit relationships – i.e. based on adultery – must be long-term and as a yardstick we chose one year as the minimum period of involvement.'[6] There is no mention of any financial transaction in this – British – definition; indeed, James and Kedgley found their mistresses were on the whole quite averse to the idea of receiving financial support or gifts from their lovers, not wanting to view themselves as 'kept' women or as falling into what they perceived as traditional mistress roles. They also emphasise that what distinguishes a 'mistress relationship' from a casual extra-marital fling is that in the former the emotions are engaged: 'A mistress relationship assumes an emotional relationship with all its concomitant involvement, responsibilities, feelings of guilt and dissembling.'[7]

For my purposes, at its simplest, I take the word 'mistress' to mean someone who is having an affair with a man who is married to someone else.

In earlier times – no longer ago than the Victorian era – a mistress could be any woman living with or having sexual relations with a man who was not married to her; he didn't need to be married to someone else for her to qualify for the title. So, for instance, Wilkie Collins had two mistresses, Caroline Graves and Martha Rudd, though he was never

6 Wendy James & Susan Jane Kedgley, *The mistress*, p.8
7 Ibid., p.10

married to anyone; likewise the unmarried composer Franz Liszt had mistresses. While accepting the term 'mistress' for these women in the time when they lived, I would not now refer to a woman as a mistress if she were merely cohabiting with a man without having legally married him. On the other hand I might describe as a mistress a woman having an affair with an unmarried man who was nevertheless living, in an apparently committed relationship, with someone else. The relationship with the mistress is illicit in that the man is supposed to be being 'faithful' to someone else. There may be a case for arguing that the relationship need not be heterosexual, that one could have lesbian 'mistresses' in cases where a couple have pledged themselves to one another and then a third party moves in. But that is not an area which I will be examining. In some cases I have identified a mistress-type – a woman whose way of loving makes her suitable to fulfil the role of mistress, though in strict terms that is not exactly what she is doing.

There is one further categorisation to be made, between those mistresses who are known about and acknowledged, and the (far greater) number of those who have to conduct their affairs in secret. The open *ménage à trois* can be very demanding on all its participants, but they have occasionally been known to work. But as long as 'human kind cannot bear very much reality' the hidden liaison, with all its inherent deceptions of self and others, is likely to predominate over the open three- (or four- or more) some.

I have concentrated mainly on unmarried mistresses – women for whom the relationship with a married lover is the principal relationship in their life. It is true that in certain historical categories, that of 'royal mistress', for instance, the women in question were nearly always married – partly because married women are less threatening than single ones, being less likely to want the upheaval in their own lives which exposure might bring, or to demand the lover divorce his wife and marry her instead. So when a whole category of mistresses has been married, I have included them, but I

would not primarily define as 'mistress' a woman who is also
'wife'.

I used to think of myself as a feminist, albeit of a fairly mild
variety. Since investigating my motivation as a mistress, and my
place in a long tradition of mistresses, I am no longer sure it
would be fair to do so. First, there is the obvious point that by
engaging in affairs with married men, I am acting in a far from
'sisterly' way towards other women. Then there is the collusion
with Demosthenes, going along with – in fact, supporting – the
idea that some women are to be wives, others mistresses, with
the enjoyments of one denied to the other. There are likely to
be some wives who will argue, and in some cases they may be
right, that mistresses really want to be wives and are stealing, or
rather borrowing, other women's husbands because they can't
get one of their own. I don't think this is true in my case, nor in
that of most of the women examined in this book. But self-
deception runs deep in all of us, and there is nothing dis-
creditable of which human beings are incapable.

Helen Fisher, writes that out of the 853 cultures on record
only sixteen per cent prescribe monogamy, in which a man is
permitted only one wife at a time.[8] And it follows that it is
only in that sixteen per cent of cultures that the concept of the
mistress can make any sense at all. Polygamous societies may
give rise to various grades of co-wives, but not to mistresses –
though women attempting to live as mistresses, or as wives of
men who have mistresses, might learn from the rules of official
polygamists:

> The Mormon system of polygamy certainly produced
> traumas of jealousy in some women and most women
> found the whole idea, when Joseph Smith originally
> introduced it, deeply shocking. However, some women
> did find it liberating . . . The sheer mechanics of the large
> household where there were several wives made the
> expression of romantic love impractical, but even more

8 Helen E. Fisher, *Anatomy of Love: The Natural History of Monogamy, Adultery &*
   Divorce, Simon & Schuster, London, 1993

simply the 'harem' completely destroyed the idea that everybody had One True Love, which is the essence of the mythology of romantic love . . . The Mormon women were also advised not to allow themselves to become emotionally dependent upon their husbands, because otherwise the polygamous life was impossible. Even though Salt Lake City was clearly a male world and the men got the best of the bargain (women were not allowed to have several husbands) it did prove to be liberating for many of the Mormon plural wives. Certainly the fact that Utah was easily the first state in America to give women the vote and that there were more professional women in Utah at the end of the 19th century than almost any other state says a good deal for the confidence and the autonomy that Mormonism gave to its women.[9]

Finally, a paradox lies at the heart of being a mistress: on the one hand the mistress seeks to live outside and undermine the institution of marriage; on the other, she is as subject to the institution as is the wife, being defined by it. Without marriage, there wouldn't be mistresses. As people continue to marry in large numbers, it is even possible that the demand for mistresses is rising. If one looks again at Demosthenes' dictum in the light of twentieth-century developments, one can perceive an interesting shift. The role of the wife, at least in Western culture, now encompasses far more than 'the bearing of legitimate offspring'. Modern marriage attempts to be a partnership of equals and, in the struggle for her equality – including, in many cases, the pursuit of a fulfilling career outside the home – the contemporary wife has necessarily had to give up – has to some extent and in many cases *wanted* to give up – certain of her previous roles, not only that of continual and unavoidable motherhood, but also of playing the supporting role to her husband. A busy late-twentieth-

9 Karen Armstrong, *The Gospel According to Woman*, Elm Tree Books, London, 1986, pp.293–4

century wife just does not have the time, even if she has the inclination, to listen to the tales of her husband's day, to provide him with the glass of wine, the soothing music, the sympathetic ear. Far less does she have the time to offer practical help. So who steps in to fill the breach? The mistress, of course. Witness the number of secretaries and personal assistants to, for instance, male politicians, who make that easy transition from help and mainstay in the office to emotional support and sexual partnership. Wives may find themselves paying dearly for their increased independence and their concomitant lack of time and energy for their husbands. I am not suggesting this is necessarily how it should be, but I am suggesting this is how it is. Maybe it is still true – however unpalatable – that no woman can be everything to a man.

THE LURE OF FORBIDDEN FRUIT, OR WHY SOME WOMEN BECOME MISTRESSES

Now the serpent was more subtil than any beast of the field which the Lord God had made. And he said to the woman, Yea, hath God said, Ye shall not eat of every tree of the garden?
And the woman said unto the serpent, We may eat of the fruit of the trees of the garden:
But of the fruit of the tree which is in the midst of the garden, God hath said, Ye shall not eat of it, neither shall ye touch it, lest ye die.
And the serpent said unto the woman, Ye shall not surely die:
For God doth know that in the day ye eat thereof, then your eyes shall be opened, and ye shall be as gods, knowing good and evil.
And when the woman saw that the tree was good for food, and that it was pleasant to the eyes, and a tree to be desired to make one wise, she took of the fruit thereof, and did eat, and gave also unto her husband with her; and he did eat.[1]

The Hebrew story of the Fall, as recounted here in Genesis Chapter 3, is now generally regarded – except by extreme fundamentalists who misunderstand the meaning of the words 'story' and 'myth' – as an aetiological myth; that

---

1 Genesis 3: 1–6 (Authorised King James Version)

is, it sets out to explain the way things are, to provide reasons for what is perceived as the human condition. One thing which needed to be explained was death, and so the story suggests that had the first man and woman not sinned, they would have lived for ever. But they disobeyed God, and so were thrown out of the Garden of Eden and became subject to hardship, disease and eventual death. Another thing to be explained was the position of women in relation to men: to the creators of this aetiological myth, the subservience of women was a 'given', part of the natural order, so, rather than trying to correct the balance, they set out to explain the imbalance. They saw that women were not only subject to men, but had to suffer the pain and dangers of childbirth. If, as they had concluded, the unsatisfactory nature of human life with its inevitable end was the result of sin, then the fact that the lot of women was even worse than that of men suggested that woman must have either sinned worst, or first, or both. And so Eve gets most of the blame. *She* allowed herself to be tempted by the serpent, *she* was the first to bite the forbidden fruit, *she* gave it to the man to eat, *she* was the original sinner, it's *her* fault. Then, once this explanatory story had been told, it became the instrument for the continuing oppression of women. In the development and reinforcement of patriarchy, writers first describe how things are and this then has the effect of setting how things are in stone: it must be this way for a reason – here's the reason – so now things must be this way. It's a spiralling self-perpetuating process. Not only did the myth encourage man to go on punishing woman for what she was supposed to have done, but it also allowed him to externalise all the flaws and weaknesses in himself and make woman the embodiment of them, leaving himself strong and intact and morally superior. The dark side of man is offloaded on to woman. In Greek mythology a similar process happens with the figure of Pandora; like Eve, her curiosity and desire for knowledge – and thereby power – lead to her opening the forbidden box, and so letting evil flood into the world. Both these myths have been used to give women the salutary warnings to know their place, not to ask questions and to accept the way things are.

Tradition has it that sex came with the Fall. Adam and Eve became aware of their nakedness and it embarrassed them. There is no mention of procreation until after the Fall. Presumably either Adam and Eve would have lived for ever and so experienced no need for descendants, or the earth would have become further populated without the necessity for the sordid groping with which the Church Fathers equated the sexual act. At the Fall, Satan was supposed to have instructed Adam and Eve on how to copulate. And because without Eve, the woman, there wouldn't have been a Fall, she is held responsible for this introduction of sex into human life, and all man's ambivalent feelings about sexuality are thrust on to her. Woman is made to represent the lust man feels for her; the object of temptation becomes the cause. (This still goes on, particularly in certain fundamentalist traditions, with woman being made to cover herself because of man's inability to resist her.) 'Eve was the original cause of all evil and, to the men of the Church, all women were her daughters, and therefore inheritors of her disgrace.'[2] Eve, the temptress, is seen in every woman, but particularly in the beautiful woman. And man fears her because she arouses his desire, and his body responds to her whether he wills it or not. His sexuality − to be precise, his penis − is the one area of himself which he cannot control, and so he must put the blame for this on woman. She has bewitched him.

The Church Fathers Origen and Tertullian, writing in the third century AD, both blamed women for luring Christian men into sexual indulgence which they might otherwise have been strong enough to resist. Women, Tertullian declared, are the devil's door: through them Satan creeps into men's hearts and minds and works his wiles for their spiritual destruction.

2 Susan Haskins, *Mary Magdalen: Myth & Metaphor*, HarperCollins, London, 1993, p.144

Origen's condemnation of women was equally severe. He believed women to be more lustful than men and to be obsessed by sexual desire. And so it continued. 'For the Fathers of the Church after Augustine, woman is the cause of the Fall, the wicked temptress, the accomplice of Satan, and the destroyer of mankind. The fury unleashed against Eve and all her kind is almost flattering, so exaggerated is the picture of women's fatal and all-powerful charms and men's incapacity to resist.'[3]

Carl Gustav Jung refers in his *Symbols of Transformation* to 'the Jewish tradition that Adam, before he knew Eve, had a demon-wife called Lilith, with whom he strove for supremacy. But Lilith rose up into the air through the magic of God's name and hid herself in the sea. Adam forced her to come back with the help of three angels, whereupon Lilith changed into a nightmare or lamia who haunted pregnant women and kidnapped new-born infants.'[4]

The myth of Lilith arose through the attempt to reconcile the two conflicting Creation stories found in Genesis – the first story in Genesis 1, where male and female are created equally and together, and the second story in Genesis 3, where the female is created out of part of the male's body, after and inferior to him. If these accounts are seen as referring to two separate events, rather than as two variant interpretations of one event, then the inference may be drawn that two females were created, the first equal and the second inferior to the male. Lilith, who retains traces of the Sumerian figure Lil, the bright Queen of Heaven, was, according to a Judaic text of the ninth or tenth century, the Alpha Bet Ben Sira, Adam's first female companion. She was the woman who claimed equality, epitomised by her refusal to allow Adam always to be

3 Marina Warner, *Alone of all her Sex: The Myth & Cult of the Virgin Mary*, Picador, London, 1990, p.58
4 C.G. Jung, *Collected Works Vol. 5: Symbols of Transformation*, tr. R.F.C. Hull, Routledge, London, 1956, p.248

the one on top during sex. For her presumption she was banished, into the borders of creation and human conscious-ness, returning at night to haunt the minds and bodies of men as they lie beside their docile wives, appearing in wet dreams to rob the wives of their husbands' seed, proving it is she – the wild, untamed – who has the power to capture the male imagination and sexual response.

Eve was then created as the second, subservient wife. There is a tradition (sometimes to be seen pictorially, as in a woodcut by Holzschmitt of 1470[5]) that it was Lilith, disguised as a serpent, who persuaded Eve to taste the forbidden fruit, as an act of revenge and as a demonstration to God and humankind that what is forbidden is always the most tempting and cannot ultimately be resisted. By her interference Lilith wrecks the happiness of Adam and Eve, and achieves nothing more satisfactory for herself than bittersweet revenge to flavour her everlasting loneliness. To Eve she is a source of fascination, jealousy and fear; the two archetypal figures – wife/mother and *femme fatale* – forever circling the one man in a dance of mutual attraction and hatred, united in their opposition to the male, divided by their need and love of him. Both wonder at the other: to Lilith, Eve seems boring, conventional (after her one lapse in the Garden), yet also powerful and with hidden depths – she has after all managed to hang on to her man, so is deserving of some respect; to Eve, Lilith seems irresponsible, feckless yet exciting, an ever-present threat to her own stability yet holding out a tantalising promise that there is more to life than tilling the earth and bringing forth children. Eve cannot quite believe that Lilith really enjoys her independence – hence her deeply held and fearful conviction that all she really wants is to steal her husband. Lilith would indeed like to succeed in doing that, but more to prove her superior powers of seduction than because she really wants him back. Once she had made her point and had Adam in thrall, she would quickly tire of him.

★   ★   ★

5 *See* Anne Baring & Jules Cashford, *The Myth of the Goddess*, p.512

The dangerous, bewitching female, forever posing her threat
to the stability of the family and the indestructibility of the
marriage bond, keeps reappearing in different, but always
recognisable, guises. There are in Greek mythology, for
instance, the Empusae, the children of Hecate, goddess of
witches, who, disguised as beautiful maidens, suck the vital
forces of men until they die. (What fear of women resides in
the aftermath of the male orgasm, that wilting penis.) The
femme fatale appears in Arthurian legend as the Loathly Damsel,
becoming Cundrie in Wolfram von Eschenbach's *Parzival*,
and Kundry in Wagner's opera. In this role she bears a likeness
to the sinner from St Luke's Gospel who washes the feet of
Jesus and dries them with her hair and who for centuries has
been, probably erroneously, identified as Mary Magdalen. At
times belief in and fear of this figure escape the bounds of
myth and story: 'In both orthodox and apocryphal literature,
Lilith's shadow falls on women as far forward in time as the
fifteenth century AD, when, in the same imagery as was
employed for Lilith, thousands were accused of copulating
with demons, killing infants and seducing men – of being, in a
word, witches.'[6] The bewitching woman appears also as
Shakespeare's Cleopatra; later manifestations include Becky
Sharp in Thackeray's *Vanity Fair*, Rebecca West in Ibsen's
Rosmersholm and Hilda in *The Master Builder*, Tolstoy's Anna
Karenina, Zola's Nana and Frank Wedekind's Lulu. And in
the late twentieth century it is the shadow of Lilith in her role
as baby-killer that is cast on women accused of murdering or
abusing children (the vituperation meted out to them is always
greater than in the case of their male counterparts), and echoes
of Lilith-hatred can also be heard in the language of the more
extreme anti-abortionists.

All these bewitching creatures are subsumed for Jung under
the heading of 'anima': 'The nixie is an even more instinctive
version of a magical feminine being whom I call the *anima*.
She can also be a siren, *melusina* (mermaid), wood-nymph,

6 Ibid.

Grace, or Erlking's daughter, or a lamia or succubus, who infatuates young men and sucks the life out of them.'[7] What Jung called the anima was, he argues, projected by our primitive ancestors on to these mythological characters, but it is in our own unconscious that we now recognise her to reside. Jung generally perceives both positive and negative aspects in every symbol so that, while he asserts that the dangerous, taboo and magical anima may lead a man into a forbidden zone, he also suggests that it is precisely in this forbidden zone that salvation is to be found, just as the whole Christian saga of redemption could never have come about without the initial expulsion from Eden. Jung writes:

> The anima no longer crosses our path as a goddess, but, it may be, as an intimately personal misadventure, or perhaps as our best venture. When, for instance, a highly esteemed professor in his seventies abandons his family and runs off with a young red-headed actress, we know that the gods have claimed another victim . . . Although she may be the chaotic urge to life, something strangely meaningful clings to her, a secret knowledge or hidden wisdom, which contrasts most curiously with her irrational, elfin nature.[8]

Denis de Rougemont, in *Love in the Western World*, puts forward the interesting thesis that we are all, and particularly those of us who go in for passionate, unhappy love, under the thrall of a renowned myth of courtly love, the *Romance of Tristan*. That 'high tale of love and death' tells how on the voyage Tristan makes with Iseult, as he accompanies her back to the court of his uncle King Mark whom she is to marry, the pair are given to drink by mistake the love potion intended for the newly-weds. They are unable to do anything other than fall passionately in love. Nevertheless Tristan continues with his mission and duly hands Iseult over to the King, but the

7 C.G. Jung, *The Archetypes & the Collective Unconscious*, p.25
8 Ibid., p.30

affair between himself and Iseult carries on just as passionately, if not more so, after the marriage. For all the joys they experience together, the lovers are doomed to unhappiness; condemned to death, they escape and live for a time as outlaws. They seem to come to their senses when the love potion wears off after its allotted span of three years; they seek King Mark's forgiveness and Iseult returns to the court. Yet their deliberately chosen separation seems at least in part a ploy to make their love still stronger.

The denouement, as expected, is tragic. Tristan has married another Iseult (of the White Hands), having been attracted to her largely because of her name. The first Iseult had earlier promised him that if ever he needed her, she would come. He falls ill and realises that only she can save him. He sends for her, and gives instructions that if she returns with his messenger on the ship, white sails are to be hoisted.

When the ship appears on the horizon, Tristan, who is too ill to leave his bed, asks his wife what colour the sails are. But she had overheard his earlier instruction and, realising what the white sails mean, is driven by jealousy to tell him that the sails are black. So Tristan, believing that his beloved Iseult has failed him at the last, falls back on his bed and dies. Then Iseult arrives, sees her dead lover, and dies herself.

There are now hundreds of versions of the Tristan legend in existence, and in the early years of this century the French scholar Joseph Bédier discovered that they can all be traced back to a single poem, now lost, which is the fountain-head of the whole tradition and the archetype of all Tristan stories. The unique fascination of the legend, says Alan Fedrick in the Introduction to his translation, seems to lie in the central theme: the unsought passion which draws Tristan and Iseult irresistibly together and which compels them to cut across the moral code and the social and family obligations which are the framework of their existence. In the earliest versions of the story the love potion comes into the narrative suddenly and unexpectedly, and its effect is to bind together two people who have no reason to like each other and whose relations have so far been more hostile than friendly.

De Rougemont declares that the description 'a high tale of love and death' sums up all that is popular, all that is universally moving, in European literature. Romance only comes into existence where love is fatal, frowned upon and doomed. What lyric poets have always been interested in is not the satisfaction of love, the contentment of the settled couple, but passion – and passion means suffering. 'The myth operates wherever passion is dreamed of as an ideal instead of being feared like a malignant fever; wherever its fatal character is welcomed, invoked, or imagined as a magnificent and desirable disaster instead of as simply a disaster.'[9] He argues that what the Tristan legend is about may indeed be the parting of lovers, but a parting in the name of passion, for love of love itself. Parting will ensure the intensification and transfiguration of love, at the cost of happiness and even of the lovers' lives. Tristan and Iseult, he says, do not love one another; rather they love love, and what they therefore need is not one another's presence, but one another's absence.

De Rougemont concludes part of his argument by saying that, while the European middle classes are brought up to regard marriage with respect, all young people breathe in from the surrounding culture a romantic atmosphere in which passion is seen as the supreme test and it is accepted that nobody has really lived till he or she has 'been through it'. Passion and marriage, he declares, are essentially irreconcilable. Their origins and ends make them mutually exclusive. Furthermore, '[Iseult] typifies the woman a man does not marry; for once she became his wife she would no longer be what she is, and he would no longer love her.'[10] He states his reasons for his concentration on this myth as follows: 'To raise up the myth of passion in its primitive and sacred vigour and in its monumental integrity, as a salutary comment upon our tortuous connivances and inability to

9 Denis de Rougemont, *Love in the Western World*, Princeton University Press, Princeton NJ, 1983, p.24
10 Ibid., p.45

choose boldly between the Norm of Day and the Passion of Night – such is my first purpose . . . And what I aim at is to bring the reader to the point of declaring frankly either that "That is what I wanted!" or else "God forbid!" '[11]

In answer to de Rougemont's challenge, I find myself declaring: 'That is what I wanted!' – passion, the transfiguring torment, the wholly absorbing, wild delights of love, all the more delightful for their transience, their hiddenness, their breaking of moral codes. *Tristan* is a tale of people like me, full of well-managed deceit, with a hero and heroine who simultaneously believe themselves to be in the wrong, yet also right, and that somehow God is on their side, their love being greater and of more transcendent value than the social conventions they break. 'Of course it would be going too far to suggest that a majority of people today are a prey to Tristan's frenzy. Few are capable of the thirst that would cause them to drink the love-potion, and still fewer are being elected to succumb to the archetypal anguish. But they are all, or nearly all, dreaming about it, or else have mused upon it.'[12] I would rather do it than dream about it. Or so I think.

'What is forbidden is desirable . . . breaking taboos can also be attractive in and of itself; the breaking sometimes is at least as attractive as the act involved, because more happens than the sex.'[13] The mistress may well identify with what Sallie Tisdale says here in *Talk Dirty to Me*, with the idea that sex is only really interesting if it is forbidden; it is the illicit, the hidden, the wicked which stimulates. There's nothing exciting about sex if you're *supposed* to be doing it. Or as Erica Jong puts it: 'Sex, by definition, is something you have with someone other than a spouse . . . Call it *conjugal* anything and the mystery withers. Sex has mystery, magic, a hint of the forbidden.'[14] The half-hidden desire to do something of

11 Ibid., p.25
12 Ibid., pp.286–7
13 Sallie Tisdale, *Talk Dirty to Me: An Intimate Philosophy of Sex*, Pan, London, 1996, p.215
14 Erica Jong, *Fear of Fifty*, Chatto & Windus, London, 1994, p.143

which the world – that is, conventional society, the upholders of law and order, other women, the father (in the sense of an archetypal image of fatherhood), maybe even God – disapproves, implies that disapproval itself is desired. Disapproval, which may result in exposure and humiliation, will simultaneously represent triumph over the world of convention and the undifferentiated masses. Even as I write this, I recognise it doesn't make much rational sense, that it's probably immature – the little girl seeking to draw attention to herself – and may ultimately be self-destructive, about as satisfactory as suffering from an eating disorder or a tendency to cut one's arms. But such things as the desire for punishment, for discovery, are in any case part of the fantasy world associated with sex. The mistress may have no real desire for her affair to be discovered, but she may like to imagine a dramatic denouement.

Sigmund Freud's identification of what he terms 'moral masochism' gives weight to the idea that there is a link between desiring what is forbidden and desiring punishment – at least in fantasy – that in fact the motivation to do the forbidden thing *is* the desire for punishment:

> . . . masochism creates a temptation to perform 'sinful' actions, which must then be expiated by the reproaches of the sadistic conscience (as is exemplified in so many Russian character-types) or by chastisement from the great parental power of Destiny. In order to provoke punishment from this last representative of the parents, the masochist must do what is inexpedient, must act against his own interests, must ruin the prospects which open out to him in the real world and must, perhaps, destroy his own real existence.[15]

This can become such an obsession that the unforbidden, the socially sanctioned, that which carries no threat of exposure, consequent humiliation and punishment cannot, act as an

---

15 Sigmund Freud, 'The Economic Problem of Masochism' in *Freud on Women: A Reader*, ed. Elisabeth Young-Bruehl, Hogarth Press, London, 1990, p.292

erotic stimulant and cannot provide the impetus for the experience of falling in love. This attitude of mind may also be a way of warding off true intimacy, in that any persistent fantasy may act as a barrier through which no partner can penetrate.

So the mistress, identifying herself with Lilith rather than with Eve (though she joins with Eve in her desire to taste the forbidden fruit) and caught up in the tumultuous and fatal passion of Tristan and Iseult, forever lures man out of the realm of the conventional and socially acceptable into the forbidden zone, out of the Garden of Eden and through the devil's door. Perhaps. She does this partly because she's addicted to it herself and loves to court disaster, partly because it's her role, anima-like, to lead the man out of innocence into deeper self-knowledge – and partly for none of these high-falutin reasons but because she feels like it, or falls suddenly, inexplicably and inappropriately in love, or just wants to add to her score. Or else she thinks this time it'll be different and he'll leave his wife. There is somewhere in the whole mistress business the desire to pit oneself against everyone else, to test the strength of one's seductive powers – can I wrest him from his old life? (The answer in nearly every case is 'No'.)

According to Jung, women are in danger of four kinds of mother-complex – maternal hypertrophy, Eros hypertrophy, identification with the mother or resistance to the mother – and all of these are the results of overconcentration on the female parent. The Eros hypertrophy, or 'overdevelopment of Eros', Jung argues,

> . . . almost invariably leads to an unconscious incestuous relationship with the father . . . Jealousy of the mother and the desire to outdo her become the leitmotifs of subsequent undertakings, which are often disastrous. A woman of this type loves romantic and sensational episodes for their own sake, and is interested in married men, less for themselves than for the fact that they are

married and so give her an opportunity to wreck a
marriage, that being the whole point of her manoeuvre.
Once the goal is attained, her interest evaporates for lack
of any maternal instinct, and then it will be someone
else's turn.[16]

Though I have no recollection from my childhood of an
'overconcentration on the female parent', much of Jung's
description of symptoms rings remarkably true, even though I
tell myself I don't really want to wreck marriages. It is also
very noticeable that a sizeable proportion of the mistresses and
mistress-types considered in this book had either very close or
problematic relationships with their fathers, and it seems
entirely feasible that they were unconsciously motivated by
'jealousy of the mother and the desire to outdo her'. Some
form of Oedipus complex – the desire to oust the mother in
order to enjoy an exclusive relationship with the father – does
seem to come into play in a large number of women who
become, or have become, mistresses. Wendy James and Susan
Jane Kedgley throw an interesting light on one thing which
may be happening here:

> Because of the uncertainty of the relationship she has
> with her lover, a mistress can find herself re-creating that
> stage of adolescence where she becomes aware of having
> to deserve love. She plays out the game which she has
> learnt from her father – fulfil my expectations and I will
> love you. This fatherly love, unlike the unconditional
> motherly love, relies on being loved because of one's
> merits. In the mistress, as in the child, it causes doubts,
> fears: if I do not please him perhaps love will disappear.[17]

Is it possible, to take this a step further, that women who in
their childhood felt they had to earn their father's love are
more likely to end up as mistresses, in another situation where

16 C.G. Jung, *The Archetypes & the Collective Unconscious*, pp.88–9
17 Wendy James & Susan Jane Kedgley, *The mistress*, p.128

the perception on the part of the woman is that if she does not continue to earn his love, the lover will leave? Whereas wives who, from the mistress's point of view, seem to take their husbands for granted and do not make the same effort to 'earn' love, experienced more unconditional fatherly love in their childhood? Obviously this is an enormous generalisation to which there are bound to be many exceptions, but I think there may be something in it all the same.

Jung's identification of the type of woman characterised by resistance to the mother also seems apposite: 'The motto of this type is: Anything, so long as it is not like Mother!'[18] Resistance to the mother can manifest as resistance to everything connected with her (as archetype rather than individual) – family, convention, society, any form of 'belonging', in fact – as well as towards mother as *matter*. (In me this seems to manifest as antipathy towards gardening, 'grown-up' cooking, house ownership – in short, everything wives and mothers are supposed to do.) Of course, despite these resonances I feel with Jung's typologies, it may all be the other way round. Rather than being a mistress because I have a negative mother complex, I may be anti-family because I am a mistress. Having always, or nearly always, formed 'unsuitable' and secret relationships, I have resented and feared the (my) family's power to penetrate my secrets and make demands which conflict with my freedom.

18 C.G. Jung, *The Archetypes & the Collective Unconscious*, p.90

THE GODDESS AND HER COURTESANS,
AND HOW THEY DIFFER

*Aphrodite, Goddess of Desire, rose naked
from the foam of the sea . . . Grass and
flowers sprang from the soil wherever she trod
. . . Some hold that she sprang from the
foam which gathered about the genitals of
Uranus, when Cronus threw them into the
sea; others, that Zeus begot her on Dione,
daughter of either Oceanus and Tethys the
sea-nymph, or of Air and Earth.*[1]

Thus Robert Graves summarises the variant myths of the birth of Aphrodite. Though ancient sources may be divided as to her origin, there is no disagreement about what she was born to do: 'The Fates assigned to Aphrodite one divine duty only, namely to make love.'[2]

It was in the fourth century BC that Plato and the group of thinkers who comprised his Academy first divided the goddess Aphrodite into two distinct figures. Aphrodite Urania, the heavenly Aphrodite, representing intellectual, divine love, removed from daily concerns; and Aphrodite Pandemos, the Aphrodite 'of all the people', who symbolised earthly, physical love, and was known as the patroness of prostitution. Prostitutes who provide a one-night-stand for money do not fall within the terms I have laid down to define 'the mistress', but the women who came at the top end of the scale, so to speak – the *hetairai* who were 'companions' to men, the courtesans, and the 'kept women' – frequently do. Until comparatively recently, being a mistress was one way to make a decent living.

1 Robert Graves, *Greek Myths*, Cassell & Co, London, 1958, p.49
2 Ibid., p.70

This sort of woman first came to prominence in Ancient
Greece, the most famous of the hetairai in fifth-century
Athens being Aspasia, who lived with the political leader
Pericles. Two other famed 'companions' were Phryne and
Lais. There has been and continues to be much discussion as to
whether the hetairai were self-made women enjoying an
enviable lifestyle filled with culture and high-minded conversation, or whether they were ultimately as much at the
mercy of men as their sisters soliciting on the streets, and
whether all their 'culture' was but a veneer to entertain their
male clients. They would certainly appear to have enjoyed a
greater freedom of movement, a wider sphere of activity, than
their married counterparts; as Reay Tannahill points out:
'What Athenian men liked about the hetairai was that they
excelled at all the things those same men prevented their
wives from learning, which must have been extremely galling
for the wives.'[3] Similar patterns of elegant and expensive ladies
at one end and inhabitants of brothels at the other existed in
the Roman sex trade. Then the next great flourishing of the
courtesan – or at least the next time we hear a great deal about
her – was in Renaissance Italy, and again such women were
contrasted with wives and seem to have had a better time of it:
'Like the earlier Greek *hetairai*, the *cortegiane* of Venice,
Florence and Milan were educated, influential and talented
beauties who specialized in catering to the sexual and social
needs of men who had excluded their wives from fully
participating in their lives.'[4]

In Venice, ever a law unto itself and always extraordinary,
the lives of young nuns seem to have been particularly
interesting. Upper-class girls were regularly placed in convents
when their parents could not afford a dowry, with a tacit
understanding that solitary spiritual contemplation did not
necessarily have to be their only activity. Marriage, it was
agreed by the Church and society in general, was the only

3 Reay Tannahill, *Sex in History*, Abacus, London, 1981, p.90
4 Nickie Roberts, *Whores in History: Prostitution in Western Society*, HarperCollins,
London, 1992, p.101

place sexually mature women really belonged, but if they couldn't be married then something else had to be done with them, both for their own good and for the stability of society. The importance of marrying well and the increasing cost to the bride's family meant that many young women were in need of a way of life outside the family structure, and convents came to offer an alternative. 'In many ways this convent life was the ideal institutional placement for young women who were too costly to dower, too dangerous to be left single, yet too dear to be abandoned. They were allowed to live with a certain style and grace as long as they were discreet, and in the process they were placed and thus maintained their families' status and dignity.'[5]

It is hardly surprising that this influx of high-class young women into these institutions had an effect on the nature of the institutions themselves. Guido Ruggiero describes some of the convents concerned as taking on a tone 'reminiscent of a cross between the courts of love of the High Middle Ages and the temple prostitution of the ancient world'.[6] In 1428, for instance, there was a great scandal at San Nicolai di Torcello involving, among others, the Abbess, whose 'affair with a scribe, Pietro Blanco, paled before the wide range of contacts that her noble sister, Filipa Barbarigo, was found to have preserved behind the walls of the cloister. Ten males were prosecuted for having had sexual relations with Filipa over a considerable period of time. Her list of lovers reads like a *who's who* of Venetian leading noble families.'[7] Another young woman, Liseta de Buora, made the easy cross-over from nun to courtesan after being thrown out of the convent of Sant' Angelo (which was itself closed by the Pope in 1474 after running up an impressive record of sex crimes).

The on-going connections between nunneries and mistresses could form the subject of a book in itself. In the early

5 Guido Ruggiero, *The Boundaries of Eros: Sex Crime & Sexuality in Renaissance Venice*, OUP, New York & Oxford, 1985, p.162

6 Ibid., p.77

7 Ibid., p.80

eighteenth century, for instance, a Catholic nunnery in Ghent provided a refuge for the Englishwoman Teresia Constantia Phillips on more than one occasion 'as a welcome, temporary respite from a life of fashionable gaity, extravagance, and sexual excess'.[8] In this nunnery she moved into the opulent quarters of the former mistress of a duke. Claudine du Tencin was another woman who used a nunnery as a base for her intrigues. Born in Grenoble in 1685, she first fled to a nunnery in order to avoid an arranged marriage, but she went on to use it as a training ground until she took up with the Duc de Richelieu. She left him in order to pursue an intellectual and literary career. 'The rewards of a life of prostitution enabled her to set up her own *salon*, which became a favourite haunt of the brightest lights in French cultural life and where the former whore nurtured such talents as the philosopher Montesquieu.'[9]

Continuing her survey of whores through the ages Nickie Roberts writes: 'Thanks to the continued expansion of both the bourgeoisie and its finances . . . the Victorian era became another classical age of the courtesan. These ladies referred to themselves as "great horizontals"; and they were certainly that.'[10] The real *grandes horizontales* flourished in nineteenth-century France, though one of the most famous of these was an Englishwoman, Emma Crouch, born near Plymouth in 1836, who changed her name to Cora Pearl. Cora graduated from an early life of prostitution, after having been seduced at the age of fourteen, through the position of gentleman's mistress, until she succeeded in becoming the mistress of Prince Jérome Bonaparte, cousin of the Emperor Napoleon III. 'Cora Pearl's personal style was *outré*; one of her favourite little pastimes was to invite her most "respectable" clients for supper, disappear just before the desert was served up, then reappear a few minutes later, carried in on a silver platter, reclining naked on a bed of Parma violets.'[11]

8 Lawrence Stone, *Uncertain Unions: Marriage in England 1660–1753*, OUP, Oxford, 1992, p.236
9 Nickie Roberts, *Whores in History*, p.152
10 Ibid., p.217
11 Ibid., p.219

But it would be a mistake to assume that the life of a courtesan, or kept woman, in any age, was all a bed of Parma violets. For a start, there was never any guarantee that male protection would not be withdrawn, the absence of a legal bond meaning a woman must never take her lover for granted.

Both courtesans and their 'trainers' were well aware of the golden rule that governed their profession. Amphis, a poet of the Middle Comedy, expressed it as follows: 'The *hetaira* should always be more obliging than a wife, for the very good reason that however disagreeable a wife may be the law compels the husband to keep her. The courtesan, however, knows that she can only retain a lover by lavishing attentions on him. For otherwise he will get another mistress.[12]

For the same reason it was inadvisable for the courtesan to fall deeply in love. There has also always been in the sex trade, no matter how high-class, the potential for physical abuse. But the principal enemy of the courtesan as of the prostitute, and where she differs so fundamentally from her patroness Aphrodite, is the ageing process, bringing with it the loss of her charms and consequently of her earning power. Of what use in old age is the patronage of the youthful Aphrodite who renews her own virginity every year by bathing? If her devotee has had any sense, she will have put by some savings when her face and form could still bring in the money (or she will have come to appreciate the spiritual consolations of life in a convent). 'The hetairai were well aware that their attractions would not last forever and that money in the bank was the thing to aim for.'[13]

Money in the bank is still a thing to aim for, but one of the differences about being a mistress in late-twentieth-century

12 Robert Flacelière, *Love in Ancient Greece*, tr. James Cleugh, Frederick Muller, London, 1962, pp.131–2
13 Reay Tannahill, *Sex in History*, p.91

Western civilisation, as compared with other eras, is that one no longer feels easy about being 'kept'. Indeed one of the reasons why a woman may decide not to marry is the desire never to be financially dependent on – or even financially entangled with – a man. The modern woman is unlikely to allow herself to make a profession out of being a mistress, however much the illusorily romantic idea of the life of a courtesan may appeal.

Today women do not need to make a profession out of being a mistress, as every other profession is (in theory, at least) open to them. But are there ways, other than financial, in which the mistress may say to her lovers, 'If you love me, pay up!' (an ultimatum attributed to Philumena, a Greek courtesan)? Principally, the mistress expects a quality of attention from her lover which might not be so necessary – or possible – if they were together all day every day (and all night every night). Perhaps the mistress demands more energy in his lovemaking than his wife does. Yet these hardly amount to extortionate payments, particularly as the mistress pays him in equal measure, *giving* him a quality of attention he doesn't generally get from his wife, responding to him sexually in a way that perhaps his wife does not. I am reminded of something I noted in *The Times* on 1 September 1995: 'A French study has found that four out of five heart attacks during sex involve people who are not married to each other. Dr Jean-Paul Broustat, the Paris cardiologist who conducted the study, said: "A middle-aged man who has sex with his wife receives the same cardiovascular workout as climbing three flights of stairs. With a mistress it's like running up a skyscraper." '[14]

But what if it is Aphrodite herself who says, 'If you love me, pay up!'? What if she demands payment from her adherents, if

14 On the same day *The Times* also carried a story about the resignation of the headmaster of Charterhouse school over a sex scandal, which included the following immortal remarks: 'The playwright and political speechwriter Sir Ronald Millar said: "In my day this was inconceivable. What is happening to the world I know? It is turning upside down. Prostitutes? In Godalming? I can't believe it." '

love which is passionate and arguably irresponsible must in some way be paid for? I am reminded now of a television documentary about H.G. Wells, presented by his admirer and biographer Michael Foot, who was clearly in sympathy with Wells's multiple relationships. Michael Foot's wife, Jill Craigie, was also being interviewed – they were talking about Rebecca West, one of Wells's mistresses – and Jill Craigie expressed the view that mistresses always had to pay – and, indeed, as a wife, she thought it quite right they should pay – and that the payment consisted in knowing that the husband (that is, the mistress's lover) would always put his wife first. It is one of the rules of any marriage which runs successfully alongside extra-marital liaisons: the core relationship of husband and wife needs to be given priority amid whatever other relationships are in operation. The mistress who understands this dynamic and accepts it is the 'successful' mistress.

Another payment Aphrodite demands from the mistress is a way of life which combines maximum availability with minimum expectations or demands. For example, I hardly ever tell my lover I'm too busy to see him, and I very rarely ask to see him at a particular time. I put him first, while knowing he cannot fully reciprocate – not practically, even if he does emotionally. At the moment this is a price I'm prepared to pay; maybe that's because I never have been very good at budgeting. Such behaviour might also suggest, according to the Renaissance philosopher Marsilio Ficino, that I am *too much* under the sway of Aphrodite/Venus, that I need to become more aware of other archetypes to achieve a better balance in my life.

A very significant payment is the additional grief and logistical difficulties to be expected in the event of death, illness or accident. Even if none of these things actually happens during the course of an affair, one is not spared the anxiety that they might. If the lover doesn't show up or is late, all the mistress can do is worry. She can hardly go looking for him or call his wife to ask where he is. In recent years life for illicit lovers has been made considerably easier in this respect with mobile phones, e-mails and pagers, yet these devices entail their own risks: an e-mail being read by the wrong person (or even disclosed as evidence in court when you thought it had been deleted) or a pager left lying around in the bedroom at home, bleeping or buzzing away until the wife picks it up and reads 'I love you – can't wait till this afternoon'.

Another payment is that the nature of the mistress's relationship with her lover – the way she will drop everything for him, the tendency not to make plans in case he is suddenly free to see her, and the greater or lesser need for secrecy – can play havoc with her other relationships. Friends have to be very understanding to put up with it. Or she may have several half-friends, from whom she keeps a large part of her life secret, a fact they may or may not suspect. There may also be unwanted attentions from men who do not realise she is already committed elsewhere.

Yet whatever the payment which may be demanded of me, I think I would say it was worth it to have known, made love with and been loved by my beloved. I imagine many people might say, 'And what of his wife? What payment are you and he exacting from her?' To which I can only say, 'I don't know.' That's Hera's affair, not Aphrodite's.

For a while at least, the followers of Aphrodite may appear younger than their contemporaries; the mistress, with her outwardly independent and carefree lifestyle, can seem to retain her youth longer than the harassed wife and mother, with all her additional responsibilities. For it must be admitted that the perennial youthfulness of Aphrodite goes hand in hand with – may in her followers even be partly caused by – a certain irresponsibility, a lack of concern for likely consequences. For a goddess not to concern herself with consequences is one thing; for a mortal it is quite another. As Robert Flacelière points out, the love affairs of the immortals cost them nothing; nothing is irreparable when life goes on for ever. 'Death changes all. It gives weight and duration to human destiny, above all to human love. Among the Immortals love is merely a kind of game, without serious after-effects. But among men it is always an important, sometimes a tragic business.'[15]

So Aphrodite needn't consider consequences, but gives herself to love – and sex – here and now, when desire, sensuality, passion claim her. Hera, the wife, thinks in terms of families, the future, legal arrangements, security, but Aphrodite goes with the moment. And as she is renewed every year, her amorous intrigues leave no mark. Whereas for a mortal woman, no action is without its consequences, no matter how much she may try to ignore it. And the woman who habitually falls for married men may be particularly practised at ignoring consequences. Or maybe – just maybe – she has learnt to anticipate those consequences and deal with them appropriately.

If I listen to the irresponsible side of myself, I hear a train of thought which goes something like this: We won't be discovered. And anyway his wife wouldn't really mind – she's not all that fond of him after all. I have no effect on his family life. I won't grow old. I won't get ill. I will never be lonely. Some of these thoughts are more ludicrous than others and, at the same time as thinking them, I can recognise that most of them aren't true – if indeed any of them are. We may well one day be 'discovered'. When I think of my lover's wife my imagination fails me; she's a closed book, partly through her own personality, partly through my lack of empathy. I must have some effect on his family life if only because he can contrast it with the less stressful times he spends with me – and then there is, of course, just the amount of time he spends with me when he could be at home. I will inevitably grow old. What sort of relationship will we have when our physical delight in one another is past? I may become ill and, if I do, who will look after me? One day maybe I will be lonely, even if now I seem always to be busy and interested in life, for I

15 Robert Flacelière, *Love in Ancient Greece*, p.19

know that a large part of my present contentment comes from seeing my lover regularly. Hanging over everything is the knowledge of mortality, the consciousness (though I may try to keep it *un*conscious) that if he were suddenly to die, not only would I have to cope with the loss of my love, but there would be no support, no recognition of my loss. I might not even be informed until I read about it somewhere. Or if the death were not sudden, but preceded by a lingering illness, would I be able to visit him? Even if I could, it would have to be brief and not necessarily private; the family – his rightful owners – would take precedence. Prudently, I have certain friends lined up, at least one of them mutual, who know about us and to whom I could turn in an emergency. But prudence is an enemy of Aphrodite, and Aphrodite urges me to set all such fears aside, and live – and love – for the moment. It is Aphrodite who springs up in joy when my lover rings the doorbell, who makes me abandon all my plans for a work-filled morning if he suggests meeting for coffee, who urges me to cancel any appointment in order to make love in the afternoon, who encourages me to go on spending money on meals and holidays with no thought of the morrow, who says, 'You only live once, and loving like this is the most important, the only thing really worth bothering about.' Hang the consequences.

The most famed of Aphrodite's vassals, both her mortal embodiment and her will-less puppet, was Helen of Troy. Promised to Paris by Aphrodite when he singled her out above Hera and Pallas Athena, progeny of the immortal Zeus and inheritor of Aphrodite's curse on Tyndareus her step-father, what hope did she have? She was never in a position to make a decision, she merely had to play out her destiny and then watch in a kind of detached horror as the Greeks and Trojans destroyed one another over her. In Homer's *Iliad*, not even the old chiefs of Troy, as they watch the clashing of their sons over Helen, can find anyone to blame for what has happened; rather, it is Helen's beauty, as irresistible as Aphrodite's famous girdle, and over which

Helen herself has no control, which has brought about the fatal events:

> So they waited,
> the old chiefs of Troy, as they sat aloft the tower.
> And catching sight of Helen moving along the ramparts,
> they murmured one to another, gentle, winged words:
> 'Who on earth could blame them? Ah, no wonder
> the men of Troy and Argives under arms have suffered
> years of agony all for her, for such a woman.
> Beauty, terrible beauty!'[16]

At one point Helen tries to defy her goddess, objecting when Aphrodite summons her to join Paris in bed after she has rescued him from the midst of the conflict:

> 'Maddening one, my Goddess, oh what now?
> Lusting to lure me to my ruin yet again?
> Where would you drive me next?'[17]

But her momentary rebellion is to no avail; Aphrodite is not to be resisted.

In the following of her destiny, Helen experienced no sense of responsibility whatsoever, no conception of any possible consequences, when she eloped with Paris, leaving behind all her previous life, including not only a husband but a daughter. Later, much later, after years of actually witnessing the consequences of her action, she comes to recognise the role she has played, yet at the same time she realises its inevitability. It has been pointed out by Jack Lindsay[18] that Helen never actually repents; she never asks herself whether she might have acted differently. She feels that the only way she could have avoided acting as she did would have been not to have been born at all. Yet even the limited sense of responsibility Helen

16 Homer, *The Iliad*, tr. Robert Fagles, Viking, New York, 1990, p.133
17 Ibid., p.141
18 Jack Lindsay, *Helen of Troy: Woman & Goddess*, Constable, London, 1974

eventually acquires is something her controlling goddess could never experience.

The differences between the gods and humankind, in terms of both the power which can be exercised and the consequences which ensue, constitute one of the themes of the *Iliad*. Bernard Knox, in his introduction to Robert Fagles' translation, provides a good summary of these differences and the way they are eventually recognised:

> To be a god is to be totally absorbed in the exercise of one's own power, the fulfillment of one's own nature, unchecked by any thought of others except as obstacles to be overcome; it is to be incapable of self-questioning or self-criticism. But there are human beings who are like this. Preeminent in their particular sphere of power, they impose their will on others with the confidence, the unquestioning certainty of their own right and worth that is characteristic of gods. Such people the Greeks called 'heroes' . . . there are some human beings who can deny the imperatives which others obey in order to live . . . And sooner or later, in suffering, in disaster, they come to realize their limits, accept mortality and establish (or reestablish) a human relationship with their fellow-men.[19]

Women, like Helen, who live under the sway of Aphrodite – and I think this includes many of the kind of women who become mistresses – tend not to act in a way respectable society terms 'responsible', and also tend to feel they have no choice in how they act. And the men, like Paris, who fall for these women can also appear to lose their will-power. To both it may feel as though gods are impelling us to our loves, so there is nothing we can do but fall. Is Aphrodite continuing to have her way with us mortals – or are we just using her as an excuse, a means to avoid our responsibilities? And do I, in my

19 Bernard Knox, 'Introduction' to Homer, *The Iliad*, tr. Robert Fagles, pp.45–6

on-going affair, sometimes forget that I am no goddess? Do I believe nothing can touch me, no harm come to me, my lover, his wife or his children? Do I believe I am free 'to deny the imperatives which others obey'? Yes, I probably do.

CUPID AND PSYCHE

[Psyche] showed [her sisters] all the riches of
the golden house and made known to their
ears the great household of voices that waited
on her. Then she refreshed their weariness in
the fairest of baths and with all the rich
dainties of that celestial table till, their senses
sated with the affluence of her heavenly
wealth, they began to foster envy deep in
their inmost hearts.[1]

O nce upon a time there was a king and queen who had three beautiful daughters, and the youngest of them was so beautiful that she was beyond the power of human speech to describe. People worshipped her as though she were Venus herself; this infuriated Venus (whom hitherto we have met in her Greek incarnation as Aphrodite), which was hardly surprising as her worshippers were deserting her for this young girl, Psyche. So in a campaign to punish Psyche the goddess enlisted Cupid: 'that winged son of hers, that most reckless of creatures, whose wicked behaviour flies in the face of public morals, who armed with torch and arrows roams at night through houses where he has no business, ruining marriages on every hand, committing heinous crimes with impunity, and never doing such a thing as a good deed'.[2] Venus's plan is that Cupid should cause Psyche to fall in love with some absolute down-and-out, the dregs of humanity.

---

1 'Amor & Psyche' based on translation of H.E. Butler in Erich Neumann, *Amor & Psyche: The Psychic Development of the Feminine*, tr. Ralph Mannheim, Routledge & Kegan Paul, London, 1956, p.15
2 Apuleius, *The Golden Ass or Metamorphoses*, tr. E.J. Kenney, Penguin, Harmondsworth, 1998, p.73

Psyche, meanwhile, was not having a particularly good
time. Her goddess-like beauty, while drawing men to worship
her as a statue, repelled them from approaching her as a
woman; in short, no one would propose to her. Both her
sisters had been successfully married off, but poor Psyche
'stayed at home an unmarried virgin mourning her abandoned
and lonely state, sick in body and mind, hating this beauty of
hers which had enchanted the whole world'.[3] Eventually her
father consulted the oracle of Apollo, and was instructed to
dress the girl for a wedding with death and then to abandon
her on a mountain crag. Reluctantly, the instructions are
obeyed, but Psyche then finds herself wafted down from the
crag by the Zephyrs, soft and gentle breezes. Sensibly enough,
on landing she goes to sleep.

Waking, she finds herself in the vicinity of a beautiful
palace. She enters it, and a disembodied voice tells her it is all
hers to enjoy. She sits down to a feast, then to a concert (all
those who serve and entertain her remain invisible) and that
night her marriage – if that is what it is – is consummated:
'Now there entered her unknown husband; he had mounted
the bed, made her his wife, and departed in haste before
sunrise.'[4] Before long Psyche gets used to her new way of life,
and settles into her 'married' state. But after a while she
becomes bored. There is, after all, no one to keep her
company during the day, no one to whom she can show
off the amazing palace, the wealth her 'marriage' has brought
her. Like many another kept woman, she has to keep her
good fortune to herself. But eventually she persuades her
invisible lover (who continues to lie with her every night and
to leave every morning), against his better judgement, to let
her have her two sisters to visit – with the proviso that she
must on no account allow them to persuade her to find out
who he is or try to make him visible. So her sisters arrive and,
predictably enough, are jealous of Psyche's good fortune and,
equally predictably, are quite sure she can't have come by it

3 Ibid., p.74
4 Ibid., p.78

respectably. And, of course, they attempt to make up for their own dissatisfaction by stressing how very respectable they are themselves. One can hear the self-righteousness in their tone: 'Now let us return to our husbands and go back to our homes – poor but decent – and then when we've thought things over seriously let us equip ourselves with an even firmer resolve to punish her insolence.'[5]

The sisters make several more visits; their envy increases and they plot to bring about Psyche's ruin, all the time questioning her about 'her husband, his family, his class, his occupation'.[6] Psyche makes a bad mistake by inventing different stories about him on different occasions; one needs to learn consistency in lying, if it is to be successful. And the sisters succeed in sowing seeds of doubt in her mind. One can imagine the questions: Who is this man? What has he got to hide? A wife, perhaps? If it's all above board, why won't he marry you publicly? Why won't he let us meet him? What do you mean, you don't know who he is yourself? Psyche, you naïve, silly, ignorant girl – you've been seduced by a philanderer, at the very least. Perhaps he's a criminal, a murderer even. Come on, Psyche, if you've got any self-respect, at least ask him his name. And if you won't do it for yourself, then do it for your family. Think what it means to Mum and Dad. How can they tell the neighbours you're living off some man, in his house, and you don't even know who he is? And so on, finishing up with: '. . . if a country life and musical solitude, and the loathsome and dangerous intimacy of clandestine love, and the embraces of a venomous serpent, are what appeals to you, at all events your loving sisters will have done their duty.'[7]

Psyche is sufficiently disturbed by her sisters' insinuations to disobey her lover. That night she lights a lamp while he is sleeping and sees that her mysterious lover is none other than Cupid himself. Then, even worse, she inadvertently pricks herself on one of his arrows: 'Thus without realizing it Psyche

5 Ibid., p.82
6 Ibid., p.85
7 Ibid., p.86

through her own act fell in love with Love. Then ever more on fire with desire for Desire she hung over him gazing in distraction and devoured him with quick sensuous kisses, fearing all the time that he might wake up.'[8] And then, worst of all, a splash of oil from the lamp falls on him and burns him. Cupid wakes, and in horror flies away. Psyche clings on to his leg, but eventually falls off. She has lost him.

She sets out in search of him – but first takes revenge on her sisters by tricking them into jumping off the crag (in expectation that the breeze will once more waft them down to Cupid's dwelling) and so falling to their deaths. Meanwhile a gossiping tern has informed Venus, in the most purple prose, of how her son, instead of carrying out her instructions, has made her rival his mistress. Venus is beside herself with rage, and determined to find Psyche to punish her. Eventually realising the hopelessness of her position and that there is nowhere else in the world for her to go, Psyche delivers herself up to Venus.

The goddess first hands her over to Care and Sorrow to be tormented, and then sends her off on a series of impossible trials, each of which she is helped to accomplish by, respectively, an ant, a reed, an eagle and a tower. Even now she has not really learnt prudence, for at the conclusion of her fourth and greatest trial, which has been to go to the underworld and bring back a box of Proserpine's beauty for Venus, she cannot resist disobeying Proserpine's stern instruction not to open the box, hoping for a share of the beauty herself. But all that emerges from the box for her is a death-like sleep, from which she is only rescued by Cupid, now sufficiently recovered from his wound to start reasserting himself against his mother. He decides to enlist his father Jupiter in his cause. Jupiter tells him off for so frequently getting his father into trouble by making him fall in love with young girls and commit adultery; then he promises to help him provided he finds him another young girl . . . So he calls a council of the gods and declares 'the hot-

8 Ibid., p.88

blooded impulses of [Cupid's] first youth must somehow be bridled; his name has been besmirched long enough in common report by adultery and all kinds of licentious behaviour. We must take away all opportunity for this and confine his youthful excess in the bonds of marriage.'[9] Accordingly Psyche is given ambrosia to drink and becomes immortal; Jupiter tells her: 'Never shall Cupid quit the tie that binds you, but this marriage shall be perpetual for you both.'[10] They sit down to the wedding-feast.

So what are the implications of this story for the mistress?

The existence of Psyche's carefree and pampered life as Cupid's mistress depends on her acceptance of its invisibility, both to herself and to the outside world, as well as of the part-time nature of her relationship with her lover. Invisibility as far as she is concerned means she cannot know all there is to know about her lover; she can know him insofar as he relates to her sexually at night and provides for her during the day, but she cannot know anything about the rest of his life or indeed anything at all about him except what he chooses to reveal. The relationship is run entirely on his terms, and when Psyche attempts to assert herself, the relationship is jeopardised; he leaves her, and it all appears to be over. A twentieth-century mistress is unlikely to be kept in such complete ignorance of her lover's 'other' life, but there are often boundaries which it may be safer not to cross, questions it is better not to ask, areas in the lover's life on which it is best not to shine too bright a light, if the mistress wants the relationship to continue. Affairs between mistresses and their lovers are usually – though not invariably – run on the lover's terms. Invisibility in relation to the outside world involves the practice of deceit, or at least of a refusal to tell the truth or the whole truth. The practice of deceit as a way of life is arguably the most damaging aspect to the self of being a mistress. Another way of looking at it is to view it merely as the playing of different roles at various times and with various people –

9 Ibid., p.105
10 Ibid.

something we all do, but which the skilled mistress does to perfection. In which case, the most important – and most impossible – task for her is to try not to deceive herself.

Cupid is thwarted by Psyche's refusal to maintain darkness and secrecy. It is possible that agreeing to keep everything secret is merely playing into the male's hands to have everything his own way and to keep his mistress firmly in the position of a toy with which to amuse himself. But if the mistress wants to end the secrecy, she will have to be prepared to lose everything.

Psyche, though mildly bored and wanting someone to show off her good fortune to (she may be the kind of person who will always find something to moan about – she is probably moaning this minute in the heavens), is happy with her lot as the mistress of her invisible lover, until the arrival and interference of her sisters. These respectably, though rather unhappily, married women are envious of her luxurious life as a kept woman, and so set out to destroy her; they begin by encouraging her to question whether she is really contented, whether she is really loved, whether her lover should behave as he does. As I intimated in the Introduction, it is frequently the reaction of other people which threatens to make the mistress unhappy with her situation, by suggesting to her, from the context of their more 'normal' lives, that all is not well in the way she lives – that, in short, she should be more like them. Left to herself, she might have been quite contented as she is.

Moral indignation, such as that voiced by the sisters, is often a mask for envy. If, after all, they were happy with their own lives, they would hardly need to come poking their noses into Psyche's. The prurient condemnation one comes across in the present-day tabloid press, always on hand to lambast any figure of high office, any celebrity who falls foul of what the masses call morality, and the popularity of these condemnatory 'stories', demonstrates, to my mind, the boredom of both the journalists' – and, more particularly, of the readers' – own lives. Resentment fuels righteous indignation: 'If we can't live like them, let us make them live like us' and 'How dare they take their enjoyment without paying the proper price like we have?' and, perhaps at the heart of it, 'Why are they braver than us? Why do they dare to step outside our conventions and live apart from the crowd?'

So Psyche, goaded by her sisters, is no longer content to live the life of a mistress, the secret life of a kept woman, to live within the terms and conditions set down by her lover. Behind her intention to 'unmask' him, to see his true nature, lies her desire to have their love come out into the light – in short, to marry him properly and be his wife. But in the act of trying to take more than is on offer, she appears to lose all she has. Nevertheless, after all the trials she endures at the hands of the jealous Venus, which are presumably partly a – not wholly successful – attempt to make her grow up and become suitable for wifehood, she does attain what she wants. How soon she becomes bored with eternal wifehood is a matter for speculation.

Erich Neumann, in his commentary on the story, seems at least partly to be taking the side of the sisters, as he asks: '. . . with all its rapture is this existence in the sensual paradise of Eros not an unworthy existence? Is it not a state of blind, though impassioned, servitude . . . ?'[11] The eventual transformation of the relationship between Cupid and Psyche from affair to marriage, however, can be seen merely as exchanging one form of servitude for another. Once the marriage has taken place, it is Cupid who is imprisoned, in the 'bonds of marriage'. He will probably find himself in the sort of relationship where the wife takes on the role of a bossy mother, forever chiding her husband and seeking to 'tame' him. Just the kind of relationship to make a man desire a mistress.

On the surface, the story of Cupid and Psyche and its respectable denouement seems to be a telling of the triumph of legal monogamy. Yet there are subversive elements, such as

11 Erich Neumann, *Amor & Psyche*, p.74

the fate of the two sisters, and the beautiful depiction of Psyche's life as a mistress, as well as the presiding at the wedding-feast of the notoriously adulterous Jove. Perhaps people like me want to remain in the early part of the story, being irresponsible and self-indulgent and having a good time (outside conventional society), resisting the imposition of the rest of the narrative, and prepared to put up with not knowing about or sharing in the rest of the lover's life. We are the kind of people criticised for not contributing to the stability of society, to the maintenance of family networks, for being fiercely individualistic.

Like Heloise (see next chapter) I resist the idea of drinking the ambrosia of immortal life with its concomitant notion that the man is now bound to me as husband for ever. It takes away the freedom of the offering of love, devaluing it. If someone is free at all times to leave me, I know that when he is with me, that's where he really wants to be.

HELOISE, WHO LONGED
TO BE A MISTRESS

The name of wife may seem more sacred or more binding, but sweeter for me will always be the word mistress.[1]

Heloise, born in 1100 or 1101, was seventeen when she first met the great scholar and teacher Peter Abelard. He was in his late thirties. 'Abelard was immensely gifted, an immortal teacher and the towering intellectual figure of his age. He was restless, unquiet, disturbing, as many great teachers are; and he was exceedingly self-centred and arrogant. He collected enemies with the abandon of a philatelist.'[2] Heloise was living in Paris, the ward of her uncle Fulbert, a canon of Notre Dame, and had been brought up as a child in the convent of Sainte Marie of Argenteuil. She was famed for her learning, so unusual for a woman. Abelard, ripe for an affair, heard of her and desired her, and her uncle played into his hands by suggesting Abelard should become Heloise's tutor and move in with them. In his *Historia Calamitatum* or *Story of His Misfortunes* Abelard makes no bones about the fact that he deliberately and methodically set out to seduce Heloise; neither is there any suggestion that she put up a struggle. What began, at least on Abelard's part, as purely physical desire, developed into an overpowering love of which sex continued to be a vitally important component. These two were destined never to experience the waning of desire through familiarity.

---

1 Betty Radice (ed.), *The Letters of Abelard and Heloise*, Penguin, Harmondsworth, 1974, p.113
2 Christopher N.L. Brooke, *The Medieval Idea of Marriage*, OUP, Oxford & New York, 1989, p.109

The bare bones of the story are that eventually, as was inevitable, Heloise's uncle discovered their 'affair' and felt grossly insulted. He throws Abelard out, but the lovers continue to meet secretly. Then Heloise discovers she is pregnant, a fact which delights her. Abelard now makes two inexplicable decisions: first, apparently worried about the insult to Fulbert, that he should marry Heloise; second, that the marriage must be kept secret. Heloise objects strongly to the idea of marriage, and also believes that a secret marriage won't serve to pacify her uncle. Abelard holds sway, but Heloise was right about Fulbert who finally takes his revenge by having Abelard castrated.

After the disaster (Heloise meanwhile has given birth to their son Astrolabius, who now drops out of the story), Abelard decides he has no alternative but to enter a monastery, and he insists his young wife should likewise enter the cloister, which she does without demur. Abelard, incidentally, makes sure she is safely sequestered before taking his own vows. His life continues to be full of controversy. He rarely settles anywhere for long, and his great gifts as philosopher and theologian ensure a stormy relationship with the Church authorities. Heloise's life, on the other hand, appears outwardly far less troubled. A few years after entering the convent at Argenteuil she becomes its prioress; subsequently, after the sisters are forced to leave Argenteuil, Abelard installs her and some others at the oratory of the Paraclete where he had at one time established himself as a hermit. Here Heloise 'remained until her death in 1163–4, abbess of a growing community which came to be the centre of a small Order; from the start respected by her neighbours and by the great figures of the contemporary monastic world, especially by Peter the Venerable of Cluny and even St Bernard of Clairvaux himself, notorious for his persecution of her husband'.[3] Abelard had died at the Cluniac priory of St Marcel at Chalon-sur-Saône in 1142, and his body had

3 Ibid., p.108

eventually been returned to the care of Heloise. She was
buried next to him.

This poignant story, briefly told, raises infinite questions, and
has become a fable whose mysteries and interpretations can
never be exhausted. What was the nature of the love between
these two, and how did Heloise's loving differ from Abelard's?
Why did Abelard think marriage would ease the situation,
why did he want it kept secret, and why did Heloise object so
strongly? How did they reconcile their love for one another
with their love of God, or did they never manage to do this?
How far were they products of their time and culture, and
how far were they completely outside it?

Our knowledge of the working of the minds of these two
lovers comes from the preservation of a brief but intense
correspondence between them, initiated by Heloise's apparently accidental receipt of Abelard's *Historia Calamitatum*. This
was written in 1132 or soon after and purports to be a letter to
an unnamed friend. It sets out Abelard's career to the age of
about fifty-four, being a record of his life from his entry into
the monastery of St Denis in 1119 and the events leading up
to it. Heloise's reading of this document provoked her into
writing to Abelard, and they exchanged two letters each
concerning the history of their love, before passing on to
more monastic matters. From these letters it is clear that, while
Abelard appears to have undergone a genuine conversion and
now repents of their former passionate loving, Heloise has
never experienced such a change of heart and has remained as
committed as ever to Abelard.

Questions have arisen at various times over the authenticity
of the correspondence. Some commentators have been unable to believe that a woman in the twelfth century could
have thought and expressed herself as does the Heloise of
these letters; so, they have wondered, could the correspondence be entirely fictional? Or could Abelard have written all
the letters himself? As what concerns me most is the Heloise of
my imagination, historical authenticity is only of secondary

importance, but I will nevertheless quote Christopher Brooke as giving some of the most sensible evidence in support of it. It must be remembered that marriage law and custom was in much disarray during the years of Heloise's childhood. It was a time when, particularly in northern France and England, clerical concubines were still socially acceptable despite the (so far ineffectual) condemnation of the Church, and such women had opportunities for learning which would be denied them once clerical celibacy was enforced. 'Now Heloise on any showing was one of a rare breed: the world of learning was a man's world. But there was one milieu in the early-twelfth century in which ladies freely mingled, where many or most clerical households contained concubines and children – and that was in the cathedral closes; and nowhere was education more advanced and more effective than in Paris.'[4] Brooke also points out the contrast between 'the ebullient, self-centred egoist' who narrates the *Historia Calamitatum* and the blundering male evoked by Heloise's letters; hence it is unlikely that Abelard wrote all the letters himself. And finally: 'I find it hard to conceive of any imaginative writer before the great novelists of the nineteenth century who would have attempted such a character as Heloise.'[5]

Much has also been written about Abelard's reasons for the marriage and for its secrecy; the confused state of Church law at that time concerning the marriage of clerics, combined with uncertainty as to Abelard's clerical status when he met Heloise, has led to endless scholarly debate on these issues. The Church's position was on the verge of attaining clarification. In 1123, only a few years after Heloise and Abelard had taken their vows, the First Lateran Council declared that clerics in major orders (that is, priests, deacons and subdeacons) could no longer marry and any unions they were currently in were stripped of legal status. Clerical concubinage was banned by this Council as well. From the early 1120s it was also decreed that both marriage partners would need to take vows simul-

4 Ibid., p.91
5 Ibid., p.102

taneously if either one of them wanted to enter a religious order. Again, as I am here more concerned with Heloise than with Abelard, I will not dwell on his legal position, other than to say it would appear that although, in the year in question (*c.*1118), he was able validly to marry Heloise, the politician and careerist in him could see which way the wind was blowing and decided it would be safer to keep the marriage secret. Yet it might have been considered more normal at the time and far less trouble to keep Heloise as a concubine. He seems to have been motivated principally by the desire to appease Fulbert, while apparently blind to the fact that a secret marriage would not go far enough.

As reported in the *Historia Calamitatum* and in her letters to Abelard, Heloise sets forth various arguments against marriage, some of which are apposite to my considerations about the differing roles of mistress and wife. Her main arguments can be summarised thus: first, that marriage demeans true love, by depriving it of its disinterestedness; secondly, that the joy and freedom of love are lessened by the bonds of marriage; and thirdly, that marriage for a man of Abelard's calibre can only deflect him from his true purpose.

Heloise is anxious to express to Abelard the disinterested nature of her love, and she does this by emphasising her lack of desire for any monetary or practical gain: 'At your bidding I changed my clothing along with my mind, in order to prove you the sole possessor of my body and my will alike. God knows I never sought anything in you except yourself; I wanted simply you, nothing of yours. I looked for no marriage-bond, no marriage portion.'[6] For Heloise her love would be demeaned, sullied, if she had hoped to get something out of it, which she believes is frequently a factor in marriage. She goes on to say: 'And a woman should realize that if she marries a rich man more readily than a poor one, and desires her husband more for his possessions than for himself, she is offering herself for sale.'[7]

6 *The Letters of Abelard and Heloise*, p.113
7 Ibid., p.114

Such opinions show remarkable independence of spirit on the part of a young woman in the early twelfth century. Most of her contemporaries would not even stop to think about the question – what options would most young women have in any case? They had to find some man to marry them or continue to be dependent on male relatives. And once she had securely got her man, a woman would pay for her position by a lifetime of servitude and the production of, preferably male, children. That is what women were for. In such a context marrying a rich man would make more sense than marrying a poor one, because then at least the woman could be comfortable in her bondage. And marriage would be preferable to concubinage, because the woman – entirely dependent on the man – would be less likely to suffer eventual abandonment.

Heloise's concern is not with these practical matters, but only with love itself. She speaks as the forerunner of the tradition of 'courtly love', for her words are echoed some sixty years later by Andreas Capellanus in his treatise *The Art of Courtly Love*:

> Real love comes only from the affection of the heart and is granted out of pure grace and genuine liberality, and this most precious gift of love cannot be paid for at any set price or be cheapened by a matter of money. If a woman is so possessed by a feeling of avarice as to give herself to a lover for the sake of pay, let no one consider her a lover, but rather a counterfeiter of love, who ought to join those shameful women in the brothel . . . For a woman who is really in love . . . does not expect anything from [her lover] except the sweet solaces of the flesh and that her fame may increase among all men because he praises her.[8]

Marriage is no longer, at least in the Western world, so clearly only a matter of property and inheritance rights (though the

8 Andreas Capellanus, *The Art of Courtly Love*, tr. John Jay Parry, Columbia University Press, New York, 1941, pp.144–5

concept of woman as chattel of the male lingers in such conventions as the woman taking the man's name, and in those forms of wedding ceremony in which the woman is still 'given away' by her father to her new owner). But Heloise's words 'I never sought anything in you except yourself' continue to speak in their purity against our contemporary conservative politicians and popular moralists who would encourage couples to marry by 'incentives' like tax breaks. My imaginary Heloise would say 'but if you love someone, you need no incentive to commit yourself to him'. If one marries to gain some material benefit and not only out of love of one's partner, it may be that the truly disinterested position continues to be that of loving without marrying. The conscious and primary motivation behind two people's decision to marry may be – and in our society usually is – that they love one another but, in Heloise's view, love is necessarily contaminated by other, more worldly considerations when it is bound up with marriage. Heloise clearly felt that to remain as mistress, rather than wife, would allow her to love Abelard without asking for any return, and her love would not only be pure but would be seen to be so.

For despite her independence of mind, appearances mattered to Heloise; not in any conventional sense of wishing to appear 'respectable', but in her wanting the world (at least as much of it as was contained in the cathedral close of Notre Dame) to acknowledge the nature of her love for Abelard. She couldn't bear the thought of other people thinking she loved him for the sake of a 'marriage portion', and it is even possible to detect a note of exhibitionism in some of her declarations: 'Yet you . . . are the deeper in my debt because of the love I have always borne you, as everyone knows, a love which is beyond all bounds.'[9] This raises the question as to whether love (or indeed any human action or feeling) can ever be fully disinterested. Heloise may genuinely have wished for no material benefit from loving Abelard; she loves

9 *The Letters of Abelard and Heloise*, p.113

him for himself alone and in that sense her love is disinterested
– yet she clearly derives great satisfaction from her exemplary
love, her self-image including some pride in her ability to love
in this way. The other shadow on the nature of disinterested
love, particularly where there is an imbalance of both power
and love itself, is that 'disinterest' may become confused with
'submission' which in turn, particularly when the submissive
lover has a tendency toward exhibitionism, may slip almost
into masochism: 'I have finally denied myself every pleasure in
obedience to your will, kept nothing for myself except to
prove that now, even more, I am yours.'[10]

The best kind of loving a mistress can offer is disinterested
(with this proviso that no human motive is entirely pure), not
only in the sense that this love is separate from marriage, but
also that, provided the mistress is secure in herself and values
her independence, she can love without tying the lover to
vows of eternal fidelity. The love is unconditional, and he can
be free to come and go as he pleases. This is of course an ideal;
the mistress, like Heloise, will at times – possibly most of the
time – fail to be her best self, and make emotional demands.
And there is a very fine tightrope to be walked between freely
offering love and allowing oneself to be used, between the
disinterest which comes from strength and independence, and
the refusal to ask for anything which comes from lack of self-
worth and the belief that one does not 'deserve' a whole
relationship. But disinterested love still seems to me an ideal
worth striving for.

Heloise's sense of marriage being opposed to the freedom
of love is made clear, according to Abelard, in her declaration
that 'it would be dearer to her and more honourable to me to
be called my lover than my wife so that her charm alone
would keep me for her, not the force of a nuptial bond; she
also stated that the joys of our meeting after separation would
be the more delightful as they were rare.'[11]

10 Ibid., p.117
11 Peter Abelard, *Historia Calamitatum*, tr. J.T. Muckle, Pontifical Institute of
   Medieval Studies, Toronto, 1964, p.37

To take the first part of this declaration: Heloise, like all mistress-types, revels in the knowledge that she is loved, and realises that marriage – because of the 'force' of its 'bond' – threatens to deprive her of that knowledge. For the mistress assumes that when her lover is with her, he's there because he wants to be; whereas the wife – at least this is how the mistress imagines it – knows her husband has little choice but to be with her. He may still love her, or he may not; but in any event he's there because he's married to her. This won't do for the mistress; she wants to know 'her charm alone' is still working its effect. To her, the very illicit nature of the relationship can be seen as proof of love; he must adore her, because otherwise he wouldn't take such risks. She may be deluding herself – perhaps he's as addicted to risk-taking as she is to seduction – but she can tell herself he is exercising complete freedom of choice in being with her. The greater the obstacles, the more his love is proved.

Then there is the question of sex itself. Things may have changed legally now that it's possible for a man to be convicted of raping his wife, but the element of free will still seems to the mistress to be much reduced in marriage and the threat of boredom much increased. How many spouses give in to the other in order to 'get it over with'? How can any spouse be sure his/her partner really wants sex at a particular time? There is likely to be far less doubt in the case of voluntary lovers.

Again, these sentiments are expressed by the adherents of courtly love: 'We declare and hold as firmly established that love cannot exert its powers between two people who are married to each other. For lovers give each other everything freely, under no compulsion of necessity, but married people are in duty bound to give in to each other's desires and deny themselves to each other in nothing.'[12]

Next, to take Heloise's statement that 'the joys of our meeting after separation would be the more delightful as they

12 Andreas Capellanus, *The Art of Courtly Love*, pp.106–7

were rare': it's far more *exciting* to be the mistress than the wife, another aspect of the 'affair' understood by the courtly lovers. 'Now in the first place [love] is said to increase if the lovers see each other rarely and with difficulty; for the greater the difficulty of exchanging solaces, the more do the desire for them and the feeling of love increase.'[13] There is far less chance of a relationship going stale when meetings are separated by gaps, or at least it will take much longer to reach that point. This is the positive side of Simone de Beauvoir's comment, 'The woman in love is one who waits':[14] the waiting attains its fulfilment, the lows are made up for by the highs.

When we consider Heloise's view of marriage as antithetical to 'higher' concerns, we fall into the murky waters of misogyny − not that we are ever far from their shores. 'For Heloise there was nothing honourable about marriage. She set before Abelard a long list of authorities − Paul, Jerome and Augustine figuring importantly − to show why marriage was an unworthy state for a great man.'[15] The arguments of these 'authorities' have been largely ignored in the recent past, until it's become possible for priests and politicians to assert that Christianity is 'the religion of marriage and the family'. Since when? Certainly not at its outset or during the centuries when it had most influence on the development of human behaviour. In the *Historia Calamitatum* Abelard sets out Heloise's arguments against marriage for a philosopher and scholar of his calibre, from which it is clear that she was drawing particularly on Jerome's *Adversus Iovinianum*, a piece of writing which Christopher Brooke describes as 'the basic medieval textbook for antifeminism'.[16] There are several strands to her argument. First, Heloise feels guilty at the thought of depriving the Church and Philosophy of Abelard's undivided services. If he does not marry, he belongs to the whole world as a

---

13 Ibid., p.153
14 Simone de Beauvoir, *The Second Sex*, Picador, London, 1988, p.671
15 Karen Armstrong, *The Gospel According to Woman*, p.268
16 Christopher N.L. Brooke, *The Medieval Idea of Marriage*, p.62

philosopher and to the whole Church as a theologian. If he marries, he must belong to his wife alone. Such servitude to a woman would prove a disgrace to him. Secondly, Heloise is pervaded with horror at the thought of Abelard's 'high', masculine, calling being dragged down into the 'low', feminine, world of domesticity: 'Who is there who is bent on sacred or philosophical reflection who could bear the wailing of babies, the silly lullabies of nurses to quiet them, the noisy horde of servants, both male and female; who could endure the constant degrading defilement of infants?'[17] Or, to remove for a moment the question of gender, we have here the split between the domains of Mary and Martha as described in the Gospels, the latter absorbed in household chores while the former chooses the 'good part' of listening to the words of Jesus. Clearly Abelard should be on the side of Mary; but would Heloise the scholar really have seen herself in the Martha role? Perhaps her vehemence here is motivated as much by a horror of being trapped in domesticity herself as of seeing Abelard so trapped. And thirdly, there is an awareness of the irrevocability of marriage. Though throughout her letters, Heloise maintains her own inability to repent of the physical expression of her love for Abelard, she nevertheless views their affair as technically sinful and as deflecting Abelard from his true purpose. While they remain unmarried, however, there is always the possibility of repentance, and that Abelard will eventually return to the dedicated life of philosopher and cleric. But marriage, rather than cancelling out the sin, would set a seal on it, making it permanent. And it would forever bar Abelard from advancement in the Church. 'If a man was so craven and weak-willed that he yielded to sexual desire, then as Jerome suggested to one correspondent, he might do better to keep his sweetheart as a concubine rather than marry her. After all, he declared ironically, your union with a wife may prevent you from receiving holy orders when you finally come to your senses, whereas a dalliance with a concubine will

17 Peter Abelard, *Historia Calamitatum*, p.33

not.'[18] Perhaps Heloise suspected that one day Abelard would indeed 'come to his senses'. Here was one area in which Heloise was unable to free herself from the prevailing conventional wisdom: that women are the ruin of men.

It is a measure of the disinterestedness of Heloise's love that the object of her affections did not, at least to modern eyes, remotely deserve it. One can't resist the conclusion that Abelard cared far more for himself than for Heloise. In his report of his first reactions to his castration, the one person he never mentions is his wife. He seems to lack any imaginative ability, at any point in the story, to put himself in his lover's place. Here he describes his thoughts prior to the marriage, and his sense of responsibility towards Fulbert:

> After a while I began to sympathise with him in his extreme anxiety and blamed myself for the deceit which love had wrought which was, as it were, a base betrayal . . . I told him that whoever had felt the force of love or recalled to what a crash women from the beginning have brought even the greatest men would not be surprised at my fall. And further to appease him, I made an offer beyond his fondest hopes to make satisfaction by marrying her whom I had defiled, provided this be done secretly so that my reputation would not be damaged.[19]

Abelard and Fulbert are in a male world at this point which bears no relation to and takes no account of Heloise's feelings or interpretation of events. She is seen here as Fulbert's property, 'defiled' by Abelard; Heloise would never use such a word of their physical love. One feels insulted on her behalf by such an account. But Abelard is acting, speaking and thinking entirely within the conventions of his society. (And he's so arrogant – 'beyond his fondest hopes' indeed.)

In her letters Heloise reproaches Abelard for his neglect of

---

18 James A. Brundage, *Law, Sex, and Christian Society in Medieval Europe*, University of Chicago Press, Chicago & London, 1988, p.101
19 Peter Abelard, *Historia Calamitatum*, p.31

her; she must have been so lonely on first entering the convent, according to Abelard's instruction, and then hearing nothing from him. 'It was not any sense of vocation which brought me as a young girl to accept the austerities of the cloister, but your bidding alone, and if I deserve no gratitude from you, you may judge for yourself how my labours are in vain. I can expect no reward for this from God, for it is certain that I have done nothing as yet for love of him.'[20] Here is the kernel of Heloise's confession – her vows are not to God, but to Abelard. Had Abelard been possessed of imagination and empathy, he might have known this at the time of her profession, but he was thinking primarily of himself. The truly loving act on his part would have been to offer her freedom – which she would not have taken. By imposing his will on her, he took away her opportunity to prove to him the extent of her love. This has always been the mistake of the possessive lover. Abelard made the further mistake of insisting Heloise take her vows before he took his, an insult from which she never recovered: 'Your lack of trust in me over this one thing, I confess, overwhelmed me with grief and shame. I would have had no hesitation, God knows, in following you or going ahead at your bidding to the flames of Hell. My heart was not in me but with you, and now, even more, if it is not with you it is nowhere; truly, without you it cannot exist.'[21] Abelard's lack of trust revealed his misunderstanding of the nature of Heloise's love for him; he was judging her by his own standards, as she sees all too clearly.

Even in Abelard's second letter of reply to Heloise, he still seems more concerned with Fulbert than with her: 'Need I recall our previous fornication and the wanton impurities which preceded our marriage, or my supreme act of betrayal, when I deceived your uncle about you so disgracefully, at a time when I was continuously living with him in his own house? Who would not judge me justly betrayed by the man whom I had first shamelessly betrayed?'[22] Again, this is a man's

20 *The Letters of Abelard and Heloise*, pp.116–7
21 Ibid., p.117
22 Ibid., p.146

world, to which women are only incidental. When Abelard
goes on to talk about their joint entering upon the enclosed
life, he reveals how little he *still* understands Heloise and her
love for him: 'Had you not been previously joined to me in
wedlock, you might easily have clung to the world when I
withdrew from it, either at the suggestion of your relatives or
in enjoyment of carnal delights.'[23] Heloise must have wondered at this point whether she had been wasting all her
words. How could he be so insulting, so extraordinarily
dense? Haven't her previous letters made it clear? He still
judges her by his own standards, and shows himself one of the
most unimaginative lovers in history. As if 'wedlock' could
have any effect on Heloise's total love. She's already told him
she would follow him to Hell. One feels at this point she must
have given up trying to make him see – what more could she
possibly say or do? – hence the letters now take up the themes
of monastic life and rule.

'[Heloise] was leading a double life. She was pretending to
be at the same time the passionate lover of yore and the abbess
of a Benedictine convent.'[24] Actually she *was* both these
things – not *pretending* at all. Was her every action as an
abbess vitiated by the fact that mentally and spiritually she was
still Abelard's lover? Does this negate, or contaminate, all she
did to help others, especially the example she must have set to
her sisters? I don't think so – but I may be wrong.

By Abelard's own testimony Heloise was very successful in
her so-called double life: 'And the more rarely she presented
herself to the public, that she might without distraction within
her cloister give herself to prayer and meditation on holy
things, the more eagerly the world outside demanded her
presence and the advice of her spiritual conversation.'[25] Or is
he fooling himself in order to make himself feel better? But
there are other, more reliable, accounts of Heloise's excel-
lence as an abbess. A few months after Abelard's death in

23 Ibid., p.149
24 Etienne Gilson, *Héloise and Abélard*, Hollis & Carter, London, 1953, p.76
25 Peter Abelard, *Historia Calamitatum*, p.69

1142, Peter the Venerable, abbot of Cluny, wrote a long and friendly letter to Heloise; in this letter he evinces more understanding of the nature of Heloise's love for Abelard than the latter ever displayed. It also stands as evidence of Heloise's excellent reputation: 'Him, therefore, venerable and dearest sister in the Lord, him to whom after your union in the flesh you are joined by the better, and therefore stronger, bond of divine love, with whom and under whom you have long served God: him, I say, in your place, or as another you, God cherishes in his bosom, and keeps him there to be restored to you through his grace at the coming of the Lord.'[26]

Heloise herself addresses the question of hypocrisy on more than one occasion: 'Men call me chaste; they do not know the hypocrite I am. They consider purity of the flesh a virtue, though virtue belongs not to the body but to the soul . . . I am judged religious at a time when there is little in religion which is not hypocrisy, when whoever does not offend the opinions of men receives the highest praise.'[27] Heloise examines herself ruthlessly and continues: 'It was your command, not love of God which made me take the veil . . . For a long time my pretence deceived you, as it did many, so that you mistook hypocrisy for piety; and therefore you commend yourself to my prayers and ask me for what I expect from you.'[28] From this it could be inferred that Heloise's 'hypocrisy', like every-thing else in her life, was an act of love towards Abelard, not letting him see the extent of her suffering, as there was little enough he could do to relieve it. Heloise in her letters reproaches him for not even having done that little.

Here she is at her most clear-sighted and uncompromising: 'How can it be called repentance for sins, however great the mortification of the flesh, if the mind still retains the will to sin and is on fire with its old desires?'[29] Heloise is no hypocrite, because she never pretends to herself, or to God. She is brave,

26 *The Letters of Abelard and Heloise*, pp.283–4
27 Ibid., pp.133–4
28 Ibid., p.134
29 Ibid., p.132

and proud, and makes the best of a bad job, whatever the underlying anguish.

Though Heloise's views on the respective natures and appropriate spheres of men and women place her firmly in a medieval world, her understanding of love and the questions she poses about the institution of marriage make her a figure of timeless, universal appeal. She makes a good model for a mistress to follow, from her rejoicing in a love unfettered by official contract, to knowing how to love for the lover's sake and without hope of reward. And another thing she knows, which the mistress does well to learn, is how to wear the mask of propriety for the sake both of her lover and of other people – in her case, her sisters and those who came to her for counsel – who might not be able to cope with the idea of lawless loving, who do not share the freedom of her soul.

HERA, WHO HATED MISTRESSES

'If I'm not wrong,' she thought,
'I'm being wronged.'[1]

To begin with, the girl enjoyed the carefree nature of her loving and the excitement of short but intense sexual encounters. She knew her lover was married and after a few weeks she realised he was a god and his wife the queen of the gods. This made her very proud; she relished the consciousness that the husband of such a woman – or, rather, goddess – wanted *her*, confided in her, loved her. She almost wanted Hera to know about the affair, to add to her – Semele's – triumph, but the more sensible part of her realised this was only fantasy, that if Hera were to find out, she – Semele – would be afraid and would hide if she saw Hera in the distance. It was well known that Hera had no toleration for her husband's peccadilloes, though she ought to be used to them by now. Semele, of course, considered herself different from all of Zeus's former conquests; he loved her in a way he hadn't loved them; she imagined she fulfilled him in every way and always would. She tried not to let herself think of the possibility of his leaving Hera for her, but every so often a vision of herself in queenly robes ordering all the other gods about would slip into her mind. After all, it wasn't as if Zeus's and Hera's children couldn't look after themselves. There'd be a bit of a scandal, of course, but the press office on Mount Olympus should be able to handle it tactfully. Zeus had never mentioned leaving Hera, it had to be admitted, though he had said they didn't sleep together any more. But in the early days of their affair, Semele felt no serious need to explore Zeus's

1 Ovid, *Metamorphoses*, tr. A.D. Melville, OUP, Oxford & New York, 1986, p.19

marital relations further. She enjoyed the way he would just turn up; she would drop what she was doing and they would make love. He usually arrived during the afternoon, in casual dress. Occasionally Semele wondered whether she would ever see him in a business suit or dressed to go out to a formal dinner. She imagined he would look wonderful in white tie and tails. But she loved him in his linen jacket and stone-coloured trousers too; she even loved him in his boxer shorts, and loved him best of all stark naked. She sometimes wished she could phone him, and the afternoons when he didn't turn up could be very tedious, but she considered the pros greatly outweighed the cons and most of the time just got on with enjoying loving and being loved by the greatest god of all. Until, that is, the inevitable happened.

Meanwhile Hera had noted all the tell-tale signs that her husband was indulging in another of his intrigues. He seemed more than usually cheerful and full of energy, but occasionally absent-minded, and he wasn't showing much interest in her sexually. He was being outwardly discreet; there were no strange phone calls and he wasn't neglecting his social or godly duties; if anything, he was being particularly polite and attentive to his wife at official gatherings. They looked the perfect married couple, she standing supportively at his side and smiling approval in the photographs (it took a goddess to cope with being photographed beside him), he helping her out of the celestial chariot and giving her his arm as they proceeded along the Milky Way, rolled out for them on state occasions. But she had noticed he'd developed a habit of changing into casual clothes after lunch and 'going for a walk' – even when it was raining. She'd offered to go with him once, but he'd said, 'Oh no, dear, I walk too fast for you. Anyway I like to think when I'm walking – it's when I make my decisions, so I need to be alone.' Then one day she noticed an unfamiliar scent when he returned from his 'walk'; another time she saw a stain on his stone-coloured trousers. She considered sending them to the lab for DNA testing but decided that wasn't really her style. Instead she disguised

herself as an old crone and followed her husband on one of his
'walks'. He did indeed walk, for about five minutes, and
straight to a cottage in the local village. He let himself in with
his own key. Two minutes later the curtains were drawn.

Hera wandered up to a threesome of old crones, sitting on a
bench on the village green. They shuffled up and made room
for her. She waited, knowing the habits of old crones on
village benches.

'I see Semele's at it again,' said First Crone.

'Disgustin', I call it,' said Second Crone. 'In broad daylight
too!'

'They have drawn the curtains,' said Third Crone.

'It's more than they did last week,' cackled Second Crone.
'Kissin', they were, and doin' somethin' with a cigar. My
niece was with me and I said to her, I said, if I ever see you
doin' that with a man who's not your husband, you'll have me
to answer to, I said. And don't blame me if you get in the
family way, I said, you'll be no niece of mine if you carry on
with a married man and get pregnant, I said.'

At this, Hera gave a start.

'You all right, dear?' asked First Crone.

'Is Semele pregnant then?' Hera asked, taking care to sound
nosy but not too concerned.

'Ooh, haven't you heard?' said Third Crone gleefully. 'My
friend, Mrs Argus – you know, the one whose husband's got a
hundred eyes – ooh, he does give her a hard time, he keeps
losing his contact lenses and poor Mrs Argus has to spend
hours and hours on her hands and knees looking for them and
then when she finds one he can't remember which eye it goes
in – well . . . where was I? What was I telling you about Mrs
Argus for?'

'Semele?' said Hera, faintly.

'Oh yes, silly me. Well, Mrs Argus lives next door to
Semele – ooh, and she does hear terrible goings-on . . .'

'Yes, bangin' and creakin' every afternoon – disgustin', I
call it,' said Second Crone.

'Yes, but now, *now* . . . she said to me, she said, *now* she's heard Semele being sick! In the morning,' brought out Third Crone, portentously, with triumph.

'Disgustin', that's what I call it,' said Second Crone.

Hera stood up. 'You off, dear?' said First Crone. 'Don't you fancy a nice cuppa tea? We always go to Mrs Argus for tea in the afternoons.'

Back home, Hera considered her options. One: ignore the whole thing and wait for Zeus to get over it. Semele could just be having fun, idling away her afternoons for want of any-thing better to do. She was no real threat. Zeus would never jeopardise his official position for the sake of a young village girl. The marriage was intact and would stay so. But no – not if Semele was pregnant. That changed everything. If Zeus had a son by Semele, the mother would bask in reflected glory, he would never abandon his son so he would end up having a permanent liaison, Semele would make demands, Hera's position be undermined and, when the son became a man – or, rather, half-god/half-man – who knows what power he might wield? So option one, the way of deliberate blindness, had to be rejected. Option two: confront Zeus. Charge him with his infidelity, threaten to leave him if he didn't give up his latest mistress. This option presented various problems. First, Hera knew from experience that Zeus didn't react well to her anger. Instead of contrition, as in the early days of their marriage she had naïvely expected, her fury spurred him to greater fury; he could even assuage his guilt with violence. She would never forget the day he had strung her up in the sky, hanging her from the stars and pinning down her feet with anvils. The humiliation, being strung up there for all the world to gawp at, had been even worse than the pain. It made her think twice about threatening him. Then there was the awful possibility that he might accede to her demand – but to the wrong one. What if he were to say, 'Fine – leave me then. Semele can be queen instead.'? If he thought Semele was about to bear his son, it was just possible he might say that. What would Hera do then? She had absolutely no intention of relinquishing her position as Zeus's consort, whatever he might get up to. No, this situation would have to be managed some other way. Her target would have to be Semele, not Zeus. Somehow Semele had to be prevented from bearing Zeus a child.

First, Hera wondered if she might poison Semele and induce a miscarriage. It would be easy enough to get the girl to drink something disguised as a herbal remedy for morning sickness. But Zeus would be the first to suspect foul play if Semele aborted – and he would know exactly whom to blame. Being strung up in the sky would be the mildest punishment he'd inflict on his jealous wife if she dared harm Semele or the unborn child in any obvious way. Perhaps she could frighten Semele into going away, just disappearing. She could give her a catalogue of all Zeus's former lovers and the dreadful ends they met once the liaisons were public knowledge, which this one was bound to be now a child was in the offing. But then Semele might, in her distress, talk to Zeus, and again he'd recognise the informant, no matter how clever her disguise. Perhaps she could convince Semele Zeus was even now unfaithful to her, that she might be his love in the afternoon but that he could pack plenty more loves into the remaining twenty-one hours of every day. But still there was no guarantee Semele wouldn't blab, and cutting out her tongue or otherwise rendering her speechless would again be a too obvious Hera-trick. Maybe she could borrow Aphrodite's girdle and seduce Zeus herself and get pregnant by him too, but he was as suspicious these days of her displays of affection as of her anger and hatred. He would be bound to suspect an ulterior motive. And even such a desperate measure wouldn't guarantee he'd give up Semele. No, the problem had to be solved in such a way that it would seem as though there had been no outside interference. The relationship would have to be blown apart by the participants themselves. Hera would have to identify the weak spot of either Semele or Zeus (and preferably of Semele, as the weak spots of mortals can prove fatal whereas those of the immortals, by definition, cannot). Then Semele must be made to bring about her own destruction.

Hera betrayed nothing when Zeus came home that evening. She asked him about his day as usual, said hers had been nothing special; she was neither overly attentive nor remote, and kissed him goodnight as usual. Zeus began to snore almost as soon as his head hit the pillow. Hera lay awake for hours, and by morning she had made her plan.

As soon as Zeus had left for work (he had an important meeting that morning on Mount Olympus), Hera donned her old crone's guise and set off for the village. She went straight to Semele's cottage and knocked. Her first sight of the girl's fresh beauty and blooming glow of pregnancy almost made her drop her guard – she involuntarily raised her fist to punch Semele on the nose, knock her teeth out and give her a black eye – but remembered herself in time, and forced her hand to unclench and pat the girl on the shoulder instead.

'Semele, isn't it?' she croaked. 'I'd heard about your trouble and thought you might like some advice. I've seen it all in my time.'

'Oh, I'm not in trouble, auntie,' said Semele with innocent happiness. 'On the contrary. I'm in love, and I'm going to have my lover's child. He supports me all the way.'

'That's good,' hissed Hera through gritted teeth. 'Most men run away as soon as they make a woman pregnant – especially if they've got a wife back home.'

'Oh, my lover's not like other men. He's quite godlike, to tell the truth.'

'He is married though, isn't he?' said Hera, trying to sound offhand. 'At least that's what I'd heard.'

'Oh, he's married for the time being. But his wife's not really important to him, she's just a habit, really, like the furniture,' said Semele airily. 'He doesn't love her any more . . . I don't think he ever did really.'

There was a pause, Hera leaning rather shakily on her old crone's stick.

'Oh, how rude I'm being, auntie,' exclaimed Semele. 'Here I am talking away about my darling Zeus, while you're standing there looking exhausted. I think *you're* the one who needs looking after. Do come in and have a coffee. I'm on decaff because of the baby, but I can make you some specially – or there's herb tea if you prefer.'

'Thank you, dear,' Hera managed to enunciate. 'I'd like to see inside your little cottage.'

While Semele went off into the kitchen to make the coffee, Hera took in the details of the living room. She noticed various ornaments, replicas of ones in her own house – Zeus must have been buying two of everything on his business trips. And there were a few framed photographs, including one of Semele with another girl (Hera later discovered this was Ino, Semele's sister), but none of Zeus.

When Semele came back into the room with her tray of coffee and biscuits (Hera recognised the cups and plates as other presents from Zeus), Hera asked her, 'Have you got any pictures of your Zeus, then? I've heard he's very handsome.'

'Oh, he is,' agreed Semele enthusiastically. 'But he doesn't like being photographed. Something about the flash not working properly when it's pointed at him. I don't quite know what he means – I think he's just afraid a photograph won't do him justice.'

'Sounds a bit odd to me,' said Hera. 'A bit fishy, I'd say. And has he ever written to you?'

'No,' said Semele, a shadow of doubt crossing her face. 'Why should he? I see him nearly every day.'

'Hm,' said Hera.

'What?' said Semele. 'What are you saying "hm" for?'

'Oh, come on, Semele,' said Hera. 'You think it's odd too. He won't write to you and he won't be photographed. Have you got anything that proves he's actually been here?'

'A baby,' said Semele. 'Nearly a baby, anyway.'

'Could be anyone's,' said Hera.

'What do you mean? It's his! He knows it's his . . . How could you?'

'Of course *he* knows it's his,' said Hera, patiently. 'The point is, dear, you can't prove it to anyone else. You can't even prove your mythical lover's been here, can you? He's been very careful to leave no evidence.'

'But all these things he's given me . . .' Semele gestured bewilderedly at the ornaments and brandished a hat pin.

'*You* know who gave them to you. *I* might believe he did. But you can't prove it. Have you got the receipts?'

'No, of course not, they were presents.'

'Well, did he pay by cheque or cash, I wonder? I bet he had more sense than to use his credit card.'

'Well, if he paid by cash, he's only being discreet,' protested Semele. 'His security people are very particular. Or his wife might go through his pockets.'

Hera did her best not to look indignant. 'Well, well, maybe I'm wrong. Maybe this time my old crone's wisdom's misleading me. Never been wrong before, mind. Still there's always a first time. I could be wrong about your Zeus. Doubt it, but I could be . . .'

'Oh, do stop it, auntie. Look . . . tell me exactly what you suspect and then I'll put you right,' said Semele, trying to sound firm and calm.

'Well, if you put it like that, if you absolutely insist, what I think is —'

'Yes? Do get on with it, auntie.'

'What I think is he's intending to run out on you any day now, he enjoyed having a fling but he doesn't like the thought of being tied to you and a baby and he doesn't want his wife, or the rest of the immortals, to find out, so he's been very careful to leave no trace of himself here, nothing that could be used as evidence to connect the pair of you. Any day now he'll hand over an envelope of cash, tell you to look after yourself and the baby, and that'll be the last you see of him.'

Semele had gone pale. 'No, auntie, you've got it all wrong. Zeus loves me. He's going to stay with me and the baby. He'll probably leave his wife once he's got things sorted out.'

Hera spluttered on her mouthful of coffee. Then she looked Semele straight in the eye. 'Prove it. Prove he loves you.'

Something in Hera's expression silenced Semele's further protests. 'How?' she asked.

'Insist you get a photo taken, you and him together. To put on your mantelpiece. You in your best frock, and him in his best suit.'

'I've never seen him in a suit,' said Semele wistfully.

'Hah! There you are, then!'

'Where? Where am I?' asked Semele.

'He keeps you separate from his real life, doesn't he? You're just a plaything for his afternoons off. It's his wife he takes to official functions, his wife he goes to the opera with, his wife —'

'All right, all right,' said Semele, in tears now. 'There's no need to rub it in. But the real Zeus is the one I see.'

'Is that so? That's the trouble with these philanderers, dear. You don't know what's real and what isn't. They'll say anything to keep a pretty mistress happy. But they never leave the wife. Oh no.'

'Zeus will,' sobbed Semele.

'If you show me a photograph of the pair of you next time I come, then I'll believe you. I'm off now, Semele. Cheer up, you'll find someone else to marry you, you're pretty enough . . . even with a squealing brat in tow.'

After Hera had gone, Semele lay on the bed and wept. She tossed to and fro, and so did her thoughts. One moment she was convinced the old crone (who was she anyway?) was wrong; she remembered all Zeus's tenderness towards her and his joy when she told him she thought she was pregnant. The next she found herself wondering why he was so averse to having his photograph taken with her and why he had never written to her, not so much as an e-mail. She admitted to herself that these were very trivial things to worry about, but something else the old crone had said had lodged in her mind and disturbed her more – it was that business about 'only being Zeus's plaything' and 'it's his wife he takes to official functions' and her own admission she'd never seen him in a suit, let alone a dinner jacket. Then the thought of being seen in public with her lover, of being acknowledged as his partner – even if initially only by a few waiters in a restaurant – began to get a hold on her, as did the thought of getting dressed up to go out with him. Surely he wouldn't deny her such a treat, especially if he noticed she'd been crying. Then it would be easy enough to find a way to fulfil the old crone's wish for a photograph, to shut her up. She's probably just jealous, thought Semele – or else she wants the photo to drool over herself.

Semele went into the bathroom and splashed her eyes with cold water. She was too vain to let Zeus see her looking a total mess, but she made sure there were still some traces of her tears – just enough to make her look beautifully fragile and irresistible. She had just finished drying her face when she heard Zeus's key turn in the lock.

'Hello, Semele, love. Are you all right, my sweet? You haven't been crying, have you?'

'Oh, just a little, sweetheart. I expect it's my condition. They say being pregnant can make you a bit emotional.'

'Oh, poor little Semele,' said Zeus. 'You shouldn't get upset. What can I do to cheer you up?'

'Let me unzip you,' said Semele, kneeling down before him . . .

'Better now, sweet?' said Zeus.

'Much,' said Semele. 'But —'

'Yes? But what?'

'I still feel a bit depressed.'

'Come now, Semele, you must cheer up. Is there a present you'd like? A new dress, or something? Are you worried your clothes are getting too tight for you? Is that it?'

'There is something I'd like, Handsome.'

'What's that, then? Tell me, little one.'

'Promise you'll give it me.'

'I can't promise till I know what it is, now, can I?'

'Yes, you can. Please promise, Zeus. Please.'

'Semele, I can't. I have to keep my promises. You don't understand . . .'

'Oh yes I do. You don't love me any more. That's why you won't promise.' And Semele burst into tears again.

Zeus was torn between concern and exasperation. I suppose she can't want anything too impossible, he thought. I expect it is a dress or something, probably a very expensive one. Aloud he said, 'Semele, don't be silly, of course I love you.'

'Then promise,' sobbed Semele.

'All right, all right, I promise, whatever you want, you can have it.' At this there was a clap of thunder. 'Oh heavens!' thought Zeus. 'Now what have I done?'

Semele was startled by the thunder on a perfectly mild and sunny afternoon, but she didn't let it spoil her victory.

'Take me out to dinner, Zeus. That's what I want. On Saturday night, to an expensive restaurant, where you have to wear a suit. You must, Zeus – you promised.'

Semele couldn't understand the sadness in Zeus's eyes as he said, 'Very well, Semele, if that's what you want. I did, as you say, promise. But for the gods' sake, be discreet. Don't let anybody know, we mustn't be seen by anyone with a camera.'

Semele pouted. 'Why not, Zeus? Are you ashamed to be seen with me?'

'No, of course not, Semele. But I've told you before . . . the flash does funny things to me. It's very important you do what I say. Let me choose the restaurant, and don't tell anyone where we're going.'

'All right, Zeus, I'll be good. Oh, I'm so looking forward to going out with you. Whatever shall I wear?' So next she persuaded Zeus to buy her a new dress as well as take her out to dinner.

On Saturday evening Zeus arrived to collect Semele in a small chariot which he drove himself. She was disappointed he hadn't brought a larger chauffeur-driven carriage, but was consoled by his resplendent appearance. He looked better in his evening suit than any man she'd ever seen – he seemed to glow, almost to sparkle. She felt the strangest sensation of pins and needles all up and down her body when he put his arm round her. They set off. He seemed rather nervous and almost spoilt the mood by saying, 'Now, Semele, you haven't told anyone where we're going, have you?'

'How could I, Handsome?' she said. 'I don't know where we're going.'

After about half an hour they arrived outside a lantern-lit building beside a lake. Zeus helped Semele out of the chariot and a bow-tied manager stepped forward to greet them. 'Good evening, madam, sir. Everything is ready for you, the private room as requested.' The couple were led through the dimly lit restaurant and into a cosy and comfortable room at the back, furnished with one table, candles and two large chairs, and where champagne already awaited them. Semele allowed Zeus to toast her and then announced that she had to find the restroom immediately. Zeus looked rather annoyed but could hardly object and, before he had time to call a waiter to ask him the way (there was a bell-pull to summon service), Semele had left the room. She could see the sign to the restroom immediately in front of her, but headed instead for the front desk to ask where it was and, while there, she picked up a card giving all the restaurant's details – for it was somewhere she had never previously known existed. Once ensconced in the restroom, she took her mobile phone out of her handbag and pressed a few buttons.

'Hello? Is that Eroticograms? This is Semele. I spoke to you earlier. Yes, that's right. The restaurant is the Slopes of Parnassus, by the Lake of the Muses. Do you know it? Oh, good. We're in a private room at the back, so you'll just have to burst through, never mind the manager – yes, I'm sure you're used to that – then as soon as you're through the door, take a photograph of me and my lover. He may look a bit cross at first, but don't worry about that, I'll sort him out. OK. So I'll see you in about an hour.'

Back in the private room, Zeus and Semele ate and drank and gazed into one another's eyes. Zeus had begun to relax after his second glass of champagne and was becoming dreamily romantic. He stroked Semele's arm as it lay on the table, and she wondered whether now was the right time to ask if he would leave his wife once the child was born. 'Zeus, darling,' she began, then there was a scuffling outside, raised voices and the door burst open. Semele just had time to notice the horror on Zeus's face as a large rosy-cheeked boy, naked except for a posing pouch and a quiverful of arrows, pointed a camera lens at them, before the flash went off. The light that shimmered and burst around Zeus blinded her; the electric shock she received as he crackled killed her instantly.

Hera was already in bed before Zeus got home. She heard the chariot pull up, and Zeus letting himself in; then she heard him stumbling around the kitchen and groaning. Satisfied, she turned over and fell fast asleep.

Semele's sister Ino was no great favourite with Hera either. For after Semele's sudden death her body was rushed to hospital and the foetus cut out alive. He was put in an incubator, survived, and was subsequently brought up by Ino, with some financial assistance from Zeus. So Hera's plan to rid herself of all future threat to her position had not proved entirely successful.

Maybe some things run in families because Ino got involved with a married man as well. His name was Athamas and his excuse was that his wife neglected him or 'held him in disdain'. She was never much of a wife, he claimed, more like a shadow of a woman than a real one. The wife's name was Nephele and she was in fact a phantom, having been created by Zeus in the image of someone else during one of his elaborate war-games with Hera. The latter regarded Nephele as something of a protégée, so it was naturally to the queen of the gods that Nephele turned to complain when she found out about Ino. Hera tried telling Ino's neighbours not to speak to her, to send her to Coventry or whatever the Olympian equivalent is, but the neighbours all preferred Ino to Nephele, because Ino took the time to be nice to them and listen to their concerns whereas Nephele went by with her nose in the air – so they ignored Hera's instructions and if anything talked to Ino all the more.

But Ino's problem was that she wasn't content just to be the mistress, not even a publicly acknowledged mistress with no necessity for concealment. She wanted Nephele out of the way; she wanted to be the wife herself. And so she started plotting, using the neighbours' affection for her to get them to spoil the harvest; then she bribed the messengers, sent by Athamas to the Delphic oracle to find out why the harvest had failed, to bring back a false message. And the message she instructed them to tell was a terrible one – that the harvest would only be fruitful if Nephele's son were sacrificed. Well, to cut a long story short, the plan didn't work out quite as she intended. She never succeeded in getting rid of Nephele, and in the end Hera drove Athamas mad (a frequent condition of the man torn between two angry and scheming women) until he turned against Ino herself and the children she had borne him. She had to run away from the palace with her son Melicertes; they fell off a cliff and were drowned. The mistress should think more than twice before taking on the wife.

Yet another girl who fell foul of Hera was Io, not to be confused with Ino. Now poor Io, like many other girls, was seduced by Zeus. There is no evidence she encouraged his advances but, once the king of the gods has decided he's going to copulate with you, there's not a great deal you can do to prevent it. Better just to lie still and let him get on with it. Maybe after a few times Io began to enjoy it, despite herself – Zeus was, after all, a very experienced lover – but it certainly wasn't her idea in the first place and she had no intention of ousting Hera. She was Zeus's 'bit on the side' and she knew it.

But for Hera jealousy had become rather a habit. So had her tendency to think all young girls should be married or invisible, tied to the kitchen by either husband or father. She spent several hours a week lecturing on the importance of marriage and the maintenance of 'family values', insisting that a woman's true fulfilment was to be found in the home. She proved such a popular speaker that she spent less and less time at home herself which suited her very well. Some days she hardly saw Zeus at all, which also suited her. But if he got home later than he said he would, or if he went out in the evening unexpectedly, forgetting to load the dishwasher before he left, there was hell to pay. And when some well-meaning 'friend' began to drop hints about Io, Hera decided she had better take steps immediately. No pussy-footing around this time, no pretending to be a crone. She was a powerful woman in her own right – she practised affirmations in front of the mirror every morning – and Io was a little hussy who deserved to be taught a lesson. So the next time she suspected Zeus of having an assignation, she followed him.

As Zeus looked up from kissing Io and saw his angry wife storming towards him, he did what every man would do in the circumstances – he turned his mistress into a cow.

'What a pretty cow!' said Hera, ominously.

'Yes, isn't it?' Zeus replied, with a nervous smile. 'I just bumped into her, never seen her in my life before, she just, sort of, attached herself to me. Nothing I could do about it. Neurotic sort of cow, really.'

Io bellowed reproachfully.

'In that case,' said Hera, 'you won't mind giving her to me, will you? I've always wanted a cow of my own, to do what I like with.'

Oh dear. What could Zeus do? If he protested he wanted to keep the cow himself, it would look very suspicious. But it seemed cruel just to hand Io over to Hera. He handed her over.

'Come on, you cow, you bitch, you trollop,' said Hera cheerfully. 'That'll teach you to make cow-eyes at other people's husbands.' She picked up a twig and smacked Io on the rump as she ambled along in front of her. Thus in high spirits Hera drove Io along to the village where she knocked on the door of Mrs Argus. 'Hello, Mrs A., is your husband at home?'

'Yes, your ladyship, he's in the garden, just having 2,000 winks. Shall I wake him up?'

'Please do. I've got a little job for him. I'll make it worth his while.'

'Ooh, I'm sure he'll be ever so pleased, your ladyship.'

Hera arranged to leave Io in the Arguses' garden, with strict instructions to Mr Argus to keep at least ten eyes on her at all times of the day and night. He could, with minimal effort, rest all his eyes in rotation.

The cow in the Arguses' garden soon became the gossip of the village, especially as she could be heard lowing pitifully almost round the clock. Some found the noise very irritating indeed, while others said it made them want to cry, the cow sounded so sad. It was inevitable that Zeus would get to hear about the cow and that he would realise who she really was. He didn't dare try to rescue her himself – he was very aware that Hera was observing his every move at the moment – but he did feel some sense of responsibility for the plight of his former lover. So he did a deal with Hermes, his paratrooping friend, to dangle an array of theatrical lighting equipment from his helicopter one night, thereby temporarily blinding Argus in all his hundred eyes. Meanwhile Hermes' accomplices opened the garden gate and shooed Io out into the street, giving her a kick to set her galloping off. She needed no further prompting.

Hera was predictably enraged when she heard of Io's escape. She made life very difficult for Zeus by refusing to speak to him or take his phone messages for a month, and she summoned Mr Argus and tore him off a strip. Then she despatched a stinging insect to chase the poor cow round the world. So Io continued to suffer, Hera nursed the insult to herself, and Zeus carried on much as before.

Another of Zeus's – or Jupiter's – so-called conquests was Callisto. This was more than seduction on his part, more even than sexual harassment: it was rape. Callisto was one of the nymphs of Diana who, in emulation of their goddess, were all sworn to chastity, and spent their days jogging through the forest, riding mountain bikes, doing weight training, t'ai chi and hunting. Jupiter caught sight of Callisto one day, as she was exercising alone in a glade. Her lycra shorts and sports bra proved irresistible; he felt he must have her – it would be worth all the trouble that would ensue if Juno (that is, Hera) found out, which he considered unlikely. This was, after all, a very secluded glade. He lolled against a tree, watching Callisto doing her stretches. He realised that if she caught sight of a man peering at her from the bushes, she'd run off immediately. It was a hot day and he didn't feel like giving chase, so decided to transform himself into an image of Diana. This done, he came up behind Callisto, touched her on the shoulder, looked into her eyes and said, 'Hi.' 'Oh, hi Di,' replied Callisto. 'I wasn't expecting to see you today.'

'My breakfast meeting was cancelled,' said Jupiter, inventively. 'So I decided to go for a stroll and then I stopped to watch you exercising. You're getting a lovely pair of quadriceps, if you don't mind my saying, and as for the gluteus maximus . . .'

Callisto blushed. She had quite a crush on Diana, as had most of the nymphs. She was nevertheless surprised when this Diana began to stroke her cheek. 'Come on, Callisto, don't be shy,' said Jupiter. 'Haven't you ever done it with a woman? There's a first time for everything.'

Callisto's heart was beating fast. She was alarmed, and unsure what to do – there seem to be no manuals on how to perform same-sex sex, or at least you have to know where to go to get them, in which case you probably already know how to do it – but in the midst of her panic was the delightful thought of how jealous all the other nymphs would be that Diana had chosen *her* for this woodland romp. So she closed her eyes and let 'Diana's' tongue prise apart her lips. Then she felt a hand slide inside her lycra shorts and she toppled over on to a mossy bank (which are often conveniently placed in these sorts of stories). She kept her eyes closed as her shorts were pulled down. Then she heard heavy breathing and felt a most unfemale-like object being pushed inside her. She opened her eyes and gave a loud scream at finding a man – albeit a very handsome one – on top of her. But by now there was no escape. She used all her force to try to push Jupiter off; she hit him round the head, tears were pouring down her face, but her opposition only excited him more. He thrust again and again, then after he climaxed he quickly pulled out and disappeared before she had time to recover and give chase or before any of her friends turned up. Callisto sobbed into the mossy bank, her carefree nymphhood wrecked.

In those days there were no rape crisis centres, no trained counsellors, no understanding of post-traumatic stress syndrome, so Callisto was forced to face the consequences alone. As often seems to happen to victims of violence, *she* felt guilty. When the real Diana and some other nymphs eventually turned up on the scene, Callisto couldn't confide in them. She felt soiled, dishonoured and unworthy of being a nymph of Diana. Soon she discovered she was pregnant and was evicted from the glades and forests where she used to hunt and be happy. To cap it all, when jealous Juno heard of the escapade, she turned Callisto into a bear.

Not all mistresses came to such a bad end in Greek and Roman mythology, but to play the role with panache and without unhappy consequences to yourself, it helped if you were a goddess. The one who played the role to perfection was Circe, the enchantress, turner of men into swine (some say she merely brought out their true character) and lover of Odysseus. In later life Odysseus would make out he never really wanted to have an affair with Circe, that all he desired was to get home to Penelope and help her with the shopping, but it's hard to take such protestations seriously. He spent a blissful year with Circe, during which he clearly forgot all about his obligations and the need to find his way home, as his companions had to rouse him to his duty after the year had elapsed. No doubt Circe was a wonderful lover and gave Odysseus great pleasure, but where she really excels as a mistress is in her letting go. She isn't interested in keeping any lover with her against his will; hers is not the language of contracts and vows, but of freely offered love and the enjoyment of its mutuality.

Odysseus reminds Circe (once his companions have re-minded *him* that he's supposed to be on his way back to Ithaca) that she promised at the start of their relationship to help him on the next stage of his journey. She doesn't demur at this, though if she did make such a promise, Homer doesn't say so. She immediately starts preparations for helping Odys-seus on his way, though he has to undergo various trials before he can finally leave her, including a trip to the underworld. So he won't be unscathed through having indulged in this relationship, but he will grow through it and through the ending of it. She, of course, as a goddess, is unchangeable.

One of the first things Circe does to prepare Odysseus for the next stage of his travels is to warn him of other women (and who better to do this than an 'other woman'?) and, in particular, of the Sirens. These two woo passing mariners by their singing; those who hear them are drawn irresistibly towards them and thence to their deaths. What is so special about this singing? The Sirens themselves, like the serpent in the Garden of Eden myth, claim to be offering knowledge. Circe, who knows Odysseus well, understands he is capable of benefiting from hearing the song of the Sirens but that, without help, he will be destroyed by it like any other mortal. So she tells him he must instruct his companions to tie him to the mast and on no account to let him go, though when he hears the Sirens he will plead and plead, remonstrate and insist that he should go to them. Meanwhile his companions must have their ears plugged; otherwise they too would follow the song of the Sirens to their deaths. So Odysseus becomes the only man to hear the Sirens and survive, a feat he would never have accomplished without the help of his former mistress, Circe. Mistresses, especially goddess-mistresses, can open up paths of knowledge and disclose opportunities which a man would not otherwise encounter.

Circe is supremely generous in this act. It would be impossible to imagine Hera, for instance, actually arranging for Zeus to have the treat of witnessing the beauties of some other woman; she might conceivably do such a thing as a test of his fidelity, or as a trap, but never without ulterior motive, just because she thought he might like it. But Circe doesn't depend on Odysseus for her self-esteem; one gets no sense that she feels diminished by his decision to leave her. She is independent; she has loved him and enjoyed his company for a year; she would have been happy for him to stay longer, but she doesn't *need* him. Hera, on the other hand, is clearly dependent on Zeus, both for her official status and her sense of self. His wanderings make her feel personally under attack.

It is interesting that the woman about whom Circe doesn't warn Odysseus is the one with whom he next has an affair. Did she expect him never to meet Calypso? Or was Calypso the one woman (whether she was a goddess is unclear; she is generally referred to as a nymph) whom Circe knew Odysseus would not resist and therefore she couldn't bring herself to mention her name? Could thoughts of the beautiful Calypso get through the chinks in Circe's armour, suggesting that even the most independent of women retain their vulnerabilities? Be that as it may, Odysseus stayed with Calypso for seven years and again, in later life, he would recount the tale of this affair as though it were entirely one-sided. To hear him talk, you could be forgiven for thinking he spent the entire seven years sitting wailing on the seashore, longing for home. Yet every night he still went to Calypso's bed – not, of course, Odysseus tells his hearers, because he *wanted* to. Oh no, she forced him. She just wouldn't let him go. She absolutely refused. Poor man, it must have been terrible. Strange, considering such behaviour, that Calypso responds so reasonably when Hermes arrives to tell her Odysseus is to depart. She isn't nasty to her rejecting lover, just makes the perfectly valid point that she has certain attributes – immortality, principally – to which Penelope the wife can never aspire. Odysseus agrees with her – how could he not? – but he seems to have been well drilled by the patriarchal propagandists (who include plenty of women – witness Hera) and trots out all the old arguments for marital fidelity. He later dismissively describes his two most important affairs thus:

There was a time when divine Calypso kept me within her arching caverns and would have had me to be her husband, and another time when subtle Aeaean Circe confined me in her palace and would have had me for husband also. Yet neither of them could win the heart within me; so true it is that nothing is sweeter to a man than his own country and his own parents, even though he were given a sumptuous dwelling-place elsewhere, in a strange land and far from his parents.[2]

Calypso, it must be admitted, doesn't handle the letting go with quite as much graciousness as does Circe – she isn't quite a goddess, after all – but she gets there in the end and bequeaths Odysseus, despite his protestations, many happy memories of his seven-year dalliance. The description of their last night together proves it can't have been all bad: '. . . the sun sank and darkness came; then the pair withdrew, and in a recess of the arching caverns they took their pleasure in love, and did not leave one another's side.'[3]

No real conclusions can be drawn from these stories. They don't lend themselves to 'conclusions' but go on repeating themselves, theme and variations running through the centuries. As I have already quoted in the Introduction: 'when something happens that seems to us an unexampled novelty, it is generally a very old story indeed.'[4]

One thing which is noticeable throughout history is that women, Hera-like, turn on one another when they're powerless to resist what men mete out to them. So a frustrated miserable wife may preach the importance of the bonds of matrimony partly because she cannot bear to see other women being free; and a betrayed wife may turn on the other woman more than on the husband whose behaviour she can never alter and on whose continuing support she depends.

2 Homer, *The Odyssey*, tr. Walter Shewring, OUP, Oxford, 1980, p.99
3 Ibid., p.60
4 C.G. Jung, *The Archetypes & the Collective Unconscious*, p.280

But perhaps the clearest lessons to emerge from these stories is that the mistress, if she is to survive and prosper, must cultivate her independence, not attempt to become the wife, and practise the gracious art of letting go.

GEORGE ELIOT,
MISTRESS DESPITE HERSELF

She called it marriage
And by that word sought to disguise her sin.[1]

It is difficult to see Marian as a home-breaker, siren,
husband-stealer; and yet in some way she was, probably
because of her intense need for emotional support,
affection, sympathy, even sensual satisfaction. Unlike
most other women of her class and time, she acted on
her feelings and she suffered the outrage that ensued, as
she would later endure the outrage created by her
attachment to Lewes.[2]

Although George Eliot lived for twenty-four years with a man
who was legally married to another woman, she would never
have accepted the title 'mistress' in relation to herself. As far as
she was concerned, she was 'Mrs Lewes'. Yet I would suggest
that, throughout her life, this eminent Victorian displayed
certain marked characteristics of what I have termed the
'mistress-type' and for this reason an examination of certain
aspects of her life can yield some insight into the figure of the
mistress.

The first problem anyone encounters in writing about
'George Eliot' is what to call her. Variously Mary Ann, Mary
Anne or Marian Evans, Mrs Lewes, George Eliot, Mary Ann
Cross – she had a name for every season. Apart from when I
am discussing her choice of the title 'Mrs Lewes', I will refer to
her either as Marian Evans (or sometimes Miss Evans) or

1 Virgil, *The Aeneid*, tr. C.H. Sisson, Carcanet, Manchester, 1986, p.88
2 Frederick Karl, *George Eliot: A Biography*, HarperCollins, London, 1995, p.120

George Eliot, depending loosely on whether I am referring to her as woman or novelist, though the two cannot always be legitimately separated. And because she found her voice as a novelist fairly late in life, this in practice means that 'Marian Evans' tends to cover her pre-George Henry Lewes life and 'George Eliot' her life from 1854 onwards.

Marian Evans evinced a pattern, from her early adulthood, of falling for married men. There are the well-documented cases of Dr Brabant and, particularly, John Chapman. There are questions about her marked friendships with Charles Bray (married to Cara) and Charles Hennell (who married Dr Brabant's daughter, Rufa). There was the deformed Frenchman, Monsieur D'Albert Durade; although she also formed a friendship with his wife, he was clearly the main focus of her interest. Then there was Herbert Spencer who, though not married, was decidedly 'unavailable'. Finally there was George Henry Lewes who, though available, was decidedly married. (Then really finally there was Johnny Cross, unmarried, available but still, arguably, unsuitable.)

Various attempts at explanation have been presented for this pattern of behaviour. Frederick Karl portrays Miss Evans as akin to a man-eating spider:

> We must . . . reject the point stressed by previous biographers that Eliot 'depended' on men. Instead of depending on them, she assimilated their power before moving on to the next, from Bray and Brabant to Chapman and Herbert Spencer, and finally to Lewes. Accordingly, her relationship to each man was a form of absorption into herself of their place in the masculine world denied to her directly. And from that, she could gather her forces, then move on: not dependent on them, but rather like the warrior who consumes his adversary's flesh in order to ingest his strength.[3]

3 Ibid., p.xviii

Phyllis Rose strikes a similar note, though in more measured tones:

> In the face of all these terrified wives and families, of men who realize with dismay that this gentle woman who has captivated them wants even more than they thought – we are supposed to see a woman who cannot stand alone. What I see is a woman of passionate nature who struggles, amidst limited opportunity, to find someone to love and to love her; a woman who goes to quite unconventional lengths and is willing to be unusually aggressive – almost predatory – in her efforts to secure for herself what she wants.[4]

I would posit three other possible explanations or partial reasons. Two contradictory forces are at play: first, a sense of superiority on Marian Evans's part – superiority over most other human beings, in fact, but particularly over the figure of 'the wife'; secondly, a fundamental lack of self-worth, which betrays itself both in the need for the validating concern of a respected man and the acceptance of a less than 'whole' relationship for herself. A mask of superiority is frequently the cover for an underlying sense of inferiority. And thirdly, there is the largely unconscious desire to avoid marriage while at the same time wishing to experience the joys of intimacy.

Marian's first experience of the literary world, and of wider horizons than she had previously known, came about through her friendship with Charles and Caroline (Cara) Bray, Cara's sister Sara Hennell, and their brother Charles Hennell. They lived in Coventry, where Charles and Cara Bray enjoyed what would now be called an 'open' marriage, Charles eventually having six children by the household's cook, for one thing. The other Charles, his brother-in-law, had written *An Inquiry into the Origins of Christianity*, published in 1838.

It was through the Brays that Marian met the 62-old Dr

4 Phyllis Rose, *Parallel Lives*, p.211

Robert Brabant. The initial reason – or excuse – for her to join the Brabant household was the marriage of Rufa Brabant to Charles Hennell. It was apparently Dr Brabant's idea that Marian should perform something like the role of a surrogate daughter. Marian and the Doctor soon became inseparable and Marian was quickly perceived as a threat by Mrs Brabant and her sister. The most lively account of events is provided by John Chapman in his diary entry for 27 June 1851, in which he recounts what 'Mrs Hennell' (i.e. Rufa née Brabant) had told him:

> . . . Mrs Hennell repeated exactly what Miss Evans had told me previously as a great secret . . . that in 1843 Miss Evans was invited by Dr Brabant (she being then only 22) to visit his house and to fill the place of his daughter (then just married) she went, the Doctor liked her extremely, and said that so long as she had no home she must consider his house as her permanent home. She in the simplicity of her heart and her ignorance of (or incapability of practicing) the required conventionalisms gave the Doctor the utmost attention; they became very intimate, his Sister in law Miss S. Hughes became alarmed, made a great stir, excited the jealousy of Mrs Brabant, <who insisted> Miss Evans left. Mrs B. vowed she would never enter the house again, or that if she did, she Mrs Brabant would instantly leave it. Mrs Hennell says Dr B. acted ungenerously and worse, towards Miss E. for though he was the chief cause of all that passed, he acted towards her as though the fault lay with her alone. His unmanliness in the affair was condemned more by Mrs Hennell than by Miss E. herself when she (a year ago) related the circumstances to me.[5]

There are several points of interest in this narrative of Chapman's. There is the reference to Marian's either ignorance of or

---

5 Gordon S. Haight, *George Eliot & John Chapman, with Chapman's Diaries*, Yale University Press, New Haven, 1940, pp.185–6

incapability of practising 'the required conventionalisms' – an indication, perhaps, that she already considered it unnecessary in her own case to follow the standards of behaviour laid down for the majority. It is through this refusal, or inability, to conform, that she rouses the ire and jealousy of the wife. Though nothing strictly 'immoral' is likely to have occurred, Marian clearly enjoyed some kind of exclusive intellectual relationship with the husband, and the exclusion of the wife, I would suggest, constituted part of the enjoyment. Frederick Karl notes this exclusivity: 'What makes the relationship so problematical – and Mrs Brabant perceived more was at stake than a research assistant with her mentor – was that Mary Ann craved affection from or closeness to a male figure. When she was with Brabant, they apparently closed out the world; they walked with arms or hands clasped, conversing in German.'[6] Yet this element may well have been unconscious. Her letter to Cara Bray of 20 November 1843 describes how she is spending her days; it sounds as though she has indeed commandeered the Doctor's time and attention, but there is no sense that she is deliberately depriving Mrs Brabant of anything: 'Mrs Brabant is a most affectionate amiable being, too forgetful of herself to talk of her loss, but really feeling it as much as any one. Of the Dr. what shall I say? for the time would fail me to tell of all his charming qualities. We read, walk and talk together, and I am never weary of his company.'[7] Also noticeable in Chapman's account is Marian's unwillingness to lay much blame on the Doctor for what amounted, ultimately, to a rejection of her in favour of domestic tranquillity.

In 1845 Marian almost became engaged to an unidentified picture restorer near her own age (twenty-five) or possibly even younger. It is arguable that the very availability of this young man was one reason why Miss Evans's relationship with him came to an abrupt end. His youth probably counted against him as well.

6 Frederick Karl, *George Eliot*, p.66
7 Gordon S. Haight (ed.), *Selections from George Eliot's Letters*, Yale University Press, New Haven & London, 1985, pp.28–9

The relationship with Brabant lasted only a few weeks, though he didn't disappear entirely from Marian's life, as he would make a point of occasionally visiting her when she was living in London. The publisher Dr John Chapman was to be a far more significant character, Marian's relationship with him demonstrating both her continuing tendency to be a disruptive influence in a household and her ability eventually to transform a difficult love into valued and valuable friendship.

When Marian Evans first encountered John Chapman (he was publishing her first literary work, a translation of David Friedrich Strauss's *Leben Jesu*, a task which Rufa Brabant had devolved on to her when she married Charles Hennell and which proved to be rather longer-lasting than the surrogate daughter job), he was living at 142, The Strand, with his wife Susanna and their children, and also the children's 'governess' – and, more to the point, his mistress – Elisabeth Tilley. Susanna was older than her husband and was becoming prey to various infirmities. Part of the family's income was obtained through taking in lodgers, and it was as a lodger, though also as an assistant to Chapman in his publishing endeavours, that Marian took up residence. She stayed at the Chapmans' for the last two weeks of November 1850, and then returned there on 8 January 1851. The addition of another woman to the household proved explosive.

Marian was immediately useful to Chapman as an editor but Elisabeth Tilley became extremely jealous. She goaded Susanna, with whom she seemed to have a working arrangement, into hostility too. Chapman played into their hands by going up to Marian's room for German lessons and to listen to her play the piano. His wife insisted the piano-playing take place in the parlour.

Here is an entry from Chapman's diary, dated Wednesday, 22 January 1851, which gives a flavour of day-to-day life at 142 The Strand ('E' is Elisabeth Tilley, 'S' is Susanna Chapman, and in general in these diaries, phrases between the brackets (<>) were originally scored through by Chapman but have been restored sufficiently to be deciphered):

. . . Invited Miss Evans to go out after breakfast, did not get a decisive answer, E. afterwards said if I did go, she should be glad to go, I then invited Miss Evans again telling her E. would go whereupon she declined rather rudely, Susanna being willing to go out, and neither E. nor S. wishing to walk far I proposed they should go a short distance without me, which E. considered an insult from me and reproached me in no measured terms accordingly, and heaped upon me suspicions and accusations I do not in any way deserve. I was very severe and harsh, said things I was sorry for afterwards, and we became reconciled in the Park.
Miss Evans apologised for her rudeness tonight, which roused all E.'s jealousy again, and consequent bitterness. S. E. and Miss Evans are gone to spend the evening with Mr and Mrs Holland.[8]

Poor Mr and Mrs Holland, one can't help thinking. A month later Elisabeth and Susanna are definitely ganging up on Marian (now referred to by Chapman as 'M'):

I presume with a view of arriving at a more friendly understanding S. and E. had a long talk this morning which resulted in their comparing notes on the subject of my intimacy with Miss Evans, and their arrival at the conclusion <that we are completely in love with each other. E. being intensely jealous herself said all she could to cause S. to look from the same point of view, which a little incident (her finding me with my hand in M.'s) had quite prepared her for>.[9]

The next day Chapman does what he can to keep the situation on the boil:

---

8 *Chapman's Diaries*, pp.135–6
9 Ibid., pp.140–2

. . . Sat in the dining room to write in the morning where M. joined me, we talked of course of the excited feelings of S. and E. I gave her an account of what had passed and urged her to talk with S. on the subject to give her an opportunity of dissipating her uncalled for hatred by expression. E. made some bitter remarks on account of our being in the dining room (i.e. together), and I therefore passed the afternoon in S.'s room without a fire. S. had a long talk with M. before dinner unsatisfactory to S. from the high tone M. took. Conversation renewed after dinner in my presence when M. confessed S. had reason to complain, and a reconciliation was effected.[10]

Chapman's actual conduct with Marian when alone can never be known, his otherwise intimate diaries revealing nothing beyond the hand-holding incident. Marian herself appears to have become fascinated by Chapman and probably to have 'fallen in love' with him. As in the case of Dr Brabant, she began to take up more and more of his time – even if in the entirely legitimate pursuits of editorial assistance and German lessons – and one can infer from the diaries that, as again with the Brabants, she was for some time blithely unaware of the resentment she was creating in the minds of the other two women in the household. Or, if not completely unaware, she would not stoop to concern herself with it – for, after all, she and Chapman (who noted her 'high tone') had important intellectual work to attend to. For his part, it is also clear from the diaries that Chapman loved to be embroiled in emotional disturbance, to have several women clamouring for his attention and falling out with one another over him – for, as much as he complains about the absence of domestic tranquillity and how hard it is to get on with his work, he does all he can to keep the emotional temperature turned up.

A later entry from Chapman's diary (Tuesday, 24 July 1860) suggests that Susanna was just the type of wife to

10 Ibid., p.142

whom Marian Evans would inevitably feel herself superior, assuming that the characteristics described here were already in evidence ten years earlier: '. . . If her personal unattractiveness were the only fact I had to deplore we might at least live together in a friendly or even affectionate relationship; but alas there are almost no elements of satisfaction: As a housekeeper she is utterly inefficient; under her rule disorder reigns everywhere . . . Her chief reading is novels. Real study of any kind she has never applied herself to since her marriage.'[11]

The reconciliation between Marian and Susanna appears to have been short-lived, for a month later Marian is departing for Coventry and the Brays:

M. departed today, I accompanied her to the railway. She was very sad, and hence made me feel so.- She pressed me for some intimation of the state of my feelings,- <I told her that I felt great affection for her, but that I loved E. and S. also, though each in a different way.> At this avowal she burst into tears. I tried to comfort her, and reminded [her] of the dear friends and pleasant home she was returning to, - but the train whirled her away very very sad.[12]

Even with Marian away, the drama continued:

. . . <I had a short simple note from M. this morning [28 April 1851], which E. read and then flew into a great passion, and begged me not to speak to her. We separated all morning, she came to me after lunch, expressed her regret, and observed that I was so cruelly calm. I wrote a short proper note to M. which she did not see, in answer to her question I said I had written which caused another manifestation of excitement, from which however she soon recovered . . .>[13]

11 Ibid., pp.245–6
12 Ibid., p.147
13 Ibid., pp.160–1

Then a few weeks later Chapman was negotiating for Marian's return to London, knowing her help with the *Westminster Review*, of which he was about to become the proprietor and editor, would be invaluable. Left to herself, Marian would not have returned, but Chapman pursued her by letter and then in person. During a visit he made to the Brays he wrote:

> Walked with M. before breakfast, told her the exact condition of things in regard to E. whom on every account I wish to stay at the Strand. She was much grieved and expressed herself prepared to atone in any way she could for the pain she has caused, and put herself in my hands prepared to accept any arrangement I may make either for her return to the Strand or to any house in London I may think suitable in October. She agreed to write the article on foreign literature for each number of the Westminster which I am very glad of. Wrote the greater part of the Prospectus today, and then gave it to M. to finish.[14]

We can note how much Chapman is now relying on Miss Evans as his fellow worker, but also how she seems prepared to accept whatever situation he cares to put her in; this extract also raises the question – which has never been satisfactorily answered – as to whether Marian had previously even understood that Elisabeth was Chapman's mistress. It is hard to believe she hadn't grasped this, but one nevertheless senses, as also in the Brabant situation, her surprise on discovering that her presence, and presumably her behaviour in relation to a man, has had an unsettling effect on women with a prior claim on him. The next day Chapman (inadvertently?) hurts her, thereby demonstrating one possible reason for her sense of inferiority:

> . . . Accompanied M. to Leamington, and while she visited her sister I went to the Dales, Susanna['s] cousins;

14 Ibid., p.172

went to Kenilworth Castle on our way back, was somewhat disappointed with the ruin, but the effect from the
Leamington side is very striking. As we rested on the
grass, I remarked on the wonderful and mysterious
embodiment of all the elements characteristics and beauties of nature which man and woman jointly present. I
dwelt also on the incomprehensible mystery and witch-
ery of beauty. My words jarred upon her and put an end
to her enjoyment. Was it from a consciousness of her
own want of beauty? She wept bitterly.[15]

A few days later (5 June 1851) Chapman's diary alludes to
some shift in the relationship between himself and Marian;
this extract also demonstrates Chapman's continuing tendency to heighten controversy by passing on what one
woman has said about another: '. . . Received an unkind
letter from Susanna regarding M. whom I told, and enquired
of her whether she would prefer living her[e] or in Town. She
became extremely excited and indignant, and finally calm and
regretful . . . <During our walk we made a solemn and holy
vow which henceforth will bind us to the right. She is a noble
being. Wrote a chiding letter to Susanna.>'[16]

From the time of the 'solemn and holy vow' Marian did
seem by and large to succeed in converting her troubled
relationship with Chapman into friendship, intellectual companionship and invaluable editorial assistance. In October
1851 she was re-established at 142, The Strand, now as the
sub-editor of the *Westminster Review*. For the next two years
while she stayed there, she was to be Chapman's most loyal and
supportive friend. The references to her in his diaries for the
remaining few months of 1851 (nothing further remains of the
diaries until the beginning of 1860) are relatively impersonal,
although they do reveal that Chapman spent a considerable
amount of time with her and that he became increasingly
dependent upon her judgement in literary and business mat-

15 Ibid.
16 Ibid., p.175

ters. She appears to have become an island of serenity in his
turbulent life. 'Not that she had quickly and easily transformed
her love for him into the calmer feeling of friendship. There
are signs that at the Strand she underwent a prolonged inward
struggle which – even while exacting its toll in the form of
depressions and psychosomatic disturbances – aroused psychic
strengths that began to give her the inner poise her later friends
assumed she had enjoyed all her life.'[17] This is a transformation
which only a certain type of woman can achieve; it requires an
ability to set aside convention, to recognise what is important
in a relationship and to salvage it, but also the willingness to be
satisfied with only a part, to stand to some extent alone and to
watch another – or others – enjoy further intimacy.

Herbert Spencer, philosopher–sociologist and one of Chapman's authors, was not married but neither was he 'available'
for a complete, reciprocal relationship. As Frederick Karl puts
it:

> In her movement among male company, Herbert Spen-
> cer was probably the most distinguished man Marian came
> close to. He was, in most respects except creative imagi-
> nation, her intellectual equal. Emotionally, however, he
> was lacking what we might call 'affect', since he appeared
> to be so self-contained, so self-absorbed, so narcissistic – a
> term apparently made to order for him – that he could not
> relate to anyone except on the intellectual level. When
> Marian came too close, Spencer retreated in fear and
> horror that she might be seeking a permanent union; a
> lifelong bachelor, he seemed to have no sexual needs, or
> else repressed them for the sake of his work.[18]

Before the horrified retreat, however, he and Marian were
seen together everywhere and friends began to wonder
whether they were engaged.

17 Ruby V. Redinger, *George Eliot: The Emergent Self*, Bodley Head, London,
   Sydney, Toronto, 1976, p.190
18 Frederick Karl, *George Eliot*, p.142

Marian Evans's fundamental lack of self-worth and the way it made her willing to accept less than a whole love from a man is given its clearest airing in this relationship. Here is an extract from her most abject letter to Spencer, written, according to Gordon Haight, on 14 July 1852:

> I know this letter will make you very angry with me, but wait a little, and don't say anything to me while you are angry. I promise not to sin any more in the same way . . .
>
> I want to know if you can assure me that you will not forsake me, that you will always be with me as much as you can and share your thoughts and feelings with me. If you become attached to someone else, then I must die, but until then I could gather courage to work and make life valuable, if only I had you near me. I do not ask you to sacrifice anything – I would be very good and cheerful and never annoy you. But I find it impossible to contemplate life under any other conditions. If I had your assurance, I could trust that and live upon it. I have struggled – indeed I have – to renounce everything and be entirely unselfish, but I find myself utterly unequal to it. Those who have known me best have always said, that if ever I loved anyone thoroughly my whole life must turn upon that feeling, and I find they said truly. You curse the destiny which has made the feeling concentrate itself upon you – but if you will only have patience with me you shall not curse it long. You will find that I can be satisfied with very little, if I am delivered from the dread of losing it.
>
> I suppose no woman ever before wrote such a letter as this – but I am not ashamed of it, for I am conscious that in the light of reason and true refinement I am worthy of your respect and tenderness, whatever gross men or vulgar-minded women might think of me.[19]

19 *Selections from George Eliot's Letters*, p.102

'I suppose no woman ever before wrote such a letter as this
. . .' She was wrong, for less than ten years previously, another
woman – also to become a novelist – wrote extraordinarily
similar words:

> I know that you will be irritated when you read this letter
> . . . So be it, Monsieur, I do not seek to justify myself; I
> submit to every sort of reproach. All I know is that I
> cannot, that I will not, resign myself to lose wholly the
> friendship of my master . . .
>
> If my master withdraws his friendship from me entirely
> I shall be altogether without hope; if he gives me a little –
> just a little – I shall be satisfied – happy; I shall have reason
> for living on, for working.
>
> Monsieur, the poor have not need of much to sustain
> them – they ask only for the crumbs that fall from the
> rich men's table. But if they are refused the crumbs they
> die of hunger. Nor do I, either, need much affection
> from those I love. I should not know what to do with a
> friendship entire and complete – I am not used to it. But
> you showed me of yore a *little* interest, when I was your
> pupil in Brussels, and I hold on to the maintenance of
> that *little* interest – I hold on to it as I would hold on to
> life . . .
>
> I shall not re-read this letter. I send it as I have written
> it. Nevertheless, I have a hidden consciousness that some
> people, cold and common-sense, in reading it would say
> – 'She is talking nonsense.'[20]

That was Charlotte Brontë writing to Constantin Heger, of
which relationship more below.

Yet Marian Evans, and far more quickly than in the case of
John Chapman, was able to 'change gear', to gain control of
her emotions – partly through the exercise of her pride – once
she perceived that her plea would never be fully answered.

20 T.J. Wise & J.A. Symington (eds.), *The Brontës: Their Lives, Friendships and Correspondence*, Vol. 1, Blackwell, Oxford, 1932, pp.23–4

Two weeks after her abject letter, she writes again, intimating that she is already beginning to be able to turn her infatuation into something more acceptable. Here again the dual mechanism of superiority/inferiority, or self-belief/self-hatred is operating: only someone of superior quality is able to turn unrequited love into friendship; only someone who believes herself innately inferior and unlovable would be prepared to try. Neither of those statements is entirely true, or tells the whole truth; yet they both express some truth and, though apparently contradictory, these characteristics subsist in the same type of person and work together to help create some extraordinary, and extraordinarily valuable, relationships.

Dear Mr Spencer, It would be ungenerous in me to allow you to suffer even a slight uneasiness on my account which I am able to remove. I ought at once to tell you, since I can do so with truth, that I am not unhappy. The fact is, all sorrows sink into insignificance before the one great sorrow – my own miserable im-perfections, and any outward hap is welcome if it will only serve to rouse my energies and make me less unworthy of my better self. I have good hope that it will be so now, and I wish you to share this hope if it will give you any satisfaction.

If, as you intimated in your last letter, you feel that my friendship is of value to you for its own sake – mind on no other ground – it is yours. Let us, if you will, forget the past, except in so far as it may have brought us to trust in and feel for each other, and let us help to make life beautiful to each other as far as fate and the world will permit us.[21]

Marian Evans is always conscious of her 'better self' and she strives, throughout all her vicissitudes, to attain and express it.

Perhaps George Eliot herself provides the best commentary

21 *Selections from George Eliot's Letters*, p.105

on this stage of her life, writing here some eighteen years later, in July 1870:

> We women are always in danger of living too exclusively in the affections; and though our affections are perhaps the best gifts we have, we ought also to have our share of the more independent life – some joy in things for their own sake. It is piteous to see the helplessness of some sweet women when their affections are disappointed – because all their teaching has been, that they can only delight in study of any kind for the sake of a personal love. They have never contemplated an independent delight in ideas as an experience which they could confess without being laughed at. Yet surely women need this sort of defence against passionate affection even more than men.[22]

Herbert Spencer was in the habit of bringing George Henry Lewes with him when he visited Marian. Lewes was estranged from, but still married to, his wife Agnes. Earlier experiments in 'free love', involving among others Thornton Hunt (a co-editor with Lewes on the *Leader*) and his wife, had resulted in Agnes having children by Hunt as well as by Lewes (as Leslie Stephen quaintly put it: 'Mrs Lewes preferred Thornton Hunt to her husband, to whom she had already borne children.'[23]). Lewes had himself accepted paternity of all these children and so would have been deemed in a court of law to have 'condoned' his wife's adultery, thereby making it impossible for him to divorce her. One night in 1853, when Spencer left, Lewes stayed behind and poured all his troubles into Marian's willing ear. At last she had found both someone who needed her and on whom she could lean. In a letter dated by Gordon Haight 16 April 1853, she wrote to Cara Bray: 'People are very good to me. Mr. Lewes especially is kind and attentive and has quite won my regard after having a good deal of my

22 Ibid., p.379
23 Leslie Stephen, *George Eliot*, London, 1902, pp.46–7

vituperation. Like a few other people in the world, he is much better than he seems – a man of heart and conscience wearing a mask of flippancy.'[24]

Marian Evans found in George Henry Lewes, I would suggest, a man to satisfy all her requirements. The fact he was married enabled her to satisfy her evident desire to act unconventionally, even to shock, and thereby demonstrate her superiority to the common herd. But secondly here was a man actually prepared to devote himself to her completely, so that her capacity for love would at last be allowed its full expression; and the more positive side to her flouting of convention was surely her ability to place her love for Lewes above the dictates of respectable society and to pay the price of exclusion from that society (a price paid only, of course, by the woman – Lewes was never excluded). The fact that some part of Marian Evans may have enjoyed – and certainly the writer George Eliot benefited from – that exclusion does not alter the fact that her decision to bind her life to that of Lewes was a brave and loving act. They left together for Weimar in July 1854, and at the time and for many years afterwards their life together was a subject of great scandal.

Marian needed love and support for herself, but she also needed to be needed by the man she loved. Lewes, in his predicament of being bound to a wife with whom he could no longer sustain relations, fulfilled this criterion. He needed her emotional support, and he needed someone prepared to abandon the conventional rewards of married life for him. Marian was thus able to maintain her position of superior being at the same time as enjoying the intimacy and devotion of a permanent lover. Frederick Karl also suggests that, in defying the codes of behaviour sanctioned by respectable society, she was attacking the men who had previously exerted authority over her: 'Her ultimate act of hostility to her dead father and her ultra-respectable brother was to become a scarlet woman.'[25] Certainly, once he was informed

24 *Selections from George Eliot's Letters*, p.121
25 Frederick Karl, *George Eliot*, p.157

of Marian's position, her brother Isaac broke off all contact with her.

Yet Marian Evans was, on her own terms and certainly by modern standards, very moral indeed. She entered into a partnership with Lewes which was quite as committed as any formal marriage could have been. She regarded herself as his wife and insisted on being called Mrs Lewes – partly to avoid embarrassment and difficulties with landladies and the like – but not only because of that. She was as determined as Lewes himself that he should maintain his responsibilities toward his legal wife and his children, and this was one of the main reasons why they both worked so hard all their lives to earn money. She continued to assume responsibility for Lewes's family even after his death. In short, she had an extremely strong sense of duty – but it had to be duty as defined by and for herself, not a duty imposed on her by society. She rejected any interpretation of her way of life which might have suggested support for 'loose' living, for affairs and liaisons: 'Light and easily broken ties are what I neither desire theoretically nor could live for practically. Women who are satisfied with such ties do *not* act as I have done – they obtain what they desire and are still invited to dinner.'[26]

In a long letter to John Chapman, dated by Haight 15 October 1854, she is concerned both to place herself above the judgement of the common herd, claiming not to care what society may think of her, but also to justify her – and particularly Lewes's – behaviour as being above reproach:

> About my own justification I am entirely indifferent. But there is a report concerning Mr. Lewes which I must beg you to contradict whenever it is mentioned to you. It is, 'that he has run away from his wife and family.' This is so far from being true that he is in constant correspondence with his wife and is providing for her to the best of his power, while no man can be more nervously anxious

26 *Selections from George Eliot's Letters*, p.151

than he about the future welfare of his children . . . Since
we have been here, circumstances (in which I am not
concerned) have led to his determining on a separation,
but he has never contemplated withdrawing the most
watchful care over his wife and the utmost efforts for his
children . . . The phrase 'run away' as applied to me is
simply amusing – I wonder what I had to run away
from . . .

I have nothing to deny or to conceal. I have done
nothing with which any person has a right to interfere. I
have surely full liberty to travel in Germany, and to travel
with Mr. Lewes . . . But I do not wish to take the ground
of ignoring what is unconventional in my position. I
have counted the cost of the step that I have taken and
am prepared to bear, without irritation or bitterness,
renunciation by all my friends. I am not mistaken in the
person to whom I have attached myself. He is worthy of
the sacrifice I have incurred, and my only anxiety is that
he should be rightly judged.[27]

In the lack of care about her own reputation and the obsessive
concern with the man's, we can again detect the two-sided
coin of inferiority and superiority. Her own reputation
doesn't matter both because she is *less* important than the
man and because she is *above* him in not requiring societal
approval. Yet again, although she is above him and society in
constructing her own morality, she still at heart wants society
to recognise that she is a highly moral creature.

She writes in a similar vein to Charles Bray, and seems
particularly concerned not to be portrayed as a 'temptress',
persuading a man to abandon his wife and children:

Of course many silly myths are already afloat about me,
in addition to the truth, which of itself would be thought
matter for scandal. I am quite unconcerned about them

27 Ibid., pp.140–1

except as they may cause pain to my real friends. If you
hear of anything that I have said, done, or written in
relation to Mr. Lewes beyond the simple fact that I am
attached to him and that I am living with him, do me the
justice to believe that it is false . . . the only influence I
should ever dream of exerting over him as to his conduct
towards his wife and children is that of stimulating his
conscientious care for them, if it needed any stimulus.[28]

Yet, as Phyllis Rose comments, Marian Evans's high-minded
account of her motivation and actions had always to compete
with less lofty interpretations:

But easy stories drive out complicated ones, and the most
familiar and vulgar version of the matter will gain the
widest currency. It was almost impossible for Miss Evans
and Mr Lewes to substitute for the popular tale of a *femme
fatale* stealing another woman's husband the much subtler
story of a husband, abandoned by his wife, refusing to
abandon his own responsibilities to her, unable to divorce her yet unwilling to live with her, unable to re-
marry yet constructing a relationship which was equivalent to marriage.[29]

There were other advantages to Marian's chosen way of life,
besides being able to indulge her sense of superiority. Principally, she acquired considerable freedom to pursue her work:
'Because they were not respectable, they were spared the
burdens of respectability. They did not have to be nice to each
other's friends. They did not have to give dinner parties. They
did not have to put up with guests for the weekend. They did
not have to appear together in public. Treated as sinful lovers,
they remained lovers.'[30] They also had no children, a deliberate choice as far as we know, and domestic concerns were

28 Ibid., p.142
29 Phyllis Rose, *Parallel Lives*, p.218
30 Ibid., p.221

kept to a minimum. In December 1860, in a letter to Barbara Bodichon, Marian reiterates her lack of concern over her irregular position. An approach had been made to a barrister over whether a divorce could be obtained under foreign law, but he had pronounced it impossible. On this verdict, Marian comments:

> I am not sorry. I think the boys [i.e. Lewes's sons] will not suffer, and for myself I prefer excommunication. I have no earthly thing that I care for, to gain by being brought within the pale of people's personal attention, and I have many things to care for that I should lose – my freedom from petty worldly torments, commonly called pleasures, and that isolation which really keeps my charity warm instead of chilling it, as much contact with frivolous women would do . . .[31]

She knew that her work and her intimacy with George Henry Lewes were the most important aspects of her life, and that they were best served in a position of exclusion from society. Also, as Jenny Uglow suggests (and as Heloise would understand), the intensity of the relationship may have come partly from their freedom from legal bonds, as this freedom strengthened the sense of voluntary commitment to each other. 'All of [her] novels emphasise how much more vital are the laws of conscience and of human community than the Law of State or Church.'[32]

In the letter to Charles Bray, quoted from earlier, there is a strange passage which almost seems to suggest that Marian *wanted* to lose her (female) friends: 'I am ignorant how far Cara and Sara may be acquainted with the state of things, and how they may feel towards me. I am quite prepared to accept the consequences of a step which I have deliberately taken and to accept them without irritation or bitterness. The most painful consequence will, I know, be the loss of friends. If I do not

31 *Selections from George Eliot's Letters*, p.254
32 Jennifer Uglow, *George Eliot*, Virago, London, 1987, p.53

write, therefore, understand that it is because I desire not to obtrude myself.'[33] Marian had chosen to inform only certain male friends, including Charles Bray and John Chapman, of her intended 'elopement' before she and Lewes left for Germany. Considering the earlier closeness between herself, Cara Bray and Sara Hennell, this lack of trust in her female friends is striking. This may be partly because she retained, on a deep level, more respect for men than for women. This is also evinced by her political views; for instance: ' "Enfranchisement of women" only makes creeping progress; and that is best, for woman does not yet deserve a much better lot than man gives her.'[34] But the loss, or expected loss, of friends also, I suspect, bolstered Marian's sense of self. Certainly Sara Hennell detected an element of boastfulness in her friend's handling of the situation, as is clear from Marian's reply to her reproaches:

> I cannot, even now, see that I did anything deserving so severe a reproach as you send me, in writing to Mr. Bray who was already in possession of the main facts, and in intimating that my silence to you arose from no want of affection, but from what I, falsely perhaps, but still sincerely, regarded as the very reverse of *pride* and a spirit of *boasting* . . . I am under no foolish hallucinations about either the present or the future and am standing on no stilts of any kind. I wish to speak simply and to act simply but I think it can hardly be unintelligible to you that I shrink from writing elaborately about private feelings and circumstances . . . But interpret my whole letter so as to make it accord with this plain statement – I love Cara and you with unchanged and unchangeable affection, and while I retain your friendship I retain the best that life has given me next to that which is the deepest and gravest joy in all human experience.[35]

33 *Selections from George Eliot's Letters*, p.142
34 Ibid., p.116
35 Ibid., p.143

This can hardly have seemed a satisfactory reply to Sara; not only does it fail to give convincing reasons for Marian's reticence, it also shows her enjoying her elevated position, in writing to her spinster friend, of one who has now known all the joys of love between man and woman.

In Marian Evans's pride at her society-defying union with Lewes and her commitment to him which did not bring the usual tangible rewards of matrimony, there is an echo of the pride of Heloise in her exemplary love for Abelard. Both these women were very conscious of themselves as lovers, and both also took 'morals' a great deal more seriously than many who appear to live by them but who are, arguably, only thoughtlessly following convention. Why then, despite all this independence of spirit, was Marian so insistent on being termed 'Mrs Lewes'? On the face of it, this would appear to be an attempt at placating society, a pretence that she was really playing by the rules, or even a piece of cowardice on her part, a refusal openly to live as an unmarried woman in a relationship with a married man. Partly it was all of these things; partly it was their complete opposite. It can be argued that styling herself 'Mrs Lewes' was the ultimate demonstration that Marian was her own law-giver, to the extent of determining her own legal status, needing recourse neither to the state authorities nor the Church in declaring herself 'married'.

In a letter to Bessie Parkes, dated by Haight 24 September 1857, she implicates George Henry Lewes in the decision: 'Secondly, you must please not call me *Miss Evans* again. I have renounced that name, and do not mean to be known by it in any way. It is Mr. Lewes's wish that the few friends who care about me should recognize me as Mrs. Lewes, and my Father's Trustee sends me receipts to sign as Marian Lewes, so that my adoption of the name has been made a matter of business.'[36] In April 1861, in a letter to another acquaintance, she seems to have claimed the title as a proof of the responsibilities she has undertaken and which she wishes to have recognised:

36 Ibid., p.178

For the last six years I have ceased to be 'Miss Evans' for
any one who has personal relations with me – having
held myself under all the responsibilities of a married
woman. I wish this to be distinctly understood; and
when I tell you that we have a great boy of eighteen
at home who calls me 'mother', as well as two other
boys, almost as tall, who write to me under the same
name, you will understand that the point is not one of
mere egoism or personal dignity, when I request that any
one who has a regard for me will cease to speak of me by
my maiden name.[37]

Calling herself 'Mrs Lewes' – as indeed the whole calling of
herself by different names for different phases of life and
purposes – is also indicative of the divisions within this
woman. George Eliot the writer is one person, Mrs George
Henry Lewes another, Miss Marian Evans a previous incarnation, and so on. The names also reflect other dichotomies: for
instance, that Marian Evans chose freedom from convention
for herself, but George Eliot granted no such freedom to the
female characters of her novels. Jenni Calder puts the case very
clearly in relation to the heroine of *Middlemarch*: '[Dorothea] is
aware of herself as an un-ordinary woman, much more so
than Maggie [in *The Mill on the Floss*], and to be judged by the
standards and expectations of ordinary women and ordinary
men has little influence on her. This is an important moral
centre of the novel. Dorothea has to come to terms with the
fact that the respect owed to her as an individual does not
exempt her from the criteria applied to the mass.'[38] Marian
Evans had no intention whatsoever of coming to terms with
such a fact.

As Virgil says of Dido in relation to Aeneas, so one can say
of Marian Evans in relation to George Henry Lewes: 'She
called it marriage.' And that very need to 'call it marriage'

37 Ibid., p.260
38 Jenni Calder, *Women & Marriage in Victorian Fiction*, Thames & Hudson, London,
   1976, p.150

betrays the consciousness of sin, the half-hidden belief that not to be 'married' to one's lover is wrong. Yet George Eliot could also write: 'A woman dictates before marriage in order that she may have an appetite for submission afterwards.'[39] If that was truly the opinion of this strong-minded, passionate and multi-named woman, no wonder she contrived to avoid the estate of holy matrimony.

'I have read Jane Eyre, mon ami, and shall be glad to know what you admire in it. All self-sacrifice is good – but one would like it to be in a somewhat nobler cause than that of a diabolical law which chains a man soul and body to a putrefying carcase.'[40] Thus wrote Marian Evans to Charles Bray on 11 June 1848, six years prior to the beginning of her union with Lewes.

Edward Fairfax Rochester asks Jane Eyre, though in veiled fashion – this is before she has discovered the existence of a mad wife – the question Marian Evans was to pose to herself in relation to her life with Lewes: ' "Such society [i.e. that of Jane] revives, regenerates: you feel better days come back – higher wishes, purer feelings; you desire to recommence your life, and to spend what remains to you of days in a way more worthy of an immortal being. To attain this end, are you justified in over-leaping an obstacle of custom – a mere conventional impediment, which neither your conscience sanctifies nor your judgment approves?" '[41] 'No,' said Jane Eyre; 'Yes,' said Marian Evans. Despite the disagreement, it is still to Charlotte Brontë (or, rather, Currer Bell) that Marian Evans turns in seeking an image for the start of her new life with Lewes; in July 1854 she wrote to Sara Hennell: 'I shall soon send you a good bye, for I am preparing to go to "Labassecour".'[42]

'Labassecour' was the name by which Charlotte Brontë

39 George Eliot, *Middlemarch*, Penguin, Harmondsworth, 1965, p.98
40 *Selections from George Eliot's Letters*, p.51
41 Charlotte Brontë, *Jane Eyre*, Penguin, Harmondsworth, 1991, p.282
42 *Selections from George Eliot's Letters*, p.135

referred to Belgium in *Villette*, her novel in which she drew upon the experience of her unrequited, unhappy love for her Belgian teacher, Constantin Heger. As previously noted, this relationship bears certain distinct parallels to Marian Evans's relationships with men, particularly those prior to Lewes.

First, there are the same feelings of worthlessness tangled up with, and compensated for by, a sense of superiority – in particular, superiority towards the wife. The hours Charlotte spent in giving private English lessons to M. Heger and his brother-in-law inevitably put one in mind of John Chapman's German lessons with Marian Evans. In both cases the wife is excluded; presumably she is in some other part of the establishment, being concerned with domestic matters, while Charlotte/Marian attend to the all-important intellectual needs of the husband. One senses that Charlotte Brontë considered herself a more fitting intellectual companion to Constantin Heger than his worldly wife could ever be. The fact she may well have been wrong about this is neither here nor there. Elizabeth Hardwick has noted that this sense of superiority is also an aspect of the heroines of both novelists, and she suggests that this is a superiority in the ability to love, as well as in affairs of the intellect: 'The heroine's moral superiority is accompanied by a superiority of passion, a devotion that is highly sexual, more so we feel than that of the self-centered and worldly girls the men prefer. (This same sense of a passionate nature is found in George Eliot's writing.) Charlotte Brontë's heroines have the idea of loving and protecting the best sides of the men they are infatuated with: they feel a sort of demanding reverence for brains, honor, uniqueness.'[43] A 'demanding reverence for brains' could also summarise Heloise's attitude towards her Abelard, in particular regarding her arguments against marriage for him.

Endless speculation has surrounded the relationship between Charlotte Brontë and Constantin Heger, but whatever differing conclusions may have been drawn, commentators

43 Elizabeth Hardwick, *Seduction & Betrayal: Women & Literature*, Weidenfeld & Nicolson, London, 1974, p.24

are united in considering it to have been of central importance in Charlotte's life and that it played a fundamental part in bringing about her creation as a novelist. 'Falling in love with M. Heger laid the ground for the emotional intensity and recklessness in Charlotte Brontë's novels. She experienced to the fullest a deep, scalding frustration. The uselessness of her love, the dreadful inappropriateness and unavailability of its object, turned out to be one of those sources of pain that are also the springs of knowledge.'[44]

In 1842, Charlotte and Emily Brontë arrived to study at the Pensionnat Heger in Brussels, with a view to acquiring the necessary skills and qualifications to run their own school. Emily, as was to be expected, held herself aloof from everyone, but Charlotte came to be fascinated by M. Heger, the husband of the proprietress and from all accounts a brilliant, charismatic teacher. Charlotte was twenty-six, Heger thirty-three. His wife was a few years older. Heger's teaching methods seem to have made use of some emotional involvement with his female pupils, if only in the sense that his frequent rages could be quickly dissipated by tears. Whatever his tactics, deliberate or otherwise, Charlotte succumbed. This was, after all, her first chance to enjoy intellectual companionship and stimulus with a man – apart from her father and brother – of equal intelligence to her own. It does appear, however, that she soon became infatuated: 'Lonely, vulnerable and acutely aware that the mental powers which estranged her from most people made her special in Monsieur Heger's eyes, Charlotte was easily won. During the course of 1843 she gradually slipped from normal feelings of respect and esteem for her teacher into an unhealthy and obsessive dependency on Monsieur Heger's every expression of approval.'[45]

After the sisters' first year in Brussels, they both returned home – their Aunt Branwell had suddenly died – and then Charlotte came back to Brussels alone. M. Heger had written glowingly of her to her father, and she was welcomed back

44 Ibid., p.21
45 Juliet Barker, *The Brontës*, Weidenfeld & Nicolson, London, 1994, p.419

now as a teacher of English as well as a pupil. That she returned to the Pensionnat primarily because of her fascination with M. Heger, to whom she continued to give private English lessons, hardly seems to be in doubt; whether she could admit this to herself – whether she realised the extent of her passion – is more difficult to determine. One person, however, was decidedly astute – and power was on her side: 'The wife soon sensed, in the way of wives and headmistresses, the disturbances and storms of an infatuation. The lessons were stopped. This enraged Charlotte Brontë for every possible reason. First it underscored her powerlessness: *that no amount of intelligence, skill, or hard work seemed to alter.*'[46]

The rest of the story is miserable. Charlotte became gradually more and more isolated and lonely. It seems that Mme Heger acted very carefully to ensure her husband had as little contact as possible with the English teacher. Eventually, defeated and depressed, Charlotte returned to Haworth. From there she wrote to Constantin Heger a series of passionate, despairing letters (from one of which I quoted earlier) – though to what extent they could be called 'love letters' is again a matter of debate. It is likely that, all along, it was an intellectual passion Charlotte was involved in and for which she craved reciprocation; certainly nothing as 'straightforward' as physical adultery was ever her aim – at least never consciously. M. Heger did not reply more than cursorily to these letters, the history of which itself is odd: it appears the recipient tore them up and threw them away, but that his wife then rescued the pieces from the wastebasket and stitched them together again. No one has ever worked out why. The letters now reside in the British Library.

Both Marian Evans and Charlotte Brontë asked explicitly for 'little', but the passionate language in which they did so, and the fact that both Herbert Spencer and Constantin Heger appear to have been petrified by the request, would suggest

46 Elizabeth Hardwick, *Seduction & Betrayal*, p.23

that the implicit demand was for quite the opposite, for an intensity of response neither man was able to approach.

Charlotte, I would suggest, had ultimately more self-confidence than Marian. She believed she deserved a far worthier place than the one accorded her by patriarchal society; and perhaps it was through the desire to attack that society that she turned on the figure of the wife. Even in Rochester's mad Bertha and her death by fire and falling, we may intuit Charlotte Brontë's revenge. Neither can one forget how Jane Eyre so greatly prefers the maimed, dependent Rochester to the earlier, all-powerful hero. It is self-belief which makes Jane reject a bigamous or extra-marital union, a self-belief Marian Evans did not possess – though in another sense she possessed it in abundance.

Marian Evans and Charlotte Brontë both eventually married – Marian at 60, Charlotte at 38; in both cases this signalled the end of their careers as novelists; in both cases they died within a few months of marriage. It seems the partly conscious belief they both held that – for them, and probably for most women during the nineteenth century – marriage and authorship could not be combined was correct. There is also the possibility in both cases that once safely married they felt no further 'need' to create works of literature. Furthermore, by marrying late and only after they had attained success as novelists, they ensured they did not enter marriage in a state of financial dependence. Marian stresses, when explaining her marriage will have no material effect on Lewes's family, that John Cross does not need any of her money; similarly, and most unusually for her time, Charlotte makes sure her earnings as a novelist do not enter into marital finances.

It is possible to view Marian's late marriage as the end of a pilgrimage towards respectability, as a final peace-making with conventional society, and certainly her brother Isaac regarded it in this light. Ruby Redinger suggests that it was the resulting acceptance by Isaac of his sister – now to be known as Mary Ann Cross – which released her from the need to justify her existence by writing fiction. Yet even at this stage in her life Marian succeeded in shocking her friends; maybe this was even part of her motivation.

> The furtiveness in her wedding plans and departure for the Continent may have been part of the pleasure, if it really is true, as one expert has said, that guilt is the cutting edge of sex. She had lived guiltily for twenty-four years with Lewes in one way. Now she had another. For although Cross was an old friend, wealthy, eligible – in all those ways a suitable person for Marian Evans to marry – he was twenty years younger than she. Again she had managed to find an object for her love which defied any social acceptance.[47]

It would appear that this woman may always have been particularly attracted to the socially unacceptable. Her whole history suggests her desire to be noticed, to be separate and superior to the herd and maybe, as Phyllis Rose suggests, unacceptability heightened her enjoyment of sex. Then there is that tantalising glimpse of strange events on her Venetian honeymoon – her husband leaping from their hotel room into the Grand Canal and having to be fished out by a gondolier. Suicide attempt? Indigestion? Sexual embarrassment? No one knows, but it's hardly the stuff of conventional respectability.

Charlotte Brontë's honeymoon took place in Ireland in July 1854, the same month in which Marian Evans and George Henry Lewes ran away – or, rather, most emphatically did *not* run away – together. Nothing as exciting as leaps into the Grand Canal here: 'Approaching an actual marriage, Charlotte Brontë was as far as possible from the purple sunset of Angrian romance. She was sober, unexcited, deliberate. She had witnessed what Victorian marriage did to wives – wiping out independent character – and with full consciousness, she allowed herself to vanish in this way.'[48]

★   ★   ★

47 Phyllis Rose, *Parallel Lives*, p.232
48 Lyndall Gordon, *Charlotte Brontë: A Passionate Life*, Chatto & Windus, London, 1994, pp.316–17

Marian Evans wrote in 1854, in an essay for the *Westminster Review* entitled 'Woman in France: Madame de Sablé', of the possible causes of the flowering of 'womanly intellect' in seventeenth-century France. Some of the conclusions she draws are apposite to her own life: 'Gallantry and intrigue are sorry enough things in themselves, but they certainly serve better to arouse the dormant faculties of woman than embroidery and domestic drudgery . . . the heart-pangs and regrets which are inseparable from a life of passion deepened her nature by the questioning of self and destiny which they occasioned, and by the energy demanded to surmount them and live on.'[49] Both Eliot and Brontë allowed passion to deepen their natures, and made use of the energy thereby demanded in the alchemical process of turning the raw material of life into the gold of art. Moreover I would contend that the unconscious artist (unconscious in the sense that it was in operation *before* either woman consciously recognised herself as an artist) in each of these women 'chose' unhappy, impossible loves – both because such raw material was necessary in their creative development as, and transformation into, artists and because happy married love would have prevented their writing; socially they would have been given no time to do it, and personally they might have felt no need, attaining at least some fulfilment in domesticity. Or possibly being driven mad by frustration.

Various oppositions have been noted in this chapter, operating in the composite figure of George Eliot as well as in her fellow writer Charlotte Brontë, and which frequently operate in the kind of woman who finds herself playing the role of mistress. There is the tendency to sink one's whole being in the other in a relationship, along with the (sometimes unconscious) fear of doing so, so that a deliberate choice (though because it can be unconscious it may feel like compulsion rather than choice) is made to fall for an unavailable man. The

49 George Eliot, *Selected Essays, Poems & Other Writings*, eds. A.S. Byatt & Nicholas Warren, Penguin, Harmondsworth, 1990, p.12

need for intimacy is thereby satisfied, while the desire to give over one's whole life to another is necessarily frustrated. The fear of giving in to that desire may be especially evident in a woman who also has the desire, or need, or vocation, to undertake some particular work in her life, maybe of a creative nature, which she knows instinctively will require more of her time and vital energy than she could give if absorbed both in another person and in the conventional demands of family life. (Both Eliot and Brontë had had ample experience of such demands, witnessing their mothers worn out by child-bearing and domesticity, and spending many years of their lives attending to the needs of their widowed fathers. Eliot escaped after her father's death; Brontë never escaped, though it was not until after her marriage that she found she had absolutely no time for herself.) Furthermore, the very frustration of a partial, part-time, to some extent unhappy, love may, if used well, actually increase the motivation and energy required to undertake whatever the work is; certainly it can feed into the creative endeavour.

Then there is the polarity of the senses of superiority and inferiority, so evident in George Eliot, and, I would suggest, familiar to many mistresses: 'I don't need to live like everyone else/I don't deserve to live like everyone else', 'I can love in a purer, more exalted, less demanding way than the wife/I am not worthy of a complete love'. (It has not been part of my purpose to investigate the origins of Marian Evans's lack of self-worth − others have done that − but just to note it is there.)

In Highgate Cemetery the obelisk mounted on the grave of 'George Eliot' or Mary Ann Cross dwarfs the monuments around it. George Henry Lewes is hidden respectfully behind; Dr John Chapman lies three graves away with his second wife, Hannah; Herbert Spencer is just around the corner, almost opposite Karl Marx. So the woman of the many names lies surrounded by at least some of the men with whom her life was intertwined; she dominates them all.

THE ROYAL MISTRESS

A man ought to be of royal blood before he
commits adultery, except in private.[1]

T wo triangles: Henri II of France, Catherine de' Medici
and Diane de Poitiers; Charles, Prince of Wales, Diana,
Princess of Wales and Camilla Parker-Bowles. Camilla and
Diane are both royal mistresses, Diana and Catherine royal
wives. In physical appearance the women line up differently:
Diane and Diana are the beautiful ones, Catherine and
Camilla more workaday. Both mistresses are expert horse-
women, and share this passion with their royal lovers. Neither
wife rides much. Both mistresses make some attempt to advise
the wives on how to handle their respective husbands:
Catherine takes Diane's advice (it concerns sexual positions)
and benefits from it; Diana, bewildered by Camilla's knowledge of her husband, takes no notice. Both mistresses are said
to have advised their lovers when it came to choosing their
respective wives – partly, at least, to ensure the wife was
unlikely to threaten their own position. Henri and Diane, to
the chagrin of Catherine, have a joint cypher made – an H
with a D on either side – and they even sign official letters
'HenriDiane'; on Diana's and Charles's honeymoon (if the
rather sensationalist biographers are to be believed), Diana was
upset to see her husband sporting cufflinks with two 'C's
intertwined, as well as being disturbed shortly before her
wedding by the discovery of a bracelet destined for Camilla,
engraved with the letters 'G' and 'F'. These have variously
been described by biographers as standing for 'Fred' and
'Gladys', reputed to be Charles's and Camilla's pet-names

1 Harriette Wilson quoted in Lawrence Stone, *The Family, Sex & Marriage: In
England 1500–1800*, Weidenfeld & Nicolson, London, 1977, p.506

for one another, or 'Girl Friday', which Charles apparently called Camilla. At least Diane, Henri and Catherine, in sixteenth-century France, were spared a running commentary on their lives by journalists and 'royal-watchers'. Interestingly, someone who has researched into the lives of this earlier triangle and to whose work I am indebted in this chapter is Princess Michael of Kent, one-time neighbour of the Prince and Princess of Wales at Kensington Palace. The parallels can hardly have escaped her. (I must also record my debt to Charles Carlton, whose book *Royal Mistresses* gives more detail about many of the women mentioned here.)

The remarkable Diane de Poitiers was born at the very end of the fifteenth century, into a world that had in a way been waiting for her. 'During the Renaissance, the courtesan in art had become, especially in the hands of Raphael, the image of the ideal woman. In Diane de Poitiers (1499–1566) she took on life.'[2] She spent her childhood in the household of a Princess of France, Anne de Beaujeu, where she was educated. Her education continued with her marriage to a grandson of Charles VII (and of Charles's mistress Agnes Sorel), as this gave her an entrée into the court of François I, France's great Renaissance king and the creator of Fontainebleau. She stayed at court after becoming a widow, and came to know Henri d'Orléans, the King's second son, when he was still a young boy; Diane was nineteen years older than him. She did not pursue him; he pursued her. For years he had worshipped her as a goddess and, once he had won her, he remained her steadfast lover, throughout his time both as dauphin (after his elder brother died unexpectedly) and as King. Diane's stepping down from the pedestal on which Henri had placed her and consenting to become his mistress happened shortly before his marriage to Catherine de' Medici. The insecurity of Diane's position as a widow at court would have reinforced her need to retain the love and loyalty of her young royal protector even after his marriage. He turned out to be

2 HRH Princess Michael of Kent, *Cupid & the King*, HarperCollins, London, 1991, p.xxii

completely indifferent to Catherine de' Medici, who had no beauty to recommend her and who was unfortunate enough to fall in love with him at once, which is something she admitted only years later to one of her daughters.

Catherine seemed unable to conceive and, as Diane realised that an annulment of the marriage and the arrival of a new queen might pose a greater threat to her own position, she resolved to help her. The dauphine had been dosing herself with various disgusting potions and wearing bits of foetus round her body, and Diane put a stop to all this and instead gave her some practical advice, including alternative positions for intercourse as Catherine's womb was unusually shaped. She also persuaded Henri to undergo a small operation, believed to have been little more than circumcision. Then, on designated evenings, Henri would spend the first part of the night in bed with Diane as usual, until she sent him upstairs to Catherine (her room was directly above Diane's). Once his marital duty was accomplished, Henri would return to Diane's bed for the rest of the night.

A son was finally born to Catherine and Henri at Fontainebleau in 1543, ten years after their marriage. And for the next twelve years, Catherine had a child every year, making her one of the most prolific royal wives in history. As a reward for her unselfishness in helping to produce an heir to the throne of France, Henri officially presented his mistress with a gift of 500 livres. As soon as the baby was born, Diane took him away from Catherine to present him to the ministers. She then supervised everything to do with him, from choice of wet-nurse to deciding what he should eat. And she subsequently treated all of Henri's children as though they were her own, leaving Catherine in no doubt as to who was really in charge. Catherine was resentful and jealous but also curious as to what it was that fascinated her husband about Diane. Accordingly, she had a spy-hole made in the floor of her bedroom so that she could watch Henri and his mistress making love.

The dauphin was crowned Henri II in 1547, at the age of

twenty-eight. On his first royal progress, it was Diane who entered the towns and cities by his side, passing with him under the triumphal arches displaying their joint cypher. Catherine's entry some days later would pass virtually unnoticed. In matters of state the new King trusted only his mistress, and many official letters were written in her hand and signed jointly with the one name: HenriDiane.

Princess Michael comments: 'By today's standards, we may sympathise with Catherine, but by the rules of the time she had only one purpose for her dynastic partner – to provide heirs to the throne. Her love for Henri, and her desire for his love in return, was seen as her personal affliction, almost as a curse.'[3] And towards the end of the twentieth century, it would appear that Charles, Prince of Wales would not have been out of place at Henri's court, whereas his Princess was completely at a loss when expected to play the role of a Catherine de' Medici. 'By today's standards', we (at least the tabloid-reading 'we') did indeed sympathise with the wife of the heir to the throne, who was expected to – and did – provide heirs, but came a decided second emotionally to her husband's mistress. No doubt we sympathised with her partly because, in appearance and deportment, she was far more a Diane de Poitiers than a Catherine de' Medici.

Diane de Poitiers kept her good looks and figure well into her fifties, bathing every day (unusual at the time) and taking regular exercise. She was dedicated to Henri and seemed able to love wisely and well.

> [She] was an intelligent though not strikingly original thinker. She was not an innovator. In outlook she was a woman of her time, a highly educated one certainly, but passionately committed to the social hierarchy and superb in her management of it. Her legend lives not only because her goddess alter-image has come down to us from the great masters of the French Renaissance, but

3 Ibid., p.62

because she was a woman of independent spirit who made an art of embracing the quality of life while preserving the youthfulness of her body and personality. She was an enchantress who inspired an unpromising youth to become a splendid king; that he loved her all his life, although she was nineteen years his senior, is proof of her enduring mystique.[4]

In her fiftieth year, illness forced Diane (who was by now the Duchesse de Valentinois) to retire from the court for a while. During her absence Henri began a flirtation with the governess in charge of the little Mary, Queen of Scots, who was then living at the French court. This governess was Lady Fleming, another beautiful widow, born Lady Janet Stuart, an illegitimate daughter of James IV of Scotland and the Countess of Bothwell. Before long she was telling everyone at court that she was carrying Henri's child. Although still unwell, Diane returned to court and is reputed to have staged, unusually for her, a tremendous scene. Henri capitulated and returned with Diane to her château at Anet. When Lady Fleming's son was born in September 1550, she made the mistake of behaving like the King's official favourite. This offended Catherine as well, so that, caught between wife and mistress, Henri had no choice but to send Lady Fleming back to Scotland. This was the only time Catherine and Diane joined forces, their intention being to avoid scandal. Although Diane was always seen to be with Henri, she did not obviously appear as his mistress — so that, for instance, the ambassador from the Vatican could report back in 1547 that, though Henri showed 'real tenderness' for Diane, 'it is not thought that there is anything lascivious about it.'[5] Catherine may have felt inwardly defeated, but her unhappiness was kept private, with Diane practising the high standards of decorum she had imbibed in her childhood from Anne de Beaujeu. In comparison with many other courts at other times, the atmosphere

4 Ibid., p.85
5 Ibid., p.51

at the court of Henri II was very sober, and neither he nor
Diane allowed any reference to be made to their relationship.
Diane had inherited the traditions of courtly love, with its
emphasis on purity, and her sense of decorum and taste set the
tone of Henri's reign.

Catherine attained her victory – though what a hollow
victory it was – when Henri was fatally wounded in a
tournament (a fitting end to someone devoted to courtly
love). As he lay dying, Catherine resumed her 'rightful'
control of him and was in charge of access to him. He called
out repeatedly for Diane, but she was not summoned. 'For the
next two days there was hope. Throughout that time a frantic
Diane waited for news in her house next to the palace; when
none came, she humbly requested to see the king. Permission
was coldly refused. At last, Henri belonged to Catherine.'[6]
Catherine professed always to love Henri, but what sort of
love is it that ignores a dying man's pleas to see his beloved for
the last time? Whatever real love she had for him must have
been contaminated by the years of bitterness, so that she
ended up hurting him as well as his mistress. Diane was also
uninvited to the funeral. She died at Anet in 1566, six years
after Henri's death.

It is difficult, at this close range and with the powerful
emotional charge it now carries, to make any objective
assessment of the second, twentieth-century, triangle. The
biographers are partisan, Ross Benson, for instance, being
even more firmly biased towards Charles in his account of the
life of the Prince of Wales, than Andrew Morton is, in his
books, towards Diana. There is disagreement between the
two factions as to when the friendship between the Prince and
Camilla became more than that. The Queen, according to
Benson, has even described Camilla as 'much maligned',
implying that she did not become Charles's mistress until
well after his marriage had irretrievably broken down. Benson
also offers quite an interesting perspective on the nature of the

6 Ibid., p.77

relationship between Charles and Camilla. He characterises her as a 'good listener', saying that once the reserved Charles had found someone he could trust and talk to, it was hard to stop him.

> 'Camilla was like a nanny to him,' one of her family observed. A member of the household explained, 'Prince Charles is a real loner. That's his basic nature and that is why somebody like Camilla is so terribly convenient, because she has got her own organized life and does not depend on him for anything but is always there at the drop of a hat for a little light chat and anything else that might imply.'[7]

Benson goes on to say: 'Given Charles's immaturity, the consequence of an upbringing that had provided him with material comfort but little emotional succour, Camilla might have been an ideal wife for him.'[8] But here he is missing the point completely: what the 'member of the household' has rather inelegantly described is the ideal *mistress*.

The late eighteenth century and another triangle, another Prince of Wales: George (later to be Prince Regent and then George IV), Princess Caroline of Brunswick, and Lady Jersey. Not to mention Mrs Fitzherbert.

When the affair between Lady Jersey and the Prince of Wales began in 1794, the former was in her early forties, the mother of seven daughters and two sons, and a grandmother, but still extremely beautiful. She was spoken of by contemporaries as exerting an irresistible seduction and fascination, and was tall, thin and elegant. Her relations with her husband, the 4th Earl, were cordial yet distant. She had for some time been the mistress of the 5th Earl of Carlisle, but by 1794 was bored of him, and decided to make a play for the Prince of Wales. He, meanwhile, was illegally (and secretly) married to

7 Ross Benson, *Charles: The Untold Story*, Gollancz, London, 1993, p.125
8 Ibid.

the Roman Catholic Mrs Fitzherbert. The 1772 Royal Marriage Act prevented any member of the royal family under twenty-five from making a valid marriage without the sovereign's permission, but Mrs Fitzherbert and the Prince of Wales had been accepted by their friends as man and wife since their 'marriage' in 1785 (when the Prince was aged only twenty-three).

Lady Jersey set to work to undermine Mrs Fitzherbert. She portrayed her to the Prince as self-seeking and duplicitous, blamed her Catholicism for his unpopularity, and insisted that the marriage of 1785 was invalid. She pointed out that, with Mrs Fitzherbert out of the way, he would be able to marry a Protestant princess, thereby securing a considerable addition to his income (he was perennially short of money). She then suggested as his bride Princess Caroline of Brunswick, knowing that such a woman would not threaten her own position at court. 'The woman chosen by Lady Jersey to be the Prince's bride was, in every sense, monumentally unsuitable. She was not dull, but eccentric, stubborn, thoughtless, full of energy, impulsive, careless, wilful and unencumbered by conventional notions of decorum.'[9] She was also rumoured to be rapacious for sex and indecent conversation. But the idea appealed enough to the Prince; he considered that, in any event, it would only be a marriage of convenience, intended to provide him with an heir as well as an increased income.

Lady Jersey next made sure that she was appointed as one of the Princess's three Ladies of the Bedchamber, a position which gave her unparalleled opportunities to torment her rival.

Once a daughter had been produced, the Prince felt he had fulfilled his obligations as far as his official marriage was concerned. He proceeded to ignore his wife as much as he could and contrived never to be alone with her. It was rumoured that one reason for his dislike of her was that she was more popular with the people than he was. When in

9 M.J. Levy, *The Mistresses of King George IV*, Peter Owen, London & Chester Springs, 1996, p.79

London he spent as much time as he could with Lady Jersey. As Princess Caroline became more popular in the public imagination, the estimation of Lady Jersey sank lower and lower. During 1798 the Prince himself began to tire of her, as he both experienced a rekindling of his affection for Mrs Fitzherbert and embarked on a short series of affairs with other women. He had never been able to forget what he owed Mrs Fitzherbert, who had not only agreed to undergo a dubious marriage ceremony with him, but had also then had to see him make an official marriage with another woman. He was now determined to get her back and – once she had consulted the Vatican who decreed, unsurprisingly, that the marriage to her had been the true one – she agreed, and they once more lived as man and wife. Until, that is, the Prince fell in love with Lady Hertford. But more of that anon; first, this Prince of Wales needs to be placed in the context of his forebears.

Courtesans have been a feature of royal courts throughout history, women prepared to use their beauty, intelligence and charm to make a way for themselves, and to provide for the future. Of all the royal courtesans, the French titular mistresses – *maîtresses en titre* – were the most powerful and prominent. The first of the great French royal mistresses was Agnes Sorel, lady-in-waiting to Isabelle de Lorraine, who attracted King Charles VII. It was for her that the title *maîtresse en titre* was created to denote the official mistress of the King of France, who rewarded and honoured her in every way he could. She bore him four daughters before dying in childbirth at the age of forty-one.

In the sixteenth century another King of France, Henri IV, reputed to have had as many mistresses as there are days in the year, fell for a young woman called Gabrielle d'Estrées. She came from a family of courtesans; her seven aunts were apparently known as the 'seven deadly sins', and her mother ran off with a lover. Henri IV fell so deeply in love with her that he decided to have his marriage to the Queen annulled and marry Gabrielle instead. She was all set to marry him – the

Papal Bull was expected, the wedding dress prepared – when she died from convulsions brought on by premature labour.

In the seventeenth century Louis XIV also had his fair share of mistresses, most notably Louise de la Vallière (who kept trying to escape her role by running off to convents and who did finally take the veil once Louis had gone on to another woman), Madame de Montespan and Madame de Maintenon. A *maîtresse en titre* to Louis XV was the famous Madame de Pompadour, unusual – and disliked by certain circles of the court – because she came from the *bourgeoisie*. Louis was married to Marie Leczinska, daughter of the exiled King of Poland, who became progressively dull and devout, finding ever more obscure saints' days as reasons for banning her husband from her bed. Louis consequently (it may be argued) began a liaison with the Comtesse de Mailly – followed by liaisons with two of her sisters, Madame de Vintimille and the Duchesse de Châteauroux. 'Madame de Châteauroux was a beauty, even nastier than Madame de Vintimille, rapacious, implacable, and very ambitious. She made the King work harder with his ministers than he had ever done before. Seeing that he was still rather fond of her sister she made him exile her from the Court; poor Madame de Mailly went off in floods of tears and was thereafter known as The Widow.'[10] Madame de Châteauroux was also nasty to the Queen. She died of pneumonia when the King was thirty-four, leaving the position of mistress vacant. The competition was fierce. 'Such was the prestige of a monarch in those days, so nearly was he considered as a god, that very little shame attached to the position of his mistress, while the material advantages to her family were enormous.'[11]

One reason for Madame de Pompadour's long tenure of the position (from 1745 to her death in 1764) was that she did not seek to make life difficult for the Queen, but rather helped to improve the King's relationship with her, thereby making his life easier all round. But a surprising element of this long-

10 Nancy Mitford, *Madame de Pompadour*, Penguin, Harmondsworth, 1995, p.14
11 Ibid., p.29

term relationship was that the sex wasn't particularly good. The King liked making love – a lot – and Madame de Pompadour found it all rather exhausting. She attempted to appear to like it more than she did, which made it all the more exhausting. Yet she must have had something, for the King remained devoted. And from this account of the daily rigours of her existence, it's hardly surprising she felt tired:

> She had many miscarriages during the first years, which pulled her down and disappointed her . . . Then the exhausting life began once more. Seldom in bed before two or three in the morning, she was obliged to be up at eight, dressed as for a ball, to go to Mass in the unheated chapel. For the rest of the day not one moment to herself. She must pay her court to the Queen, the Dauphin and Mesdames [the King's daughters], receive a constant succession of visitors, write sometimes as many as sixty letters and arrange and preside over a supper party . . . It was too much for her.[12]

Eventually she had a daughter, Alexandrine – who died aged ten, a blow from which Madame de Pompadour never fully recovered. But the King continued to come up her secret staircase at Versailles, for long or short doses of her company. And, like the mistresses of every age, she never went out, for fear of missing him when he called.

In 1751 she moved into a new and larger apartment in the palace, and was concerned to disseminate the information that her relationship with the King was no longer sexual. 'It must, however, be observed that the relationship between two human beings is seldom as cut and dried as other human beings like to imagine; the very blaze of publicity in which she left the King's bed throws a certain shadow of doubt. And Madame de Pompadour's new bedroom, like her old one, had a secret staircase leading to the King's.'[13] In any event, she

12 Ibid., p.82
13 Ibid., p.157

remained central to his life, and for subsequent flings he chose lower-class girls who could provide him with sex and no complications. These girls were kept for the King's pleasure in the Parc aux Cerfs, a small villa in the town of Versailles. Many of them did not even know their lover was the King, and Madame de Pompadour knew that none of them posed a threat to her own position.

Whenever the King became ill and seemed near to death – after, for instance, he was stabbed in an apparent assassination attempt – he would have to repudiate his mistress, in order to be able to make his confession and receive extreme unction. However much an illicit relationship might be tacitly tolerated by the Church authorities in the days of health and well-being, the imminence of death stripped the situation of any pretence and reminded the mistress how costly was her love. She would have to pay for it both in this life, once her royal protector was dead, and maybe – if the Church was to be believed – in the world to come as well. In Madame de Pompadour's case it was she who died first, and was compelled to make the act of renunciation. 'When the doctors said that she was dying, she asked the King whether she ought to confess; she was not very anxious to do so, as it meant that she would not be able to see him again. However, he said that she must. He bade her a last farewell, and went upstairs to his own room.'[14]

Nancy Mitford ends her biography of Madame de Pompadour with a telling tribute: 'After this a very great dullness fell upon the Château of Versailles.'[15]

'So far as is known, the English record for the production of bastards is held by Henry I, who begat at least twenty. According to William of Malmesbury, the procreations were acts of policy not pleasure, since the female children were used to obtain politically profitable marriage alliances with neighbouring princes.'[16] Henry ruled England from 1100 to 1135,

14 Ibid., p.257
15 Ibid., p.260
16 Lawrence Stone, *The Family, Sex & Marriage: In England 1500–1800*, p.505

and took advantage of the insecurity and dependency that mistresses and illegitimate offspring experienced. His sons could be depended upon to be loyal in the execution of his policies, while his choosing of particular mistresses cemented various political alliances. Unfortunately his strategy to avoid arguments about succession misfired when his only legitimate son, William, was drowned on the White Ship in 1120.

After Henry I came Stephen and then Henry II who married Eleanor of Aquitaine and had three legitimate sons – Henry, Richard and John. By the birth of John, the marriage had broken down. Henry consoled himself with Rosamund, the daughter of Sir Walter Clifford of Bredelais on the Welsh Borders, who became his mistress in 1173 when she was about sixteen. When she died three years later he was distraught and gave large bequests to the nuns of Godstow who buried her before their altar. She proceeded to become something of a cult figure, the nuns venerating her in such a way that Bishop Hugh of Lincoln was moved to protest when he visited the nunnery in 1191. ' "She was a harlot," fulminated the bishop as he ordered Rosamund exhumed and buried elsewhere . . . the nuns obeyed, reinterring Rosamund in their chapter house, where she remained until the Reformation, when an even greater intolerance caused her to be dug up again and scattered to the four winds.'[17] 'Fair Rosamund' then became the focus of many legends. One of the earliest, recorded nearly two centuries after her death, was that Queen Eleanor had tried to murder her by having her bleed to death in a hot bath. Another was that the Queen pursued her into a maze at Woodstock, built by Henry to protect his mistress; Eleanor accomplished this by following a silk thread from a sewing basket taken in to Rosamund. Once she had found her, Eleanor was supposed to have offered Rosamund the choice of either drinking a bowl of poison or stabbing herself.

17 Charles Carlton, *Royal Mistresses*, Routledge, London & New York, 1990, p.17

While neither of these stories was literally true, they do suggest a degree of popular sympathy for 'Fair Rosamund' that contrasts markedly with the increasingly harsh stand that the church was taking against illicit love, as well as a surprising amount of venom between Queen Eleanor and the king's mistress. Younger mistresses were an expected price that older queens paid for the position, status and wealth that marriage gave them.[18]

Leaving aside a few Edwards and Henrys we come to Henry VIII who, though best known for his wives, had several mistresses while he was married to Catherine of Aragon – to whom to begin with he was faithful, but things began to fall apart when she was pregnant as custom prevented him making love to her then. By one mistress, Elizabeth Blount, he had a son – given the unoriginal name of Henry Fitzroy. Then he had another by Mary Boleyn (Anne's elder sister). The production of a legitimate son seemed for some reason beyond him.

Queens Mary I and Elizabeth I were aware that the same standards did not apply to them as to their male counterparts. Elizabeth's court emphasised platonic love and the cult of the Virgin Queen. By contrast, the court of her successor, James, lived according to quite different morals from his increasingly puritan subjects. Next, Charles I lost his head but not to women, whereas Charles II had already become the father of several illegitimate children from various mistresses by the time of the Restoration in 1660. The most notable were Lucy Walters, mother of the future Duke of Monmouth, and Barbara Palmer née Villiers, who later became the Duchess of Cleveland and whom Charles brought with him when he returned to claim the throne. Exactly nine months later, she gave birth to a daughter, Anne, whom the King immediately acknowledged as his own. Barbara treated the Queen (Catherine of Braganza) with public disdain and also insisted on

18 Ibid.

being presented to her at court. In total, she bore Charles five children.

Her fecundity – combined with the discarded queen's barrenness – made her even more greedy and promiscuous. Apart from the king, she slept with the Earl of St Albans, and a Miss Hobart (a Maid of Honour, who was also intimate with Charles). She persuaded the king to appoint Dr Henry Glenham, her mother's uncle and a notorious drunkard, Bishop of St Asaph, and to make her old lover, Thomas Wood, Bishop of Coventry. But Barbara went too far – even for a man as tolerant of human foibles as Charles II – when she made love to both Jacob Hall, a rope dancer, in his booth at St Bartholomew's Fair, and with an anonymous footman in her bath. The last straw came when she then insisted that the king acknowledge the paternity of her children, no matter how and with whom they had been conceived.[19]

Then Charles fell for the beautiful Frances Stewart – the model for Britannia – but she was chaste. Over the next few years he had a number of affairs, none of which amounted to much. In 1670 he met Louise de Kéroüaille, when this beautiful young Breton girl came over to England with his sister, Henrietta-Anne, fourteen years his junior and always his favourite. Shortly after they returned to France, Henrietta-Anne died of peritonitis, and Charles was heartbroken. To relieve his despair – and for diplomatic ends – Louis XIV sent Louise back to England. They had a 'mock marriage' at Euston Hall in October 1671, and nine months later Louise gave birth to a son, Charles, whom the king delightedly acknowledged. He made Louise Duchess of Portsmouth, gave her a pension of £10,000 a year and a suite of twenty-four rooms in Whitehall Palace. She remained Charles's mistress –

19 Ibid., pp.68–9

though not his only one – for the rest of his life, providing him with a sense of domestic permanence and stability. She also knew, however, that he did not want to be completely free from the sense of guilt which accompanied all his affairs, so made use of tantrums and fits of hysteria to control him. She apparently did this to such an extent that Nell Gwyn, the King's other long-term and faithful mistress, dubbed her 'the weeping willow'.

In 1675 Hortense Mancini arrived in England. In her late twenties, she was one of the most beautiful women in Europe. She was the niece of Cardinal Mazarin, who had elevated her first husband to the Duke of Mazarin. He turned out to be a religious maniac, so she left him. 'After a brief dalliance with the Duke of Savoy, she turned up in England, complete with her black page, Mustapha, and a pet parrot.'[20] The King promptly installed her in Barbara Palmer's old apartments. Like Barbara, Hortense seems to have pushed her luck too far. A compulsive gambler, an athlete and a nymphomaniac, she finally alienated the King by flirting with the Prince of Monaco. Having dismissed her, Charles returned to the stability he enjoyed with Louise de Kéroüaille, spiced up by his on-going affair with Nell Gwyn. Louise seems, at least partly, to have been playing the role of the wife, in a way which Catherine of Braganza was either unable or unwilling to do.

In the public perception, Nell was the English Protestant mistress, Louise the foreign Catholic one. Though neither mistress exercised any real political power, they had a symbolic function which allowed the monarch to express his political preferences or, by maintaining both at once, assist in achieving a balance between rival factions. The corollary of this was that others might also choose his mistresses for him. None of them were liked by his subjects, with the exception of Nell Gwyn.

Charles II died leaving no legitimate children, but fourteen acknowledged bastards, by seven mothers.

20 Ibid., p.74

Charles's younger brother James, Duke of York, had likewise sought relief from the pains of exile in the arms of various women, eventually marrying Anne, the Earl of Clarendon's daughter. Though he was fond of his wife, he continued to have affairs. 'And since Anne was a commoner's daughter, she had reluctantly to put up with her husband's infidelities, and, starved of the pleasures of the bed, turned in compensation to those of the table, becoming inordinately fat. She died in 1671.'[21]

James first had a brief fling with Godotha Price, a maid of honour to his wife. Then he took Lady Elizabeth Denham, the wife of the royalist poet, Sir John Denham. Then there was Arabella Churchill, the sister of John Churchill, Duke of Marlborough. 'While James seemed to like all sorts of women, fair, dark, intelligent, Protestant and Catholic, he insisted they be young. Once they started to age he traded them in. Thus in 1678 he ditched Arabella for the young and beautiful Catherine Sedley.'[22] Catherine had been born in 1657, the only child of the poet, playwright and 'Restoration Wit' Sir Charles Sedley and Lady Catherine Savage. Her mother was mentally unstable and was eventually taken care of in a Catholic convent abroad. The daughter was placed at court, in the household of the Duchess of York. She was not, despite Charles Carlton's description of her as 'young and beautiful', known for her beauty, but she was renowned for her intelligence. In 1677 Sir Winston and Lady Churchill were interested in having her marry their son John, but she chose another avenue than that of respectability.

James had married Mary of Modena, his second wife, in 1674, and he inherited the throne (as James II) in 1685. The elevation from ducal to kingly mistress was not achieved painlessly, and might not have been achieved at all without great determination on the part of Lady (as she now was) Catherine. The new King at first resolved to lead a new, mistress-free, life. Catherine, he determined, must either go

21 Ibid., p.81
22 Ibid., p.84

and live in the country or go abroad; he would provide for her but would see her no more. But Catherine refused to go. She instead negotiated a house for herself in St James's Square, which had previously belonged to James's former mistress Arabella Churchill, and she also obtained a pension of £4,000. Before long former habits reasserted themselves and 'Catherine Sedley was being conducted up that notorious Privy Staircase leading to the King's apartments in Whitehall which had more than justified its existence during the previous reign'.[23] Charles Carlton gives another version, or further details, of how Catherine resisted this attempt to get rid of her: 'Catherine cited Magna Carta, which she claimed entitled her as a free-born Englishwoman to sleep with her king. The bribe of a house worth £10,000 and a pension of £4,000 a year managed to persuade Catherine that such might not have been one of King John and the Barons' intentions, and she left London for Dublin.'[24]

The arrival of William of Orange in 1688 brought about a complete change, but Catherine's instinct for survival again proved triumphant and, eight years later, at the age of thirty-eight, she married Sir David Colyear. She died in Bath in 1717.

William had found a companionship more congenial to him than that of his wife Mary in the company of Elizabeth Villiers. Elizabeth was no great beauty but, like Catherine Sedley, she made up for that by her intelligence and wit. She had first come to Holland in 1677 as part of Mary's household, and had attracted William's advances almost immediately. She tried to dissuade him by encouraging a Captain Wauchop instead, but William dismissed his rival. Elizabeth soon succumbed and rumours of an affair were rife by the summer of 1679.

Thence to the Georges and the odd-sounding German mistresses of George I. 'There was Ehrengard Melusine Von

23 Antonia Fraser, *The Weaker Vessel: Woman's Lot in Seventeenth-Century England*, Weidenfeld & Nicolson, London, 1984, p.403
24 Charles Carlton, *Royal Mistresses*, p.86

Der Shulemburg – a woman whose physique somehow matched the magic of her name. She was so tall and so thin that English courtiers nicknamed her "the maypole". In contrast Sophia Charlotte, Frein Von Kielmannsegge, was so fat that she was known as "the elephant".'[25] George II, who was married to Caroline, had an affair with Mrs Henrietta Howard for more than a decade. Fleshy, she had a nice nature, with a plain yet pleasing face. Every evening at nine, the King would go to Henrietta's apartments where he would stay for several hours. 'Being the royal mistress was, one courtier noted, about as regular, exciting, and physically challenging as being a mill horse plodding around its constant track.'[26] George III, who was completely faithful to his wife, decided in 1809 that mistresses should no longer live openly in royal palaces and ordered two of his sons, the Dukes of Kent and Clarence, to get their mistresses out of their official residences.

And so we return to where we left off. 'Few men have spent as much time, money, and effort in indulging themselves as George IV.'[27] We left him reunited with Mrs Fitzherbert but then, in his early forties, he discovered Lady Hertford, who became for him both confidante and nursemaid. When he was away from her he grew morbid and melancholy, sitting dumb and tearful for hours at a time. It was hard to work out the true nature of the relationship, so that many of his contemporaries wondered whether it was like his relationships with his other mistresses or whether it was merely platonic. Even during his obsession with Lady Hertford, the Prince also had his eye on – among others – his old flame Lady Bessborough. Yet Lady Hertford was the dominant influence during his forties and fifties, while Mrs Fitzherbert saw little of the Prince after he was made Regent in 1811. Under Lady Hertford's influence, he had decided she could no longer sit at his table at banquets and so on. Then, by

25 Ibid., p.88
26 Ibid., p.103
27 Ibid., p.111

the time he became King, he seems to have grown bored with
Lady Hertford as well.

His next conquest – or did she conquer him? – was Lady
Conyngham, a greedy, shrewd and very fat 49-year-old
matron, with whom he took up during the final weeks of
1819 while he was still Regent.

A few years later the infamous and impecunious courtesan
Harriette Wilson, who uttered the epigraph for this chapter,
threatened Lady Conyngham's peace of mind. Having previously had affairs both with Lord Francis Conyngham and
Lady Conyngham's own former lover Lord John Ponsonby,
Harriette decided to blackmail Lady C. She initially demanded a small payment in return for withdrawing Lady
Conyngham's name from her notorious *Memoirs* of 1825, but
inevitably she became greedier. Later that year, she wrote to
Ponsonby, threatening to publish some of Lady Conyngham's
letters to him, which had somehow fallen into her hands,
unless she was given a large sum of money. Lady Conyngham
was unsure how to proceed and the King was frantic, when a
satisfactory solution was proposed by the foreign secretary,
George Canning. He hit on the idea of offering Ponsonby a
diplomatic appointment in Buenos Aires to get him as far
away as possible; at the same time he bought up the letters
with some money from the Secret Service Fund. None of this
was good for Lady Conyngham's health but she still managed
to last till 1861 when she died at the age of ninety-one, having
apparently become pious and repentant. The King, meanwhile, had died in June 1830.

' "I resent Mrs Langtry," George Bernard Shaw told a group
of his friends. "She has no right to be intelligent, daring and
independent as well as lovely. It is a frightening combination
of attributes." '[28] Lillie Langtry, the daughter of the Dean of
Jersey, was a beautiful woman painted by Millais and Burne-
Jones. Her father, Dean Le Breton, was pious and conserva-

28 Noel B. Gerson, *Lillie Langtry*, Hale, London, 1972, p.9

tive, and her mother equally modest and self-effacing. Their six sons also grew up to be quiet and respectable. Lillie, who was born in 1853, seems to have been a different type altogether.

In 1877 Albert (Bertie) Edward, the second child and eldest son of Queen Victoria and Prince Albert, was thirty-six. He had been married for fourteen years to Princess Alexandra of Denmark. In May of that year, when the Princess was ill and had gone to convalesce at her brother's in Greece, the Prince of Wales asked friends to arrange for him to meet Lillie. She was then twenty-four, and had been married to the yacht-owning, hard-drinking Edward Langtry for three years, having married him principally in order to make her escape from Jersey. After a slow start, she finally broke into fashionable London circles as a 'Professional Beauty' after being noticed at a party. Her bored husband had to accompany her on her forays into society. No one knows precisely when she became the Prince's mistress. She was flattered by his attentions, realising her position gave her increased standing in certain circles, and she accepted the gifts he gave her. For some reason he was far less circumspect in this relationship than in many of his previous ones and seemed eager to let the world know of his attachment to 'the Jersey lily'. This shocked the respectable ladies of London society and, as they could hardly express their displeasure towards the Prince, they focused their wrath on Lillie. They continued to entertain her because they had no choice, but they were biding their time, as Lillie was well aware. An indication of what would happen if and when the Prince tired of Lillie was provided by a rather trivial incident. At a costume ball given by Lord Randolph Churchill, things got out of hand and Lillie dropped a lump of ice down the back of the costume of the Prince of Wales. This was going too far in familiarity and no way to treat the heir to the throne in public. Bertie glared at Lillie and then left, followed hurriedly by Princess Alexandra, and then all the other guests left for home too. The following day no invitations were delivered at the Langtrys' flat, but instead cancellations of various social engagements began to arrive. Even the usual at-homes were temporarily ended. Artist- and writer-friends remained loyal, and before long the Prince forgave her; her creditors therefore agreed to hold off and the invitations flowed freely again. But Lillie now saw this as only buying time while she decided how to take control of her life. She was considering going on the stage. Then she discovered she was pregnant.

She was visited by both the Princess and the Prince, who provided for her, told her husband she was leaving him and 'retired' to Jersey. Her daughter Jeanne was kept virtually a secret and, after the birth, Lillie returned to London in order to set about becoming an actress, the fame of her royal liaison helping to ensure her success.

In 1891 Daisy Countess of Warwick replaced Lillie as Bertie's official mistress. She was twenty years younger than him, good-looking and rich, and enjoyed the usual social round of balls, hunting and house parties. This affair ended in 1898 when Daisy became a socialist. It was after this that Mrs Keppel appeared on the scene.

Alice Frederica Edmonstone was born in 1869 and married George Keppel (who called her 'Freddie') in 1891. There were established links between the Keppel family and the Crown, and so from the start of the marriage Alice had access to court circles. She was known as 'La Favorita' of Edwardian high society, and her affair with Bertie, first Prince of Wales then King Edward VII, brought her social splendour and great riches. Before long her photograph was being frequently requested by magazine editors, who referred to her as the Prince of Wales's 'friend', commended her looks and clothes, and noted her presence at royal functions. She needed money to keep up this role and the King helped obtain employment for George Keppel, which both provided an income and ensured he was absent at the times the King came to call. (A milder, less murderous intervention than the biblical King David's sending of the husband of Bathsheba into the front line, but arguably in the same tradition.)

The King's death in 1910 changed Mrs Keppel's life

overnight. She had wealth but no longer a semi-royal position. Neither could she be one of the official, public grievers. She was cold-shouldered by Bertie's son and rebuffed when she went to sign her name in the visitors' book at Marlborough House.

'Wronged' queens and princesses have varied in their coping strategies. The first reaction of Catherine of Braganza, the King of Portugal's daughter, on learning she was to marry Charles II was to go on pilgrimage to a saint's shrine. Secondly, she promised her mother not to tolerate her husband's mistresses.

> Unfortunately Charles had made an equally solemn promise to Barbara [Palmer] to make her one of the new queen's ladies-in-waiting. Since she had just presented him with a son, and – unlike Catherine – did not surround herself with a dismal train of numerous confessors, a deaf duenna, a Jewish perfumer, and a gaggle of 'old, ugly and proud' servants (all badly in need of a wash), the king was much more inclined to keep his promise to his mistress than to his wife.[29]

Clearly Catherine learnt to accommodate herself to the situation, which has earned her the praise of Lady Antonia Fraser for one: 'Mary of Modena [James II's wife] never displayed any of that kindly tolerance towards her husband's mistresses which so signally marked the wise character of Charles II's wife Catherine of Braganza.'[30]

Mary of Modena's lack of tolerance was in evidence during the on-going wranglings with Catherine Sedley. Trouble had erupted when the King decided to make his mistress Countess of Dorchester and Baroness Darlington. (It has to be admitted that this was not an action likely to inspire tolerance in a wife.) The Queen was furious and refused to receive the new countess,

29 Charles Carlton, *Royal Mistresses*, pp.67–8
30 Antonia Fraser, *The Weaker Vessel*, p.402

who was already dressed to attend the formal royal reception when the refusal was conveyed to her. It seems Catherine was prevailed upon to take refuge in Ireland for a time, but returned to court in November 1686. Even after Catherine's influence with James was considered to have declined, the Queen would still be weeping at Windsor if the King were late home, convinced he had been with his mistress.

The daughter of James II by his first wife, Anne Hyde, was Mary, who married William of Orange in 1677. She was brought up on 'sentimental romances' and was longing to have someone to love. She did everything she could to please her husband, and William tried to respond, but Mary was too immature to provide him with the kind of companionship he valued. Hence his turning to Elizabeth Villiers. When his wife heard about this liaison in 1680 she was distraught. She fell ill and seemed to lose the will to live. Yet somehow she managed to survive and even accept that this is the way things often are if you marry a prince. When Mary died of smallpox in 1694, William was far more upset than might have been expected. Just before she died Mary wrote a letter to her husband, to be opened after her death, begging him to dismiss Elizabeth Villiers for the sake of his immortal soul. He complied with this request to the extent of never again seeing Elizabeth in public, giving her lands worth £30,000 a year and marrying her off to the Earl of Orkney.

The royal wife who most commonly receives accolades for her behaviour when faced with a multiplicity of mistresses is 'Bertie's' wife, Alexandra of Denmark. She was also renowned for founding hospitals, working for charity and having unusual compassion and understanding of the needs of the poor. She was enormously popular with people of every class in Great Britain. She accompanied her husband to all official functions – neither of them ever shirked their duty – but they led separate private lives. She felt at home in the court circles he was bored by, whereas he escaped into the society life of London whenever he could. They followed this routine for so many years that it came to be taken for granted that an invitation issued to the Prince need not necessarily be extended to the Princess. Then as Lillie Langtry and her successors began to appear at official functions, there was ever greater admiration for Alexandra's ability to receive them with at least a show of friendliness. She is reputed to have continued this behaviour at the time of the King's death. Mrs Keppel had sent Alexandra a letter written to her by Bertie in 1901 when he had appendicitis, stating his desire to 'say farewell' to her if he were to die. The Queen allowed Mrs Keppel to come to see him, 'shook hands with her, said, "I am sure you have always had a good influence over him," then turned away and walked to the window.'[31]

So what has changed? Clearly princes haven't. Or, as King Magnus puts it – perhaps exaggerating – in George Bernard Shaw's *The Apple Cart*: 'Our country has produced millions of blameless greengrocers, but not one blameless monarch.'[32]

Implicit in Princess Michael of Kent's treatment of her subject is the view that, during the many centuries when the wives of kings and princes were chosen for dynastic and foreign policy reasons, royalty's habit of taking mistresses was to be expected and by and large excused. She follows precisely Demosthenes' principle, in fact – wives for the bearing of legitimate offspring, mistresses for love and enjoyment. The further implication, almost made explicit, is that the habit is less acceptable now, because it is unnecessary. Princes, at least in theory, can marry the women they love (always provided, of course, that the woman in question is not already married, or – in the case of the United Kingdom – a Roman Catholic). Yet when the current Prince of Wales married, it would appear he was still making the assumptions which belonged to the old dynastic tradition: Diana would provide him with heirs, would be present as his wife at official events, but would not expect romantic love and would turn a blind eye to his having a mistress. It is not clear whether he

31 Diana Souhami, *Mrs Keppel & her Daughter*, Harper Collins, London, 1996, p.91
32 George Bernard Shaw, *The Complete Plays*, Odhams Press, London, 1934, p.1022

considered the idea that she might also take a lover. But Diana, it seems, married with quite other ends in view; she thought this really was a marriage for love, that the romantic fairy tale as presented by the media was real. The result was a terrible disillusionment for her.

If one compares the affairs of Charles with his predecessor Bertie a century ago, one first of all realises that Charles has been far more faithful to his long-standing mistress than Bertie was to any of his. Charles made the mistake (if that is what it is) of being in love with his mistress – of, in fact, being in love with her, if accounts are to be believed, at the time of his wedding to Diana. And Diana, unlike Alexandra, never played the part of the complaisant wife. Furthermore, she had affairs too, something Alexandra would never have dreamed of – the 'double standard' of one set of rules for men and another, more stringent, set for women applying to royalty as strongly, if not more strongly, as in other strata of society. Alexandra seems to have been almost as popular as Diana, seen as compassionate, in touch with 'the people'. She was also an example to all other wives of how to keep a husband and keep up appearances while not trying to deny him his freedom (which would probably have been a wasted effort anyway). But to say Diana should have behaved like Alexandra – or, indeed, like Catherine de' Medici – would be anachronistic. She couldn't have; it would have gone against the person she was and the time in which she lived.

One major change between this and most previous generations is that we 'the people' now know far more – or think we do – about royal affairs of all varieties. The respectful diffidence once shown by newspaper editors and proprietors has vanished for ever. It is not that the people were never previously interested in royal affairs – they always have been. Court artists such as Sir Peter Lely used to paint nude portraits of Charles II's mistresses to satisfy public interest, and Pepys records a dream of sleeping with Barbara Palmer. But there used to be a strong sense that the affairs of the aristocracy, of the royals, even of politicians, were private, nothing whatsoever to do with the masses – always provided they obeyed the codes of decorum, so that dalliances were not viewed in public, thus forcing a reaction from others. This sense has now gone, partly because the royals – especially the younger ones – are less concerned with being discreet, partly because the concept of 'the people' has gained greater currency, and the opinions of the people are considered to be of far greater importance than previously. And partly also because we lack a sense of history, and appear to have forgotten what an old story this is. For questions to be raised, for instance, as to the suitability of an adulterous monarch as head of the Church of England, at this late stage in its history, is laughable. Yet things have moved on, and it is clear that a completely separate world of monarchy and aristocracy, living by a different set of rules from everyone else, does not sit well with democracy. The people are too resentful, and they wield considerable power as they demonstrated after the death of the Princess of Wales. Perhaps we are witnessing the final triumph of what the ex-dustman Alfred Doolittle in George Bernard Shaw's *Pygmalion* referred to as 'middle class morality', and we are all, royalty included, expected to conform to the same narrow codes of respectability and convention, and generally behave like characters out of popular soap opera.

It is not only the press and the people who have changed, but also the way members of the royal family deal with them. (The use of that phrase – 'royal *family*' – is itself indicative of a change in attitude during the course of this century, with the stress being placed on the family rather than on the monarch alone, and fidelity to the family being expected of the monarch. Family is anathema to mistresses, and vice versa.) All the younger royals, maybe even their parents, have at least colluded with the press in making their affairs (in every sense) material for public consumption. Charles has in his time entered a confessional mode entirely foreign to Bertie. This is partly just because Charles is a child of his time, believing in personal fulfilment and the communication of feelings – even if this was not the way he was brought up.

Bertie's mistress Mrs Keppel died before the birth of her great-granddaughter Camilla. Diana Souhami opines that 'Mrs Keppel would have been delighted had Camilla married Charles not Captain Andrew Parker-Bowles, an army man like George [Keppel]. But given her respect for social appearances and discretion . . . she would have viewed with disdain the way Prince Charles, his princess and mistress made public their muddle over sex.'[33]

In fact Camilla seems to have remained far more firmly in the tradition of discretion than the other two parties in this triangle. The shadowy figure – the one we still know the least about – remains the mistress.

---

33 Diana Souhami, *Mrs Keppel & her Daughter*, p.291

THE POLITICAL MISTRESS

*I can't help it if somebody doesn't want their
husband and then somebody else besides them
decides they do.*[1]

On 5 October 1983, the Right Honourable Cecil
Parkinson, MP, Secretary of State for Trade and
Industry and a former Chairman of the Conservative Party,
made a statement to the press through his solicitors, in which
he acknowledged that he had had a 'relationship' (H. Montgomery Hyde puts this word in quotation marks on nearly
every occasion he uses it in his narrative) with his former
private secretary, Miss Sara Keays, and that she was expecting
his baby the following January. Sara Keays was then aged
thirty-six. He said he would be making financial provision for
both mother and child, and he admitted having previously
asked Miss Keays to marry him and then changing his mind.
'He added: "My wife, who has been a source of great strength,
and I decided to stay together and to keep our family
together." '[2]

On the night of 13 October Miss Keays issued a statement
to *The Times* which was immediately transmitted both to Mr
Parkinson and the Prime Minister, Mrs Thatcher, at the Party
Conference in Blackpool. It detailed the long-standing, loving nature of the relationship, and the understanding given by
Mr Parkinson and received by Miss Keays that he would
eventually marry her. It seems, at least according to her
version, that he first asked her to marry him in 1979, that

---

1 Pamela Harriman quoted in Sally Bedell Smith, *Reflected Glory: The Life of Pamela
Churchill Harriman*, Touchstone, New York, 1997, p.206
2 H. Montgomery Hyde, *A Tangled Web: Sex Scandals in British Politics & Society*,
Constable, London, 1986, p.335

he changed his mind when she knew of her pregnancy in May 1983, that he changed his mind again on polling day (9 June), asking her to marry him and telling Mrs Thatcher that such was his intention. He then changed his mind yet again while on holiday with his wife and family in the summer and decided not to marry her after all. She had meanwhile been asked by press reporters during August if it was true she was pregnant by him. She had finally decided, in issuing the press statement, to 'put the record straight'. It had the (desired?) effect of precipitating Mr Parkinson's resignation from the government. On 31 December 1983 Sara Keays gave birth to a daughter, Flora Elisabeth. In the following March a formal maintenance order was made against the father (provision being made in this way apparently for tax purposes).

Sara Keays is unusual among ex-mistresses of politicians for having written a book about her experiences (*A Question of Judgement*, published in 1985) and it is an extraordinary book, notable for what she does not relate as much as for what she does. She moves fairly rapidly over the progress of her twelve-year affair with Parkinson, the bulk of the narrative being taken up with a minute recording of all that was said and written, in the press, on television and radio, in solicitors' letters and in phone calls, leading up to and in the aftermath of the statement put out by Parkinson, with her consent, on the night of 5 October 1983.

What is immediately clear from Sara's telling of her story is that she is no natural mistress-type. That she nevertheless managed to hold such a role in Cecil Parkinson's life for twelve years resulted from her firm belief that the role was temporary, to be exchanged – at some unspecified date, but quite definitely – for that of wife. She uses this belief that Cecil wanted to and would eventually marry her as justification for having continued the affair, and she did indeed break it off at least twice and for several months when that assurance was missing. (Her lover does not emerge with much credit from this story, having several times, according to Sara – and I see no reason to *disbelieve* her story as she tells it, though I might

question her interpretation of various words and events –
prevailed upon her to resume the affair by using further
promises of marriage.) What is striking, though, for someone
who clearly holds firm views, and keeps expressing them, on
'integrity' and 'duty', is that she never explains – beyond the
non-explanation of 'I fell in love' – why she embarked upon
the affair in the first place. It is hard to believe Mr Parkinson
walked into the office one day – they met when she became
his secretary in 1971 – and said, 'Hello, Sara, I intend to marry
you so let's go to bed together.' There are, to do her justice,
more subtle ways of letting the promise of marriage hang in
the air, particularly if the man perceives that that's the way to
persuade the woman to have, and then continue, the affair.
But no woman as fixated on marriage and children as Sara
Keays reveals herself to have been is going to be contented as a
mistress.

Part of her trouble was, it seems to me, that she had no
experience of romantic and sexual relationships before she
encountered Cecil Parkinson. She was twenty-three and he
thirty-nine when they met; she says he was the first man she
ever fell in love with and he remained the only man for her
throughout the twelve years of their affair. Her inexperience
combined with naïvety and an apparent inability to analyse
why a married man might say one thing one day and something else the next – an inability somehow to put her
relationship with Cecil Parkinson into context, the context
of his family, his political life, his overriding ambition – meant
that she took everything he said at face value and that she
seemed to operate on a very simplistic paradigm, something
along the lines of 'He loves me, so he must want to marry me
– but today he doesn't want to marry me, so he doesn't love
me any more.' She appears not to understand – at least not
during the time of the affair or when she wrote the book –
that a man may love more than one woman at once, and that
loving his mistress doesn't necessarily imply a willingness to
divorce his wife. She makes the assumption that love and
marriage are always inextricably linked. 'I believed that he

truly loved me and for the first time I felt I could hope for future happiness with him.'[3] No mistress should ever make assumptions about 'future happiness'. When she describes her lover's earliest proposals of marriage to her – well before the anguished time when she became pregnant and the affair public – she never mentions questioning him as to the logistics. Maybe she has simply not recorded questions like 'When are you going to tell your wife?', 'What are you going to do about the children?', but the impression one gets reading her account is of her sitting back happily waiting and trusting while Cecil continues to go off on holidays to the Bahamas with his family, clearly not having told them a thing and not intending to. For Sara it is as though, right up until the crisis point in 1983, Ann Parkinson doesn't really exist – either as a woman capable of being hurt or as an obstacle to her own marriage plans. I don't think this was callousness – and who am I to talk anyway? – but rather a lack of perception, either an inability or a refusal to imagine her lover's life away from her or to admit that she could herself be behaving in an any less than honourable way. And her naïvety takes an incredibly long time to wear off. After months and months of appalling treatment by reporters and Tory spin doctors (it was before the term was coined, but there was plenty of spinning going on), she is still surprised each time her views are misrepresented or her words or actions misinterpreted.

Another curious aspect of this story is the extent to which Sara's family – her father, sisters, brothers and respective in-laws – embroil themselves in it and are embroiled in it by her. It is as though she is a little girl being mistreated by the nasty Tories (in whom she previously innocently trusted) and needing protection from Daddy, rather than a grown woman capable of taking responsibility for her own actions and their results. It seems to me extraordinary that in 1983 the father of a 36-year-old woman should take it upon himself to write to the Prime Minister to complain of the way his daughter has

3 Sara Keays, *A Question of Judgement*, Quintessential, London, 1985, p.13

been treated by one of her ministers – and even more extraordinary that this interference should not have absolutely infuriated his adult daughter. Instead she writes: 'If only Cecil had faced up to his responsibilities sooner, my father would not have been driven to intervene. I did not question his right to do as he did and I respected the principles which motivated him.'[4] Is this an example of 'Victorian values' in operation? It seems to me not at all surprising that Mrs Thatcher did not write fulsome replies. Colonel Keays also provides a Foreword to the book in which he says, 'My daughter Sara has had my entire support in the preparation of this book.' Why should a woman, by now in her late thirties, be in such strong need of her father's stated approval? In fact, this admiration of and dependence on her father, who in her childhood had had to spend long periods working away from his family, are possibly the only usual mistress characteristics which Sara betrays. It's not particularly surprising that she should have fallen in love with a powerful man, considerably older – and definitely more experienced – than herself.

It is clear from the mass of detail in *A Question of Judgement* that Sara Keays read every article and watched every news programme touching on her affair with Cecil Parkinson, and that the opinions of both her close friends and relatives and of millions of people whom she had never met were of desperate importance to her. At no point did she feel able to say 'Oh, let them think what they like – I know the truth of the matter, and so does Cecil.' It is also undoubtedly true that she fell victim to the old double standard that talks about – and detests – the 'fallen' woman, while tending to glorify the virile, untrustworthy, male seducer. A fallen woman who dares to stand up for herself is doubly hateful to the moralising masses. And it must have been desperately hurtful, and induced a strong desire to 'put the record straight', to have a long-term love affair, to which she had committed herself and to which she believed her lover to be committed, written off as a

4 Ibid., p.52

'peccadillo', a 'dalliance', a piece of 'foolishness' on his part.
Yet it is also true that no woman who cares about her
'reputation', and the effect of a blackened reputation on
her 'family' (and Sara Keays reiterates these words again
and again) should ever take on the role of a mistress.

A catalogue of presidential, ministerial or other ranks of
political affairs will not add anything to an understanding
of 'the mistress'. It's all been done before – and it's being done
all the time – and it is ultimately very repetitive and rather
boring. Who had sex with whom is primarily of interest to the
parties involved and their other nearest-and-dearest, and
secondly to people who haven't got anything better to think
about, who take vicarious pleasure in the doings of others and
find their pleasure heightened by describing, even condemn-
ing, those doings as misdoings. And in pursuit of an understanding of the mistress, it must be admitted that not many
women who get involved with politicians seem to play the
role to perfection. At least, not many *of those we hear about*. It is
an innate difficulty of writing about this topic that the most
successful mistresses are those we never hear about – at least
not in their lifetime or that of their lovers – for their success is
measured by the extent to which they keep their affairs secret.
It's not at all easy for the mistress of a politician to do that, but
it has been done, and probably is being done, even in these
media-infested days.

   This chapter is also about the way people believe what they
want to believe, to the extent of being able to operate a
'double-think' of believing two contradictory things at once.
So Sara Keays can conveniently forget about the existence of
Mrs Parkinson, and Megan Lloyd George can simultaneously
hate her father's infidelity to her mother and take up with a
married man herself. And Frances Stevenson can take at face
value all Lloyd George's moans to her about his wife, thereby
absolving herself from any accusations of 'stealing' his love –
for clearly his wife didn't really want him. As A.J.P. Taylor
puts it in his introduction to Frances's diary: 'Naturally he

worked off on Frances Stevenson the irritation which he sometimes felt with his family. It does not follow that they were as tiresome as he made out or as she was led to believe. Indeed it is a fair surmise that there was a Welsh side to Lloyd George which cherished life at Criccieth with his wife and children.'[5]

Of the political mistresses we do hear about, some are out to ruin their man – maybe out of anger because they have been rejected in favour of the wife, maybe for money, maybe because they crave publicity. Some, like Monica Lewinsky, have been appallingly careless and left a trail of e-mails, notes and answer-machine tapes, not to mention 'friends' ready to come forward and reveal all. Others – and probably these constitute the majority – we hear about but never see, those silent and invisible figures with whom the man in question 'made a mistake', who were never of 'real importance' compared to the supportive and loyal wife, bravely smiling beside him. Occasionally – rarely – the mistress does make it into the position of wife, as in the case of Gaynor Regan, now the second Mrs Robin Cook – but she might do well to remember the words of the late Sir James Goldsmith: 'When a man marries his mistress, it creates a vacancy.'[6]

Megan Lloyd George possessed all the qualifications to be termed a 'political mistress'. The daughter of a politician who was to become Prime Minister, a politician herself, and the mistress of a politician, she managed to keep her liaison hidden, with only a few close friends knowing the truth, throughout her life. And, as the daughter of that particular Prime Minister, she was also on the receiving end of infidelity, her loyalty to her mother outweighing even her devotion to her beloved 'Tada'.

Megan, the youngest of three daughters (her eldest sister,

5 A.J.P. Taylor (ed.), *Lloyd George: A Diary by Frances Stevenson*, Hutchinson, London, 1971, p.x

6 Quoted in *Vice: An Anthology*, compiled by Richard Davenport-Hines, Hamish Hamilton, London, 1993, p.36

Mair, died suddenly at seventeen), adored her father. She never stopped talking about him, and her sense of herself primarily as 'daughter' may have contributed to her lifelong youthful appearance and demeanour. When she first discovered his unfaithfulness to her mother, it came as a terrible shock, for she seems to have idealised her parents' relationship. It was in any event a strong one, but her mother Margaret had to employ more compromise than Megan thought acceptable. Margaret Lloyd George was never accepting of her husband's unfaithfulness, but neither could she see any point in having rows over it which she considered would be beneath her dignity.

It was indirectly through Megan that Frances Stevenson first entered the lives of the Lloyd Georges, when she came as a young teacher to coach Megan prior to her entry to Allenswood School. David Lloyd George was soon smitten and before long proposed that Frances should give up her teaching job and come to work for him instead as his private secretary. 'He offered her this job, as she put it, "on his terms". It was, in fact, a package offer as secretary and mistress, and it was irresistible.[7] She reciprocated his love, and remained his steadfast lover throughout his life.

Prior to Frances, Lloyd George had had many affairs and minor flings. By and large these dried up after he became involved with her (he fell in love with Frances in 1912, when he was forty-nine). This would suggest that she gave him what he needed – which would in turn suggest that *maybe* his wife might have done the same, if she had cared to. Margaret Lloyd George was known as a formidable woman in Wales, but she did not wish, or try, fully to share her husband's political life; she resisted the move to London, preferring Wales whenever possible for herself and the children, and she didn't provide her husband with that undemanding, constant and supportive audience he so clearly needed and relished. (Whether successful and dynamic men *ought* to need so much female adulation

7 Mervyn Jones, *A Radical Life: The Biography of Megan Lloyd George, 1902–66*, Hutchinson, London, 1991, p.21

is another question; I am merely pointing out that if they do
and their wives don't provide it, they are quite likely to find
mistresses who will.) By the time Lloyd George became Prime
Minister in 1916, Frances had become an essential part of his
life. The cement in David Lloyd George's and Frances
Stevenson's relationship was not so much their emotional
and sexual involvement with one another, though these were
important too, but the fact that they *worked* together, that they
made a good partnership in every sense.

Frances did have cravings to marry her lover though she
had more sense than to try to destroy his current marriage and
family. LG had made it clear that he had every intention of
avoiding a public scandal that would jeopardise his political
career, but he did promise that if he were ever free he would
indeed marry her, and he even agreed to give her a child.
Jennifer was born towards the end of the 1920s, and it was all
managed very discreetly. Those who knew about the relationship were few, and Frances's high reputation as a confidential
secretary protected her from being identified as a mistress.
Neither did she look like the stereotypical image of someone
with whom a politician would be having an affair. As one of
the civil servants on Lloyd George's staff said: ' "No one
would suspect her of a sexual relationship with anybody.
You'd take her to be a prim schoolteacher." '[8]

According to one of Frances's grandchildren, Ruth Longford, a motivating principle for Frances had always been to
give pleasure to people. In her childhood and youth this
meant passing exams and practising the piano. In later life it
made her an easy prey when Lloyd George expressed his need
for her. Her upbringing reinforced the message that the
achieving man needed and deserved a supportive woman.
She wasn't, however, brought up to become a mistress; the
expectation – on the parts of both herself and her conventional mother – was that she would marry respectably and
have children. Her university education was never intended,

8 Ibid., p.34

or felt by herself, to be a replacement for this. But, swept along by her devotion to Lloyd George, she found herself pursuing quite a different course. Part of the justification she would find for fulfilling her desires subsisted in, as it usually does, denigrating the wife:

> She would tell herself that Margaret neglected David. Margaret should come to the House and hear David speak. Margaret should provide him with comfortable little suppers and the admiration he needed to encourage him in his work. If she chose to neglect him, attending first to the interests of her children, and having no interest in making her home comfortable, then she should expect him to find a soft shoulder to lean on, or at least a willing listener to talk to.[9]

To begin with, LG could do no wrong as far as Frances was concerned. In later years, according to Ruth Longford, she grew to resent some aspects of her 'servitude', but she continued always to admire him and put his interests above her own.

As his private secretary, Frances was able to spend more time with her lover than is often the case for a wife. As she noted herself in her diary on 8 February 1916, 'The only thing we lack is children, but I often think that if I were married and had children, then I should not be able to keep in touch with D.'s work to the extent that I do now, and perhaps should be less happy. At present all our interests lie together; he does nothing but what I know of it; I almost know his very thoughts. I don't suppose I should see nearly as much of him if I were married to him.'[10]

In the privacy of her diary (though it has to be remembered she did agree to its publication), Frances allows herself really to let rip about Mrs Lloyd George, succeeding in being as bitchy

---

9 Ruth Longford, *Frances, Countess Lloyd George: More than a mistress*, Gracewing, Leominster, 1996, p.10
10 *Lloyd George: A Diary by Frances Stevenson*, p.96

about the wife as any mistress I have encountered. Perhaps it is not surprising the hostility was mutual:

It is extraordinary how everyone dislikes Mrs L1.G. Mr J.T. Davies [another civil servant on Lloyd George's staff] was talking to me about her this morning: he says that sometimes when he is feeling particularly unfriendly to her, he tries to find some redeeming feature about her which will compensate for all her unlovely qualities. But it is impossible to find one. I have often felt the same too. She is simply a lump of flesh, possessing, like the jellyfish, the power of irritating. But I am being very nasty. I try as much as possible to refrain from commenting upon her, as she has good reason to dislike me. But she has no pride. D. has told her time and again that he does not want her in London, that he would much prefer her to live at Criccieth – when she has been making a fuss about me. I am sure I would not remain with a man who showed so plainly that my presence was not wanted.'[11]

The sentiments Frances expresses on 20 February 1920 must have been echoed by thousands of perplexed mistresses, viewing marital relations from afar: 'Mrs L1.G. is watching him like a hawk. She is an extraordinary person. She goes away for weeks and does not bother about him, but when she comes back she is on the watch all the time. Most inconsistent.'[12]

It had taken the young Megan a while to realise what was going on (she became aware of the relationship some time in 1920 or 1921, when she was about eighteen), but once she did her hatred for Frances – of whom she had previously been fond – was deep and implacable. But what of Megan's own relationships? She had two. The first was with a popular novelist, Stephen McKenna, whom she wanted to marry (though it was unclear whether he wanted to marry her –

11 Ibid., p.122
12 Ibid., p.202

or indeed anyone), but she was too young to do so without her parents' consent and they vetoed it. The second, which was to last for about twenty years, began at the time when Megan was a Liberal MP (she became MP for Anglesey in 1929). Her lover was on the Labour benches – was in fact a fairly prominent member of the Labour Party – and his name was Philip Noel-Baker. By his own account he fell in love with Megan in 1929. There is, however, no evidence that the feeling was reciprocated or that they became lovers at that time. But from 1936, when he won the Derby by-election (with Liberal support), they were able to meet every day when the House of Commons was sitting. It must have been in fact that year that they became lovers; this can be deduced from his later letters in which he takes that year as the starting point of a new life.

Philip's wife Irene was several years older than him, and he gave Megan the picture of an unsatisfactory marriage, in which he never quite fulfilled Irene's expectations and there was no true partnership between them. According to him, Irene criticised him all the time, they quarrelled and he had often thought he ought to end the marriage. She spent much of her time in Achmetaga in Greece, from where she accused her husband of infidelity (though she never knew about Megan) while refusing to be with him herself. He was a compulsive letter writer and the tenor of the long liaison, and particularly Philip's character as a lover, can be judged from the many letters which survive. A number of these letters are quoted verbatim in Mervyn Jones's biography of Megan, with the permission of Philip's son, Francis; the Noel-Baker family have, however, refused to allow me to reproduce extracts from any of these previously published letters here. Megan's letters, of which there were far fewer in any event, have not survived, but it is still possible occasionally to hear her voice – loving, upset, exasperated or angry – behind Philip's response. From the earliest letters which survive (from 1940) it is clear this was a serious relationship, and that Philip held out – at some unspecified date in the future – the possibility of marriage, or at least that he could be interpreted in this way, if the recipient so desired. But the language is also vague and dreamlike enough for the writer to hold he never meant anything of the sort. He writes of being unable to live without Megan, and declares that he will always love her, but there is no definite promise of anything.[13]

Dreaming, besides letter-writing, was Philip's strong point, and it is as though he felt his dreaming absolved him from the need to take action, as though claiming he *wanted* something to happen (probably after being reproached by his lover) was as good as taking steps to make it happen. He asked Megan to believe, for instance, that he dreamt every night that he was married to her and that they were surrounded by her babies.[14]

They took as a leitmotif of their relationship a phrase Megan first used in 1939: 'Never love me less.' But what does 'love' mean in this dreamworld when, on Philip's side, it so clearly doesn't mean putting himself out for Megan, or considering whether his actions – or inactions – were harmful to her? Does 'Never love me less' become anything more than an emotional panacea, a sort of sticking plaster which attempts to cover up the wound of daily life lived without the other person? Letters written in July and August 1940 show Philip oscillating – sometimes offering to vanish from Megan's life, sometimes looking forward to marriage – but he throws the responsibility for actually taking decisions on to Megan. He apologises if he was selfish (though any apology which includes the word 'if' inevitably sounds half-hearted) and tells Megan that he hates the thought of being a strain on her, but insists that there is nothing he can say (and the implication is there is nothing he can *do*) unless she tells him to leave her, in which case he will obey.[15]

What is infuriating about someone like Philip Noel-Baker is the lack of honesty, as much in his dealings with himself as with others. For some reason he would not leave Irene, but he didn't

13 See Mervyn Jones, *A Radical Life*, p.138
14 See Ibid., p.258
15 See Ibid., p.143

appear to understand himself what that reason was – or even to be able to admit that it existed, and that the refusal to make a decision is a decision in itself. There were no obvious obstacles to his leaving his wife: they had one grown-up child, the relationship was, according to him, unsatisfactory – she did not seem even to like him very much – and there was no suggestion that at this stage a marriage breakup would have a bad effect on his political career. Yet for some reason he was terrified of causing marital disharmony and, as is usually the case with people who refuse to examine their own motivations and real desires, he cast the blame for his situation on 'fate'. In 1946, at the start of the second phase of this affair, there is a reference to a postcard from him which had made Megan angry. We do not know exactly what it was that had angered her, but from Philip's protest one can infer that Megan had accused him of not being whole-hearted about his relationship to her. His reply to her criticism puts the onus first on Megan herself, and secondly on fate: on Megan, by implying that she is responsible for the nature of their relationship by allowing him to be her lover; and on fate, by accusing it of placing an insurmountable barrier in his life – by which he presumably means his marriage. He assures Megan that if only the barrier were not there, everything would be perfect.[16]

The only people who definitely knew about this relationship in the 1930s were Megan's close friends, Thelma Cazalet and Ursula Thorpe, her mother and her sister Olwen. Patricia Llewellyn-Davies, Philip's secretary in the 1940s, was aware of his assignations with Megan, but was not certain that they were actually lovers; he had such assignations with a number of other women as well. Lord Jenkins of Hillhead who, as Roy Jenkins, was his Parliamentary Private Secretary in 1949–50, was completely unaware of the relationship until he read Mervyn Jones's biography of Megan.[17] The people who did know about the affair were under no illusion as to how deeply involved Megan was with Philip and to the emotional inequal-

16 See Ibid., p.187
17 Mentioned in a letter to VG of 15 September 1998

ities of the relationship: ' "It meant a great deal to her," Ursula remarked. Patricia stated with conviction: "She was tremendously in love with him." Asked whether Philip was in love with Megan, she hesitated and said: "He thought he was." '[18]

Towards the end of the 1930s Thelma Cazalet had tried to persuade Philip to obtain a divorce; it was taken for granted in their discussions that Irene would be prepared to divorce him for adultery and desertion. It also seems to have been taken for granted – at least by Thelma – that Megan definitely wanted to marry him herself. The only evidence for thinking she did is that which can be inferred from some of Philip's letters, presumably written in response to a desire articulated by her for children. But I am unconvinced, and if there is any excuse for Philip's vacillatory behaviour it may be that Megan herself gave off mixed messages, so that he could never be entirely sure that she really wanted him to leave Irene. It remains all too often the assumption of outsiders that a woman involved with a married man, whatever she may aver to the contrary, *really* wants to marry him herself and have his babies. Nevertheless, it still can't be denied that Philip used Megan's distaste for divorce, real or imaginary, as an excuse to do nothing that would disturb his own status quo. It is possible Megan was too diffident, too proud, to ask him to divorce, but that she may always have been waiting, expecting him to do so. But one can never be sure.

Both her sister and mother knew of Megan's relationship with Philip, and both disapproved. Olwen was unhappy about it not so much on moral grounds as because she had a low opinion of Philip and thought Megan was wasting her time. Margaret was far more emphatic; she took the firm view that a love affair which entailed marital infidelity was wrong. When she realised she was dying, at the end of 1940, she asked Megan to promise her that she would break with Philip. Megan gave the promise.

There was worse to come (from Megan's point of view).

18 Mervyn Jones, *A Radical Life*, p.121

After Margaret's death, Frances Stevenson decided the time had come – after a reasonable interval – for Lloyd George to make good his promise to marry her if this ever became possible. Megan found the whole idea horrifying and was still trying to argue her father out of it the night before the wedding finally took place in October 1943 in a register office at Guildford. The only guest for champagne after the ceremony was the newly married couple's daughter, Jennifer.

> Two weeks after the marriage, Frances wrote to Megan: 'My dear Megan, I hope you will read this letter through, as it is written in all sincerity, to ask if you will not reconsider your attitude towards your Father's marriage with me. I am so anxious that you will not commit yourself to a permanent and irrevocable estrangement from him, both for the sake of his happiness and your own, and that is why I am sure you would not forgive yourself if you were to be the cause of any sadness in his last years. I am depriving you of nothing in becoming his wife – neither of his affection, nor of any material benefits now or in the future.[19]

There was no reply.

Only when it was clear that David Lloyd George was dying (in 1945) did Megan relax her refusal to be in the same room as Frances; he died with each woman on either side of his bed. After his death hostilities were resumed. There was a very mean and unforgiving streak in Megan. A surround of local stone was designed for the grave and, when it was completed, there was a short family ceremony of dedication – to which Frances was not invited. But she came later, and left a bouquet of red roses on the grave. The next day, while out for a walk with Ursula Thorpe, Megan picked up the roses and flung them over the hedge into the road.

19 Ibid., pp.165–6

Philip began to write to Megan again in 1946, desiring to restart the affair. At first she resisted, but they became lovers again in 1947. And so the well-rehearsed themes and half-truths of Philip's letters are resumed. One of his most contradictory efforts was written in February 1953. He is at pains to stress that Megan is the most important thing in the world to him, that she is indeed everything to him, and that he cannot believe that she can be in any doubt about the strength of his feelings. But at the same time he is remonstrating with her, accusing her of not understanding how difficult it is for him to call her on a Saturday morning when he is not alone. (She has clearly been complaining that he did not call her at a specified time, or that he called much later than she had hoped.) Yet even after having explained, at least by implication, that he has other people's feelings to consider, Philip reverts to telling Megan that she is the only person he loves, and that he would do anything to make her believe that she matters more than anything or anyone else to him. He ends on an *almost* repentant note, but again casting the onus back on to Megan by agreeing to be penitent – if that is what she wants.[20] It is the kind of letter which a psychoanalyst would revel in. Suffice it to say that what comes across so clearly in what Philip writes – and Megan must have been aware of this, if only in the sense of unease and frustration the receipt of such a letter engenders – is that if he 'can't' phone her because of being in a house with other people then she is *not* the most important thing in the world to him. More important to him is not upsetting the domestic applecart. His declaration that he would do anything in the world – that is, if he could think of anything he could do – to make Megan believe she is his only love rings hollow, when what he will not do is ring her up when Irene is in the house. Not even his repentance is real; by agreeing to be penitent if Megan *wants* it, he refuses to accord any seriousness to her criticisms. His refusal to engage is genuine argument is also a tactic for getting his own way.

20 See Ibid., pp.255–6

According to Patricia Llewellyn-Davies, Irene never knew
that Philip and Megan were lovers. She did not imagine,
however, that Philip was a faithful husband. She watched him
with suspicious vigilance, but could not decide who, out of
various potential candidates, was his mistress. And Philip took
elaborate precautions to keep the affair secret.

On 8 February 1956 Irene Noel-Baker died from a sudden
and unexpected heart attack. Although she was seventy-six
years old, it does not seem to have occurred to Philip that she
might die, and he was completely disorientated. His behaviour in the immediate aftermath of the death was bizarre.
Megan was in London at the time – her friend Ursula Thorpe
was staying with her – and Philip phoned her and insisted that
she come round immediately. He then led her into the room
where Irene's body was lying and made her stand there with
him for several minutes. She left as soon as she could, deeply
upset and hurt.

Then Philip's letters dried up. He went to Greece for two
months, giving Megan no idea of his intentions – concerning
her or anything else. He returned to London on 18 June and
four days later wrote to Megan. This last letter told his
mistress of nearly twenty years' standing that on the day Irene
died, Philip had suddenly realised how very much he loved
his wife. It appears that on her death he suddenly became
aware of how wonderful she was. (It seems a great pity for
both women that it had taken him so long to come to this
realisation.) Philip declares that he was unconscious of how
he felt right up until 8 February, but that since then it has
been all he has been able to think of. What this means to him
in relation to Megan is – unsurprisingly, given his record –
contradictory. He claims still to love her and to have
appreciated the comfort and support she gave him in the
weeks immediately after Irene's death, but he also seems to
be regretting ever having embarked on the affair. He now
feels unable to offer Megan anything at all; he cannot be with
her, or even think of her, without also being in the presence
of dark and unhappy thoughts. He tells her that he must now

face his considerable and anxieties alone and that, until he resolved them, he believes he must not try to see her or continue to take any of the things she has given him – including her love and companionship – over so many years. In saying he can no longer *take* from her, he is of course refusing to *give* any more to her himself; he appears in fact to be negating much of their past love (based as it was on his repeated assertions that Megan was everything to him), as well as declaring that the relationship is now over. And yet he goes on to insist that he is not being disloyal to Megan, and that he still loves her, as he always has.[21]

The only really truthful word Philip uses of himself in this letter is *unconscious*, which he certainly has been, and to some extent still is. Megan received the letter at her house in Wales, ran down to the end of the garden with it and wept uncontrollably.

Several questions need to be raised at this point. First, why did Megan stick with this relationship for nearly twenty years? Was she really hanging on and waiting for Philip to leave his wife and propose to her? That sounds extraordinarily passive for a forthright woman MP, the proud daughter of a charismatic Prime Minister, and someone capable of flinging a bunch of her father's lover's roses over a hedge. No, she must have actually *wanted* to keep the relationship going for its own sake. Despite the irritation and anger Philip clearly caused her, she must have loved him enough to want him to stay around, and the good times they had together must have made her at least as happy as the bad times made her miserable. And whatever she may or may not have said about wanting children, it mustn't be forgotten that the life of a female Member of Parliament in the 1930s and 40s did not leave much time for domesticity. It is more than likely that, like many mistresses before and after her, Megan found that a part-time relationship actually suited her very well. She may well have been frustrated that she could not often decide for herself

21 See Ibid., p.269

when those part-time hours would be, Philip's timidity and indecision may well have infuriated her, but the relationship still provided her with enough of what she needed. His ultimate rejection of her hurt her so badly because that was what it was – a rejection, and a shock, telling her it was Irene he had really loved all along – and she would be lonely and miss him, but the fact he didn't want to *marry* her may not have been the point at all.

Yet there is nevertheless something far more satisfactory about the relationship between David Lloyd George and Frances Stevenson, and it rests in the greater degree of honesty. It's much easier to cope with not having all you may want of someone if that person has spelt out the terms of the relationship in advance – there is far less to get angry with them about. We are all self-deceivers, but some are worse than others. Frances could have been in no doubt that Lloyd George had no desire either for public scandal or private ructions in his family life – she was to be his beloved mistress and secretary and that was that. Yet she was clearly able to talk to him about the terms and even accomplish some negotiation – witness a daughter and the promise, eventually realised, of marriage. For Megan, on the other hand, nothing was clear-cut and negotiation was impossible. Not only did she not realise how much his wife meant to Philip, he didn't realise it himself. But I think that maybe not all of the blame for confused motives and vacillation lies with Philip. Megan was not a very 'conscious' individual either.

There is a coda to this story of two mistresses, joined and divided by the love of David Lloyd George. First, when the statue of him in the House of Commons was unveiled in 1963 the Lloyd George family sent no invitation to Frances. But the Speaker of the House did invite her. She appeared, and was duly ignored by the family. Then, just over three years later, Megan died of cancer. Her funeral took place on 18 May 1966:

★   ★   ★

Philip Noel-Baker was not there. He knew that his presence would not be welcomed by Megan's family, and perhaps he felt that he would be unable to restrain his grief. But there was someone else who did defy the hostility of the Lloyd George family. An elderly woman stood near the gate of the cemetery and did not mix with the other mourners. It was the Dowager Countess Lloyd George – Megan's teacher, Frances Stevenson.[22]

It seems fitting that an ex-courtesan – arguably the greatest courtesan of the twentieth century – should have been appointed by President Clinton as U.S. envoy to France in 1993.

Pamela Churchill Harriman was born Pamela Digby, one of the Digbys of Minterne, Dorset, in 1920. She had an aristocratic pedigree, but showed by her life that she owed even greater allegiance to another tradition. 'Her precursors included Madame de Maintenon, Ninon de Lanclos, and Madame de Pompadour in the seventeenth and eighteenth centuries, and Cora Pearl and Léonide Leblanc in the nineteenth. Pamela was the only genuine exemplar in the twentieth, renowned like Pearl for her "golden chain of lovers".'[23] Like many mistress-types, Pamela lived for the moment, seizing opportunities and not worrying too much about consequences, trusting to her inner spirit and her unfailing luck to carry her through.

She was brought up in the conventional ways of the British aristocracy, being presented at court as a deb in the final season before the Second World War. She wasn't a great success at that time, being considered rather too plump and pushy. Her career was really launched with her marriage to Randolph Churchill – precipitate, as were many marriages in the early days of the war, and disastrous in itself, but providing her with an entrée into the inner circle of power, as the daughter-in-law of the Prime Minister during the most critical years of his, and Europe's, life.

22 Ibid., p.320
23 Sally Bedell Smith, *Reflected Glory: The Life of Pamela Churchill Harriman*, p.15

Pamela's first affair after her marriage was with the American financier and diplomat, who was involved in securing supplies for the Allies under the Lend-Lease scheme, Averell Harriman. He was considerably older than her – old enough to be her father – as evinced by the fact that she became very friendly with his daughter Kathleen, who was two years her senior. (Kathleen was clearly better able to cope with the idea of her father having a lover than was Megan Lloyd George.) Averell was married to Marie, who had stayed behind in the States. Pamela was extremely useful both to Harriman and to the British leaders, as a conduit of information between him and Churchill. When Marie Harriman got to hear about Pamela, she was most annoyed that the affair was being conducted in such a public fashion.

By early November 1942, Pamela had told her father-in-law that she and Randolph planned to divorce (they had one son, 'young Winston'), and she was installed in a new flat in Grosvenor Square, paid for by Harriman, who also provided her with a yearly allowance of £3,000. Pamela had other men in her life at the same time as Harriman; he was, after all, married – and intended to remain so – and neither of the lovers felt he therefore had exclusive rights over her. He also, on his trips back to Washington, had other women.

In October 1943 Harriman was posted to Moscow, and by December Pamela, now aged twenty-three, had taken up with the 35-year-old CBS radio broadcaster Edward R. Murrow. He was also married and his wife Janet was with him in London. 'Averell Harriman may have been the most important American in London, but Edward R. Murrow was surely the most glamorous. During the Blitz, his dramatic nightly broadcasts on CBS Radio helped stir pro-British sentiment and counteract isolationists in the United States.'[24] Pamela's war effort also included affairs with a very wealthy U.S. Army captain, Jock Whitney, and Major-General Fred Anderson, the American bombing comman-

24 Ibid., p.118

der. She also had a brief fling with Murrow's boss and friend, William Paley.

In 1944 Pamela used Janet Murrow's absence, when she returned to New York in a state of mental and physical stress partly as a result of her husband's liaison, to press Murrow to divorce Janet and marry her. It was William Paley who intervened and strongly advised Murrow not to do it, on the grounds that Pamela was a great courtesan but that to marry her would be ruinous.

Meanwhile, Harriman continued to pay the rent on Pamela's Grosvenor Square flat until 1950, when Lord Beaverbrook (who had been the go-between in this transaction) urged him to terminate the agreement as he knew that by this time Pamela was being supported in Paris by Gianni Agnelli. Nevertheless, Brown Brothers Harriman paid her annual stipend for nearly three decades.

When Pamela met Gianni Agnelli, the scion of the Fiat automotive empire, he was twenty-seven, a year younger than she. He bought her an apartment in the 16th *arrondissement* of Paris, as well as underwriting a new London flat for her in Hyde Park Gardens. He also, however, despite being unmarried, resisted her attempts to persuade him towards the altar. She appeared to have got unwillingly stuck in the role of mistress. 'By becoming a perfect extension of the men who kept her, Pamela had done her job too well: no man of wealth and rank would marry her, knowing she functioned so well as a mistress.'[25] In 1950 Pamela even converted to Roman Catholicism (in the process getting her marriage to Randolph Churchill annulled – but being careful to keep his illustrious name), at least partly in an attempt to get Agnelli to marry her. But it was in vain.

So then she went on to André Embiricos, a Greek whose family had built a fortune in shipping. Meanwhile Agnelli, who had decided to marry someone else, nevertheless let Pamela keep her Paris apartment and made a

25 Ibid., p.157

substantial financial settlement on her. 'His generosity was motivated by a sense of responsibility that she actively encouraged.'[26]

Embiricos didn't last long, and next came Elie de Rothschild. Parisian society quickly came to know of this affair, which at least temporarily boosted Pamela's status, yet it was kept secret from Elie's wife Liliane for some months. 'Despite the entrenched tradition of official mistresses in France, the wife has always had a clearly defined role to which the mistress by custom deferred. At first Pamela seemed willing to live within the rules. But, after a lull, she began urging Elie to divorce Liliane and marry her.'[27] She persuaded him to tell Liliane he wanted to leave her for his lover, but when Liliane refused to be accommodating Elie gave in to his wife. Then Liliane set about making Pamela's life in Parisian society difficult, by cutting her in public and telling her friends not to mention her.

In an attempt to provoke Rothschild, Pamela took up in the mid-fifties with Stavros Spyros Niarchos, an even richer shipowner than Embiricos. Next she went on to the United States where she had a brief affair with Albert Rupp Jr who ran an automobile dealership on Long Island, but then she became involved with the Hollywood agent and producer Leland Hayward. And now at last she attained her target. Hayward was on his third wife, known as 'Slim' (he had also married and divorced his first wife twice); Slim made the mistake of not taking her rival seriously enough, and Pamela realised that here was a husband she could wrest from his wife. 'Pamela had no guilt whatsoever about her actions. "I can't help it if somebody doesn't want their husband and then somebody else besides them decides they do," she said years later. "It's not my fault." '[28]

Pamela and Leland Hayward were married on 4 May 1960, hours after his divorce from Slim became final. The marriage

26 Ibid., p.162
27 Ibid., pp.170–1
28 Ibid., p.206

lasted until Leland's death in 1971. And by this time Pamela's old flame Averell Harriman was a widower. He was also nearly eighty, but that didn't seem to worry either him or Pamela. 'He had supported her financially, so he knew her price, and he also knew that she was worth it: She would work hard, take good care of him, and not simply grab his money. She knew that he was prickly and self-absorbed, but she also knew that he was utterly dependable – and vulnerable enough to yield to her coaxing ways. Both of them had their eyes open.'[29] They married on 27 September 1971, eight weeks after their reunion in Washington and six months after Leland Hayward's death.

As Harriman's wife, and subsequently widow (he died in 1986), Pamela had an entrée into the very centre of U.S. politics, just as her first marriage had brought her into the centre of British political life. And now at last she was able to act as a political figure herself, rather than playing only as the consort of a man. 'At sixty-six, Pamela was once again on her own, but this time there seemed little likelihood that she would launch a search for a new man. Harriman had given her everything she needed, including his prestigious name . . . She had stature as well as financial security, which allowed her to break the pattern.'[30] She played a large part in Bill Clinton's election campaign in 1992, and her reward came in March 1993, when he announced her nomination as U.S. envoy to France, the first woman to be so nominated. She was sworn in as the nation's sixty-fourth ambassador to France on 17 May. So back she went to Paris, in rather a different role from her previous incarnation in that city.

Pamela Digby Churchill Hayward Harriman died on 5 February 1997, at the age of seventy-six, after suffering a cerebral haemorrhage in the Hôtel Ritz swimming pool. 'She had lived a full and eventful life spanning a remarkable half century from World War II to the end of the Cold War, and

29 Ibid., pp.261–2
30 Ibid., p.317

she had achieved all she wanted: wealth, admiration, and finally, respectability'.[31]

The cynical no-nonsense approach of Pamela Harriman arguably pays dividends in this world of shadow-boxing between wives, mistresses and men with a public image to uphold, though it is completely at odds with Heloise's view of what loving is all about, and may also be out of step with late-twentieth-century ideals of female independence. She knew what she wanted – generally someone else's husband, but also name, status and wealth – and even only a few decades ago being a political mistress may have been her best route to attaining these things. She could also usually tell when it was time to cut her losses and move on to the next prospect. She didn't go in for years of allowing herself to believe a man was about to leave his wife and marry her if he showed no active signs of doing so, and she doesn't appear to have wasted her energies in resenting the wives – rather, she attacked them head-on or not at all. The other mistresses I have considered in this chapter were considerably more deluded, both by their lovers and by themselves. This may be inevitable in a world where appearances matter so much and disguise far more than they reveal. Official photographs of politicians with their happy families present one version, sometimes the most obviously false. Other versions are proffered by husbands to wives, lovers to mistresses – and then each person also tells their preferred version to themselves. The deception necessarily involved in the outward part – the logistics – in the lover/mistress relationship can too easily spread into the inner workings of the relationship itself. The parties want to believe in happy-ever-after for themselves and so they start to feed one another's fantasies. The lover comes to his mistress, after all, for relief from the practicalities and problems of family life; it is therefore not surprising if he doesn't want to talk practicalities with his mistress, and is prepared to make her

31 Ibid., p.453

happy by running down his wife and imagining a life with her where everything is easy and love conquers all. The mistress's mistake can be to confuse this imaginary world she inhabits with her lover with the 'real' world where her lover is caught up in shared property, children, other relatives, and a complex relationship with his wife in which he is likely to have far more of himself invested than he is prepared to admit either to his mistress or to himself. And it may appear as though his wife doesn't want him but, as Frances Stevenson admitted in her diary – despite her diatribes against Lloyd George's family – 'There is always something to be said on both sides!'[32]

32 *Lloyd George: A Diary by Frances Stevenson*, p.259

THE ARTIST'S MISTRESS

*You meant – all that lay outside the dull
home, the unspeakable fireside, the gruesome
dinner table – you are the one outside who
calls a man to apparent freedom and wild
rocks and wind and air . . .*[1]

A young, naked woman, kneeling on the ground, stretches out her hands towards an older, also naked, man; their fingertips touch, but he does not look back. He leans towards the figure of an older woman, who is behind him, her hands on his arms, restraining him and beginning to pull him away. He seems tired, reluctant to leave, yet unable to resist the power of the older woman, who seems to coil herself around him, snake-like. The younger woman has the advantages of youth and beauty but, since the man is no longer looking at her, such advantages are useless. Perhaps the younger woman is the mistress, the older woman the wife. Or perhaps this is a struggle between youth and life on the one hand, old age and death on the other. There is a kind of inevitability about this trio and no doubt as to the eventual outcome – the older woman will triumph, at least partly because the man seems to exercise no will of his own. Yet the younger woman has an energy, apparent even in her pose of supplication. Perhaps she will throw herself on the floor and weep when the man – her lover? – has been borne away, as much for him as for herself. But then one feels she will pick herself up and go on with her life, lonely yet strong. For the man there is no hope.

The above is a description of *L'Age mûr* (Maturity), a

1 Ida John quoted in Michael Holroyd, *Augustus John*, Vintage, London, 1997, p.178

sculpture by Camille Claudel (1864–1943). This was a work which Camille had succeeded in getting the state to commission, but the commission eventually fell through – possibly through the intervention of Auguste Rodin – in 1899.

It has always been interpreted as representing the final stages of Claudel and Rodin's affair, as he is borne off in the clutches – as Claudel sees it – of the middle-aged Rose Beuret, who is not in fact Rodin's legal wife but who has for years played the role of one.

Auguste Rodin first encountered Camille Claudel in 1882 when he agreed to supervise a small group of students, all of whom were young women. One of the students – indeed the instigator of the group – was the seventeen-year-old Camille. 'Her brother, the poet Paul Claudel, described her in one of his essays as a headstrong and strikingly beautiful girl: "A superb forehead and magnificent eyes of a deep blue rarely encountered except in novels . . . her large mouth was more proud than sensual; her hair was of that true chestnut shade which the English call auburn, and fell to her waist. She had an air of courage, frankness, superiority, gaiety." '[2] In childhood Camille had expected everyone to do her bidding – her brother and sister, the housemaid, her schoolmates. She was fiercely determined to become a sculptor and succeeded in getting her family to move from Nogent-sur-Seine to Paris in the pursuit of her aim to study there. Once arrived, however, the Claudels had no money to spare for their daughter's education, but eventually she organised a 'colony of students' who shared the rent as well as tutors' and models' fees. It seems Auguste and Camille fell in love almost at first sight.

An interesting document has come to light in the last few years, written and signed by Rodin but apparently drawn up by Camille. It begins: ' "In the future and beginning today, 12 October 1886, I will have no student other than Mlle Camille Claudel, and she alone will I protect with all the means I have at my disposition and with the help of my friends, who will

2 Frederic V. Grunfeld, *Rodin: A Biography*, Hutchinson, London, 1988, p.211

also be her friends, especially my influential friends." '[3] Rodin goes on to promise that from the date of the document until May of the next year he will have no other woman – or the agreement will be terminated – and Camille promises to 'receive' him in her studio four times a month until the same date. In 1888 Rodin started paying rent on a studio for Camille, after she had had to move out of her parents' place where the strain between mother and daughter had become too great. Her father was inclined to take a more lenient view of her liaison with Rodin than her morally indignant mother, though the mother later insisted the father had 'suffered' too when he realised what was going on. Camille's attitudes were clearly quite at variance with those of her immediate family and background.

At the outset, Camille had recognised in Auguste Rodin a great sculptor and the best teacher; she was therefore prepared to submit to his direction and abandon her own will as a step along the road to art. Then she fell in love with him, and her submission became more complete – though, as if unconsciously aware of the damage this might do to her, as woman and artist, she embarked upon the relationship with many reservations. But most importantly she knew that, as a student, and with great ambitions for herself, she needed to assimilate as much as she could from this genius. Having an affair with the great sculptor also suited her high opinion of herself, her sense of herself as unique, and fulfilled the requirement of always getting what she wanted. It provided an affirmation of how special she was, how important to her teacher; moreover, she then used his love, or desire, to further her own ends as an artist, stipulating the conditions, the favours she required, in return for *her* favour. In the early 1890s she benefited from the special considerations Rodin had promised, especially introductions to his friends and help with commissions.

What appears to have happened next is that Rodin exhausted her, demanding all her time and energy in his service.

3 Ruth Butler, *Rodin: The Shape of Genius*, Yale University Press, New Haven & London, 1993, p.198

At first this would have been offered freely by Camille – so Rodin can hardly be blamed for taking it, until he began to take it for granted – but in time she came to resent the situation she had helped to bring about herself. 'Camille worked under Rodin's aegis for more than a decade . . . During the time she worked as his assistant he exploited her gifts . . . She modeled innumerable details for him, enlarged his maquettes and carried out his designs, his instructions.'[4] By the time she broke off the relationship, in or around 1893, and as a contributory factor to that breakup, she had become anxious to escape Rodin's overwhelming influence and devote herself exclusively to her own art.

The outward reason for the breakup – and this may have been no more than a psychological excuse presented by her conscious self to the artist in her struggling to break free – was that Camille could no longer tolerate Rodin's remaining with Rose Beuret. The relationship between Rose and Rodin seems to have been one of those partnerships incomprehensible to anyone on the outside, which appears to give little satisfaction to either party but is held together by invisible glue. Perhaps the glue is an unacknowledged need for one another, perhaps it's an unexpressed and inexpressible love, perhaps it's merely habit and a fear of the unknown – whatever it is, it sticks. But for those who can't see *why* it sticks, particularly those involved in other relationships with either party, it's nothing but a source of frustration and anger. Camille was possessive, she wanted exclusivity, and could not see the point of Rose Beuret in Rodin's life (neither could most of his friends). Considering there were no legal ties to be severed, it must have been even more mystifying and frustrating to her that Rodin refused to part from Rose than it would be for a demanding mistress faced with a genuine wife. But refuse he did, despite being passionately in love with Camille (whatever, in the circumstances, that may mean).

The object of all this opprobrium, Rose Beuret, was

4 Frederic V. Grunfeld, *Rodin*, p.220

eighteen when she met Rodin in 1864 (he was twenty-four). She had come to Paris from Champagne, where her parents owned a vineyard, to find work. She sewed clothes for a shop, and lived in a room in the rue Thiers, a ten-minute walk from Rodin's studio. 'Many years after the fact, Rodin described his meeting with Rose: "She attached herself to me like an animal." It is a forceful statement and reflects the way Rodin – so awkward and shy as a young man – experienced this fiery, determined woman who did, in fact, attach herself quite well. Their relationship would last all their lives.'[5] In January 1866 they had a son, another Auguste. The fact Rodin chose not to marry Rose was not unusual in late-nineteenth-century Paris, where some (reminiscent of Heloise) considered marriage detrimental to an artistic career. He did eventually marry her in 1917, but the wedding was planned by others who wanted to ensure Rodin's legacy to France. Rose died of pneumonia two weeks later; Rodin himself died soon after.

If the young woman, supplicating with outstretched arms in *L'Age mûr*, can indeed be interpreted as Camille herself, she did not succeed in fully rising from her kneeling position and attaining the stature she so desired of an independent artist in her own right. Something began to go wrong almost as soon as the relationship with Rodin ended; she began to neglect herself, showed signs of paranoia – in particular a fear that Rodin was trying to steal her ideas and ultimately destroy her – and became increasingly turned in on herself. There has to have been more than Rodin's refusal to part from Rose to start sending this highly talented sculptress over the edge. The fear of failure had begun to get a grip on her; perhaps she had begun to wonder if her earlier self-belief had been exaggerated. Perhaps some part of her she could not bear to acknowledge suspected that only under Rodin's influence, working to his direction, could she produce truly good work. And because this suspicion was so unpalatable, she had to turn it into its opposite, and blame Rodin for stealing her ideas and

5 Ruth Butler, *Rodin*, p.49

seeking to destroy her and her work. She feared she had allowed herself to become worn out, worn down, in the execution of the work he had given her to do, that her vital energies had been stolen, subverted to his service; that instead of learning from him in order to flower into the true artist she could have been, she had been absorbed by him and his demands so that she would never now achieve her full potential. She could not bear to admit her own complicity in this, that she had chosen to give her all to her man, so she had to heap all the blame on to him. And the perception that she had sacrificed herself for him made it even more unacceptable, infuriating and belittling that he wouldn't even give up Rose Beuret for her.

A visitor to Camille's studio in about 1904 described her thus: 'She was forty, but looked fifty . . . There was such extreme negligence in the way she dressed, a total absence of any kind of stylishness. Her complexion was doughy, fading away in the precocious wrinkles and emphasized by her general state of physical decline . . . However, there was not a trace of despondency in this woman, who was still active and charming.'[6] Despondency soon set in, however, or, more likely, was already intermittent, for from around this time onwards Camille chose a very solitary existence, cutting herself off from her family – though her elderly father continued to take an interest in her, sending her small gifts of clothing and money from time to time – and seeing no one apart from the concierge. She began to exhibit a pattern of creating her sculpture in a state of euphoria and subsequently destroying it when depressed. What she perceived as her inability to achieve in sculpture the greatness of which she had dreamt confirmed her angers and fears, and so the spiral into paranoia started to intensify, as each succeeding summer she destroyed her year's work, never satisfied, hating herself and Rodin. Then Paul Claudel stepped in to seal her fate.

Her brother Paul, to whom Camille had always been close

6 Ibid., p.282

(though his real feelings towards her remain a mystery), spent the years from 1909 to 1913 as French consul in Prague and Frankfurt, only returning to France in March 1913, in response to a telegram telling him that Claudel *père* was dying. No one informed Camille. A week after their father's death Paul Claudel had Camille legally committed, as a third-class patient at Ville-Evrard, a public lunatic asylum with 1,060 beds. We can only assume he thought he was acting in his sister's best interests, to protect her from herself, by removing her from her now squalid living conditions and the only company she periodically chose of down-and-outs. Perhaps also this Catholic poet and diplomat found it unacceptable to have a disreputable sister on the loose in Paris, besmirching the family name. One of Camille Claudel's biographers, Reine-Marie Paris, is a granddaughter of Paul Claudel and so wishes to put the most favourable interpretation on his actions, but even she has to admit that 'the haste with which Camille was incarcerated was shocking'.[7] She remained in a lunatic asylum for thirty years, until her death in 1943. Doctors attending her reported that she had a real fear of being poisoned by a gang of Rodin's followers. Convinced Rodin had plagiarised her work, she talked about him with a fierce hatred.

During the thirty years Camille spent in confinement – first at Ville-Evrard and then in the Montdevergues asylum at Villeneuve-lès-Avignon – neither her mother nor her sister ever came to visit her, though her mother did correspond with her and tried to ensure that the conditions in which she was kept were tolerable. The second asylum was no improvement on the first but it was remote from the public gaze – there had been an outcry in the newspapers at the time of her committal. She was not allowed to practise her art (Reine-Marie Paris's version is that she was given clay from time to time but did not use it), and when the staff psychiatrists wanted to release her into the family's custody, her mother refused to hear of it.

7 Reine-Marie Paris, *Camille: The Life of Camille Claudel, Rodin's Muse & Mistress*, tr. Liliane Emery Tuck, Aurum Press, London, 1988, p.71

[Camille's] letters from the asylum show that she remained lucid and self-possessed, though she could not
reconcile herself to the loss of her art. 'All that has
happened to me is more than a novel, it is an epic, an
Iliad or an *Odyssey*, but it would need a Homer to
recount it,' she wrote to her former dealer after twenty
years of silence. 'I live in a world that is so curious, so
strange. Of the dream which was my life, this is the
nightmare.'[8]

Rodin was sixty-three when he and the painter Gwen John
became lovers in the summer of 1904. She was twenty-seven
when she first visited his studio and was making a living as an
artist's model. She began to model for Rodin, translate for
him, and sleep with him. She fell so passionately in love with
him that for a time she lost interest in everything else. He
made her come alive as a sexual being and she wished for
nothing in life but to serve him. Their affair was at its height in
1905 and 1906, with Rodin taking a paternal role, encouraging his young mistress to eat properly, to read more, and
insisting she draw every day. He also helped her financially; in
short, she seems to have become completely dependent on
him. She hung around the café opposite his studio, camped in
the bushes outside his fence at night, and wrote him hundreds
of adoring letters. It is hard to know how long what could
genuinely be called an affair lasted, as it continued in Gwen's
imagination long after it had ceased to be real for Rodin. For
his part, Rodin began to lose interest in her, once he had
finished his sculpture *Muse*, for which Gwen was the model.
She would wait for his weekly visit with mounting despera-
tion and anxiety. She couldn't afford to keep her room heated
most of the time, but when she was expecting him she made
sure the fire was burning. 'The French have a name for this
kind of relationship: she had become his *cinq-à-sept*, the lover
one sees from five to seven, after work and before going

8 Frederic V. Grunfeld, *Rodin*, p.242

home. In her case the caresses lasted barely an hour: he would make love to her, give her an orgasm, and then go instantly off.'[9]

As time went on, Rodin became less and less willing to spend his energy on Gwen. He even gave instructions to his *concièrge* to stop Gwen from pestering him.

> On the one hand she was quite prepared to accept this marginal existence as a perpetually waiting woman. 'One can be more free and independent in the mind and heart sometimes when one is tied practically. The girls in some harems of I forget where I read it, are more wonderful and advanced than any other women.' Yet she was also possessed of a terrible impatience that drove her to write him three letters a day for months on end, protesting all the while that she did not want him to be hardened by her love any more than by the wind in the country or the leaves that fall from the trees.[10]

She stayed in contact with Rodin for the rest of his life, never giving up her obsessive letter-writing, while he would reply only occasionally and briefly. Yet where her work was concerned, she seemed a different person, far removed from the hopeless lover. 'When it came to her art she was as tough and inviolable as if nothing else existed. Once she was asked her opinion of an exhibition of Cézanne watercolors. "These are very good," she said in her scarcely audible voice, "but I prefer my own." '[11]

Gwen John's artist brother Augustus also had an impressive roll-call of mistresses, as well as a legal wife, Ida (née Nettle-ship). And his more or less permanent mistress came to be known as Dorelia 'John', though she never in fact married him. Dorelia was born Dorothy McNeill, in 1881, in

9 Ibid., p.481
10 Ibid., p.482
11 Ibid., p.483

Camberwell, the fourth of seven children. By 1902 she was working as a junior secretary in a solicitor's office in Basinghall Street in the City of London, while also attending evening classes at the Westminster School of Art. Since her earliest days Dorelia had been drawn to the world of art, where she felt her destiny to lie. Even in this youthful secretarial phase she was known for dressing 'artistically', in a style all her own. She and Augustus met early in 1903; one story of their meeting was that Augustus overtook her in Holborn, looked back at her in her black hat, and was unable to look away. By the summer he was already writing her passionate letters.

> What was uncommon about Dorelia was the serenity that gave her beauty its depth – a quality [Augustus] so conspicuously lacked. She was not witty or articulate; and certainly not sentimental. It was her *presence* that was so powerful, her vitality and above all her magical peace-giving qualities. People who were miserable would come to her, relax, absorb something of her extraordinary calm. All manner of disasters, tragedies, crises appeared to shrivel up within the range of her personality. She guarded her secrets well, like a cat.[12]

This and other descriptions of Dorelia are very reminiscent of the way Jung described 'certain types of women who seem to be made by nature to attract anima projections': 'The so-called "sphinx-like" character is an indispensable part of their equipment, also an equivocalness, an intriguing elusiveness – not an indefinite blur that offers nothing, but an indefiniteness that seems full of promises, like the speaking silence of a Mona Lisa.'[13]

Ida John had not only to cope with the knowledge of her husband's infidelities but with nearly all of the responsibility for deciding what to do about them. At the time of his falling in love with Dorelia, for instance, he presented Ida with the facts, introduced her to Dorelia and left her to decide what

12 Michael Holroyd, *Augustus John*, p.129
13 C.G. Jung, *Aspects of the Feminine*, tr. R.F.C. Hull, Ark, London, 1992, p.51

should be done. She and Augustus had been married for about three years and she knew that the future of the marriage depended on her decision. She also knew that she loved Augustus and liked Dorelia; at times her feelings for the latter could even be described as love. Her reason told her that a *ménage à trois* was the only sensible course to adopt, and most of the time this reason prevailed, but she could not always smother a violent jealousy, which she felt to be unworthy of herself. Neither could she help reflecting that whereas marriage meant freedom for Augustus, it meant the opposite for her. Later Ida wrote of their *ménage* to their friend Alice Rothenstein: 'You know we are not a *conventional* family, you have heard Dorelia is beautiful and most charming, and you must learn that my only happiness is for him to be happy and complete, and that far from diminishing our love it appears to augment it. I have my bad times it is only honest to admit. She is *so* remarkably charming. But those times are the devil and not the truth of light.'[14]

In August 1904, Dorelia became pregnant by Augustus. She seems to have kept this a secret for almost five months, apprehensive of the effect it might have on Ida. Shortly before the baby was due, Ida wrote Dorelia one of the most lucid and interesting expressions of a wife's feelings towards a mistress I have encountered. In it is all the jealousy of the home-bound wife for the 'freedom' of the mistress, who can – at least in theory – leave whenever it suits her, but more particularly Ida recognises the differing images called up in the man by the words 'wife' and 'mistress'. She suggests that there may be little reality to these images – the mistress represents 'apparent' freedom, the wife 'apparent' slavery – but because these are the man's perceptions, the women – in particular, the wife – find themselves trapped in these definitions.

I know you and Gus think I ought to think of you as the sufferer, but I can't. You are free – the man you love at

14 Michael Holroyd, *Augustus John*, p.168

present, loves you – you don't care for convention or
what people think – of course your future is perilous, but
you love it. You are a wanderer – you would hate safety
and cages – why are you to be pitied? . . . You are living
your life – you chose it – you did it because you wanted
to – didn't you? Do you regret it? I thought you were a
wild free bird who loved life in its glorious hardships. If I
am to think of you as a sad female who needs protection I
must indeed change my ideas . . . It was for your freedom and all it represented I envied you so. Because you
meant to Gus all that lay outside the dull home, the
unspeakable fireside, the gruesome dinner table – that I
became so hopeless – I was the chain – you were the key
to unlock it . . . Nothing can change this fact – that you
are the one outside who calls a man to *apparent* freedom
and wild rocks and wind and air – and I am the one inside
who says come to dinner, and who to live with is
apparent slavery . . .

You are the wild bird – fly away – as Gus says our life
does not suit you. He will follow, never fear. There was
never a poet could stay at home. Do not think myself to
be pitied either. I shudder when I think of those times,
simply because it was pain . . . It has robbed me of the
tenderness I felt for you – but you can do without that –
and I would do anything for you if you would ever ask
me to – you still seem to belong to us. I.[15]

The last paragraph contains a sentiment very typical of the
whole John family, that of not being able to let go (of Dorelia,
of Rodin, of whoever came within their orbit), even while
the person in question may be a source of pain. Ida can't let go
of Dorelia at least partly because she now fears being left alone
with Augustus; she knows he would take other mistresses and,
in this case, better the devil you know.

But becoming pregnant necessarily entails a loss of freedom,

15 Ibid., pp.177–8

and once Dorelia was a part of his domestic circle and another 'mother of his children', Augustus could no longer sustain his image of her as wild, free and mysterious. This had the effect of lessening his passion for her. He needed a woman around whom he could weave mysteries as a source of inspiration; when Dorelia ceased to be quite so mysterious to him he found others, and one in particular. She was Alick Schepeler, a 'paragon of boredom',[16] and for a few years she became, next to Dorelia, his supreme model. Her real name was Alexandra and she worked as a secretary for the *Illustrated London News*, while sharing a flat in Chelsea with a friend who was a student at the Slade; it was through this latter connection that she got to know Augustus and subsequently many other writers and artists. Alick sounds in some ways like a caricature of Dorelia, the mysterious muse taken to an almost senseless extreme. She seems also to have been empty, almost a non-person, so that Augustus could create her in his imagination any way he wanted; thus she became for him the perfect mistress–muse. She represents a salutary warning to any artist's mistress who wishes to be more than a figment of her lover's imagination, who wants to be related to as an actual, living, interesting person in her own right. That may not be what the artist wants at all.

Meanwhile, as Augustus amused himself with Alick's vacant mysteriousness, both Dorelia and Ida found themselves playing the role of wife, while neither felt particularly suited to it. Ida summed up the ambiguities and unsatisfactoriness of their position in another letter to Dorelia:

A woman is either a wife or a mistress . . .

If a wife, she has (that is, her position implies) perfect confidence in her husband and peace of mind – not being concerned about any other woman in relation to her husband. But she has ties and responsibilities and is, more or less, a fixture – and not free. If a mistress she has no

16 Ibid., p.213

right to expect faithfulness, and must allow a man to come and go as he will without question – and must in consequence, if she loves him jealously, suffer doubt and not have peace of mind – *but* she has her own freedom too. Well here are you and I – we have neither the peace of mind of the wife nor the freedom (at least I haven't) of the mistress. We have the evils of both states for the one good, which belongs to both – a man's company. Is it worth it?[17]

Ida died of puerperal fever and peritonitis after giving birth to a fifth son, and Dorelia subsequently took over the care of Ida's children as well as of her own. Thus the 'freedom' which drew Augustus to her in the first place completely disappeared, while her 'mystery' became debased into a kind of impassivity and fatalism, in the face of her artist-lover's strength of will. Despite occasional attempts to escape, Dorelia succumbed – completely, in the end – to the needs of Augustus.

The letters John wrote whenever he was abroad reveal his dependence on her, and it was this need that held her back. Finally it was too late, too unthinkable that 'Dodo', as everyone now called her, should not always be there. She grew more fatalistic, relying on the swing of her pendulum – a ring harnessed to a piece of string – to decide everything from the wisdom of a marriage to the authenticity of a picture. From anything that might cause pain she averted her attention, though she might seem to stare at it without emotion. The range of her interests narrowed. She had stopped drawing, now she read less, and eventually would give up the piano. Nothing got on top of her, nothing came too near.[18]

In the cases both of Camille Claudel and Rose Beuret and of Dorelia and Ida John, the mistress-v.-wife battle, though

17 Ibid., p.185
18 Ibid., pp.503–4

waged at times, seems to have been unreal, beside the point, a women's sideshow while the man in question just got on with being an artist. Rose Beuret was not even really the wife and, in any event, Camille's resentment towards her and towards Rodin for staying with her played only a part in her disintegration as an artist and a woman. Neither does it seem likely that the shadowy figure of Rose attained a great deal of satisfaction from her role as wife; Rodin kept her firmly in the background, as something akin to a dependent housekeeper, a figure rather scorned by his artistic and society friends as his reputation grew. Camille and Rose might have done better to join forces if they harboured any hope of controlling Rodin.

That's certainly what Dorelia and Ida did, not that theirs was an ideal situation either. Even in the early days of trying to establish a *ménage à trois*, and even in her occasional flashes of jealousy, Ida was aware that a simple confrontation between wife and mistress was not the real issue. Her jealousy was directed less at the objective of having Dorelia just go away, of her husband not having a mistress, than it was bound up with her desire to be the mistress herself. She felt mistresses got a better deal than wives and considered herself more suited to be a mistress than a wife. Yet she could also recognise that Dorelia's position was not so very different from her own, that the long-term mistress of a self-obsessed and driven artist, as both Rodin and Augustus John were, can be as captive as a wife, and that the freedom she represents is only *apparent*. It is a freedom the male artist colonises and uses to inspire his art; it isn't intended to be freedom in the practical sense. And once the woman, the muse, has given her freedom over into the hands of the artist, particularly once she has become part of his domestic life, she loses her 'mystery' along with her freedom and so the artist needs to go searching for other inspiring women (or so he holds). In Dorelia's case, Ida's untimely death led to her becoming the wife in all but the legal sense and ultimately she relinquished any attempt at retaining even a partial freedom.

Perhaps   the   still   mysterious   Gwen,   painting   her contemplative and inward women, writing her letters to Rodin, surely not in the hope of replies but in some way to fulfil her own purposes, has something to tell other creative women who become mistresses of an artist. What she tells them can never quite be put into words, but it's to do with using unhappy and unequal passion as base material for the transforming power of art, taking what she needs from her artist-lover while appearing only to be giving, letting her passion have free rein when it requires it in order that it may bear fruit when the time is right. It's a very risky way of loving, involving self-abandonment, and there's no room for grasping at prosaic hopes of ousting the wife, or even the other mistresses. Unless the mistress is absolutely sure of herself as an artist she'll just get eaten up. To the outsider, Gwen John's obsessive passion for Rodin must have looked embarrassing and useless, bringing her only grief; but the artist in her knew exactly what she was doing.

THE WRITER'S MISTRESS

*She was to be a lovely, wise and generous
person wholly devoted to me.*[1]

T he forte of the woman who is not only the mistress of a
writer but a writer herself is *rewriting*: the rewriting of
her own history to make it more palatable both to herself and
to her readers and admirers, the reinterpreting of her situation
as it occurs to make it conform more nearly to her wishes.

The most gifted of the rewriting mistresses was probably
Rebecca West, about whom the 'truth' seems almost impossible to come at. She is as tantalising and mystifying a
character as the heroine of Ibsen's *Rosmersholm*, from whom
she took her name – entirely, according to her, as a whim, for
no apparent reason. Ibsen's Rebecca West is, or tries to be, an
'emancipated' woman, but one interpretation of the play is
that both she and Pastor Rosmer (the man whose wife
Rebecca tried to supplant and who – the wife, that is –
has committed suicide before the opening of Act I) are
attempting to be emancipated before their time, and that
the pressures of conventional society as well as their own
doubts and sense of guilt are still binding them. It is impossible
to live in a truly emancipated and autonomous fashion when
both inner conflict and concern with external judgements
impugn their motives and distort reality with gossip, innuendo
and guilt. Similarly the 'real' Rebecca West, no matter how
much she tried to portray (to herself and others) her relationship with H.G. Wells as emancipated and bold, above the
judgement of the common herd, never managed to rid herself
of a contradictory desire for respectability and convention.

---

1 H.G. Wells quoted in Victoria Glendinning, *Rebecca West: A Life*, Macmillan,
London, 1987, p.56

George Eliot, more than half a century earlier, seems to have been far more confident in her unconventional stance. Ibsen's Rebecca, acting, according to Freud, under the domination of an Oedipus complex (there has probably been unwitting incest in this character's past), sets about – maybe unconsciously – getting rid of the wife and mother so that she might take her place with the husband and father. The 'real' Rebecca, deeply attached to her own version of the father she lost as a girl, actively pursues (according to most accounts) H.G. Wells and would dearly like to 'get rid' of his wife and mother of his children in order to take her place (and she does indeed herself become the mother of a child of his). But, she tells us, her taking of the name 'Rebecca West' was purely accidental, done in a hurry – she liked neither the play nor the character – and no significance should be attached to the choice. I would rather say that, when dealing with the unconscious, there are no accidents.

At birth 'Rebecca' was given the name Cicely Isabel Fairfield and was known as Cissie. Her Anglo-Irish journalist father and Scottish mother met and married in Australia where Cissie's two elder sisters were born. Charles Fairfield was a romantic figure to his daughters, full of tales of past family glories and of his own Irish childhood. He left home (which by this time was in England) in 1901, when Cissie was nine, and died five years later in impoverished circumstances in Liverpool. His apparent rejection of his family was so painful to Cissie that she devoted much emotional energy in later life to denying it had happened. 'The failure of this flawed and gifted man makes a pitiful story, and any daughter might wish to defend such a father from the glib judgement of strangers. Cissie, though she took her mother's side as a girl, could not, as a grown woman, reject him. She created a myth out of the wonderful father she had and did not have.'[2]

The pseudonym made its first appearance in 1912, when its owner was beginning to make a name for herself as a journalist

2 Victoria Glendinning, Rebecca West, p.24

and critic and apparently wished to spare her mother any embarrassment. H.G. Wells expressed his interest, showing up at her mother's house in Hampstead Garden Suburb after having previously met Rebecca at a lunch, at the beginning of 1913. He was then in his mid-forties; Rebecca was just twenty. H.G. had had much experience of mistresses, and also had a wife prepared to tolerate his affairs, provided she approved of the woman concerned and could tell she was no real threat to the marriage.

Though H.G. may have made the first move towards Rebecca, he seems to have backed off for some time when she reciprocated and wanted a full-blown affair, perhaps because some of his earlier experiences – notably with Amber Reeves – had taught him that very young mistresses can be harder to handle in tandem with a complaisant wife than the more mature and practised sort. Reports of the initial stages of the relationship with Amber seem very similar to those concerning Rebecca: a young woman 'chasing' the older writer who succeeds in resisting for several months but suddenly succumbs. Maybe a pattern was indeed being repeated; maybe the two accounts have become confused. According to H.G.'s own account, written some twenty years after the event, he did not rush into an affair with Rebecca because of the affair he was already having with Elizabeth von Arnim.[3]

It is unclear when Amber Reeves and H.G. first met but, according to his biographer Michael Foot, it was probably at a Fabian lecture in 1906. In the autumn of 1907, Amber went up to Newnham to read Moral Sciences. She took a first (though could not at this time, as a woman, receive a degree) in the Moral Philosophy Tripos, and went on to study at the London School of Economics. In later life she published several books on economics and political science. H.G. described her as 'a girl of brilliant and precocious promise. She had a sharp, bright, Levantine face under a shock of very

---

3 G.P. Wells (ed.), *H.G. Wells in Love: Postscript to an Experiment in Autobiography*, Faber & Faber, London, 1984, p.96

fine abundant black hair, a slender nimble body very much alive, and a quick greedy mind.'[4] Her thick and rather unruly hair earned her the sobriquet of 'Medusa', sometimes shortened to Duse or Dusa. At the age of nineteen, she began – so we are told – a rather public pursuit of H.G. This was noticed by, among others, Bernard Shaw and Beatrice Webb, but not by Amber's family. After nearly a year (and Shaw thought Wells had done well to hold out so long), Amber succeeded in capturing him. They had an active physical liaison for some months. As the affair became known – and Amber boasted widely about it – her parents became disturbed. She and H.G. continued to meet, though fearing the consequences and mainly at Amber's instigation. She then became pregnant, and real scandal ensued. Rivers Blanco-White, an earlier rejected suitor, came forward to offer to marry her and cover up the scandal in a Victorian manner. The wedding duly took place, but Wells did not disappear, as would have been the normal Victorian thing to do. Instead he maintained Amber in a cottage in Sussex where he visited her frequently. To make matters worse (in the eyes of the conventional) H.G.'s wife Jane helped Amber with buying what she needed for the baby, who was named Anna Jane Blanco-White. Subsequently H.G.'s infatuation began gradually to wane. Amber reappeared fairly often, however, throughout his life, sometimes with Anna Jane in tow. She was also credited as the partial author of one of his later books.

Almost simultaneously with the Amber Reeves affair (there must have been some overlap), Wells had a relationship with Dorothy Richardson, the feminist stream-of-consciousness novelist. This too went through a sexual phase, but continued as a friendship until Wells's death. His principal liaison at the time he met Rebecca West was with the novelist Elizabeth von Arnim, born Mary Annette Beauchamp in 1866 (making her the same age as Wells) in New Zealand. She came to London in 1871, married a Prussian count in 1891, and had

4 Ibid., p.73

difficulties with marriage and with men in general. (Her experiences on the count's Pomeranian estate are described in her novel *Elizabeth and her German Garden*.) She found herself becoming increasingly attached to various of her children's tutors, who included Hugh Walpole and E.M. Forster. Her husband died in 1910; during the same year her play *Priscilla Runs Away* was performed in London; she thus found herself with independent means and used some of the royalties to build a chalet in Switzerland. She had wanted to meet Wells for some time, and in 1911 she wrote to him to praise *The New Machiavelli*. For about three years they were seen together a good deal, to the distress of her family, who thought a liaison with a socialist and possibly a libertine would have a bad effect on her book sales as well as on her reputation. A passionate interlude ensued, which lasted for over a year, and then continued as a friendship for more than twenty years. Wells's comments about what went wrong with this affair are enlightening – not so much in regard to Elizabeth, as to his general attitude concerning the respective importance of his wife, his mistresses and his work:

> [Elizabeth] developed a queer hostility to Jane. She hated the daily letters I wrote home to England and was jealous to see that the answers often amused and pleased me. More and more did she resent the fact that I kept our love light-hearted. She began to demand depth of feeling. Had I ever wept about her or trembled to come near her? *Real* lovers did. Would I ruin myself for her? Would I even interrupt my work for her? 'Not a bit of it,' I said, 'for you or anyone.'[5]

And so to Rebecca. But how to arrive at the 'truth'? Gordon N. Ray's book about this relationship, published in 1974, relies heavily on Rebecca's recollections, recounted many years after the events they describe, and on more than eight

5 Ibid., p.90

hundred letters H.G. sent to her. The letters she had written
to him during their ten-year affair were destroyed by him long
after their separation, only five of them surviving; these had
either been returned to her with messages added by him or
were drafts Rebecca kept (or didn't send at all). In the case of
the 'drafts', how is one to know whether that is what they
really are, or whether she wrote them at a later date, and either
deliberately or unconsciously amended them to suit her
preferred version? As regards other biographers of Wells,
Michael Foot is hopelessly biased in favour of his subject,
Michael Coren as biased against him. David C. Smith may get
it about right. Anthony West, Rebecca and H.G.'s son,
presents another load of problems in his biography of his
father. He shows some understanding of both his parents'
need to 'rewrite', saying of his mother:

> Like George Sand before her, she thought of her life
> history as something that could easily be improved by
> editing, and like George Sand again, she realised that if
> her biographers were to portray her to her liking, she
> would have to provide them with suitable material to
> work upon. She consequently devoted a great deal of
> time and no inconsiderable part of her creative energy to
> building a dossier that would win her a good posthumous
> press and ensure that a future generation would see her in
> the right light. Before she was out of her twenties she had
> begun to plant the documentation for an ideal biography
> on a variety of correspondents, and she was to go on
> doing so for the rest of her life.[6]

Unfortunately Anthony may well have been suffering from a
similar affliction himself. Rebecca did not in general like her
son's version of their shared history, and would dispute his
opinion of her (*Aspects of a Life* was published the year after she
died, but she knew he was working on a biography of his father

6 Anthony West, *H.G. Wells: Aspects of a Life*, Hutchinson, London, 1984, pp.57–8

while she was alive and she had her misgivings). In the same year that *Aspects of a Life* was published, so was *H.G. Wells in Love*, H.G.'s own 'postscript' to his autobiography, begun in 1934 and edited by his (legitimate) son, Gip. Again, this is a version, a retelling of the stories; Wells himself admits as much: 'I not only rationalize but I incline to self-justification.'[7] Putting all the versions together does not enable one to arrive at a composite answer, the lowest common denominator of truth; rather, it underlines the multiple ways of viewing any one life or even one incident within a life. Victoria Glendinning, as the expert biographer she is, attempts to get as near the 'truth' as she is able, but she did not have access to material at Yale which Carl Rollyson makes use of eight years later; she did have access to Rebecca West herself, but both she and her subject were fully aware of how biography and autobiography are as much the telling of stories as is fiction. One of the epigraphs to Glendinning's *Rebecca West*, a remark made by Rebecca in 1975 in the *Sunday Telegraph* makes this abundantly clear: 'Everyone realises that one can believe little of what people say about each other. But it is not so widely realised that even less can one trust what people say about themselves.'

Once the affair began, Rebecca soon moved out of the house she was sharing with her mother and sisters, and soon also she was pregnant (Anthony was conceived on only the second time she and H.G. made love). Having a child made their relationship difficult from the start, removing Rebecca's freedom and emphasising Wells's lack of a full-time commitment to her. Later on, Anthony's existence kept them together, and hurting one another, longer than they might otherwise have lasted. H.G. describes the impact of a child on their lives thus:

And when we found ourselves linked by this living tie, we knew hardly anything of each other. We were all, Jane included, taken by surprise. We all wanted to stand

---

7 *H.G. Wells in Love*, p.142

by each other as generously as we could bring ourselves to the situation. Rebecca had never wanted anything but a richly imaginative and sensuous love affair with me, and we now had to attempt all sorts of vaguely conceived emotional adjustments.

We never achieved any adjustment of any sort. We came to like each other extremely and to be extremely exasperated with each other and antagonistic. Rebecca could produce voluminous imaginative interpretations of action and situation that dwarfed my own fairly considerable imaginative fluctuations altogether.[8]

Rebecca did not revisit her mother's house from the time she gave birth until Anthony was three years old, having decided that she would not give up Wells in return for her family's support. The attitude of the lovers in this early stage is reminiscent of that of George Eliot and George Henry Lewes: 'What they had started together needed no excuse or subsequent palliation: by her creed no less than his, what they had done was right, and the rest of the world would have to learn.'[9] What also had to be learnt, however, was how the two parties themselves had different understandings of what their relationship entailed; such learning was acquired only gradually. They used the nicknames of 'Panther' (Rebecca) and 'Jaguar' (H.G.) partly to emphasise their alienation from conventional society: '[The nicknames] stood for the whole attitude towards life evolved by Rebecca and Wells, who continued to use these names as long as their love lasted. They emphasized the ruthless withdrawal from society that the relationship entailed, the fact that Rebecca and Wells were not part of the pack and did not acknowledge its laws.'[10] Gordon N. Ray is too glib here, too ready to accept what someone has told him; for, looking at fuller versions of these two people's stories, it is clear that Rebecca found a 'ruthless

8 Ibid., pp.96–7
9 Michael Foot, *HG: The History of Mr Wells*, Black Swan, London, 1996, p.128
10 Gordon N. Ray, *H.G. Wells & Rebecca West*, Macmillan, London, 1975, p.36

withdrawal from society' easier to postulate than to practise, while H.G. did not actually practise anything of the sort. He had plenty of society every time he went home.

Much of the trouble which subsequently developed between the two resulted from his ability to keep their relationship in a separate compartment from the rest of his life, and his expectation that she could, and should, do the same. He did not want a domestic life with her; he already had that with Jane and his legitimate sons, and he did not want to jeopardise that comfortable side of his life. What he needed from Rebecca was an amusing young companion and a lover. But she needed, or felt she needed, more of a whole life from him. She knew very little of his arrangements with Jane – of his need for her and the extent to which she knew about his mistresses, nor the amount of time he spent with her. This is not surprising, as in letter after letter H.G. told Rebecca he was devoted to her alone. Yet some part of her was always aware of the hold Jane had over him and this was part of the reason for her hatred of her.

Wanting to keep them well out of the way, Wells found a furnished nineteenth-century farmhouse in East Hertfordshire for Rebecca and Anthony to live in. Attached to a working farm just outside the village of Braughing, it was on its own, surrounded by fields. Rebecca and H.G. enjoyed exploring the countryside together, but the winter could be cold, muddy and lonely. Wells was not always free to visit, and only a few trusted friends like Ford Madox Ford and Violet Hunt (of whom more below) were encouraged to stay. When Anthony was a year old, he and his mother moved to another furnished house in Hatch End. This was more convenient for Rebecca to get to London when she needed to, or to see friends; but Wells did not enjoy spending evenings there when the company included Anthony's nanny and Rebecca's companion. As their son puts it:

> Her life style had changed, and my father could never find her alone. She had become the mistress of an

establishment, and there were always people about her. There was a nurse, there was a maid, and sometimes a second maid. There was a cook, and there was, as often as not, a companion or friend in the role of chaperone. There had to be, even at that late date, to save her from a further fatal loss of respectability: a woman living on her own, without a husband, and with a young child in the house, would have been assumed to be disreputable unless there was another woman of her own class in the menage.[11]

Next Wells took rooms in Pimlico where he and Rebecca could meet as lovers and which they could use as a base for going out to theatres and so on; meanwhile, in the spring of 1917, she and Anthony moved to a modern house in Leigh-on-Sea. In 1919 she came back to live in London altogether, taking a flat in South Kensington, with Anthony and a woman called Ada Pears to look after him. Wells paid part of the outgoings and would visit her for half-days and evenings from his new London base at Whitehall Court.

Rebecca never found this divided life easy; she manifested symptoms of stress such as skin trouble and tended to console herself with – before the term was invented – 'retail therapy'. Gordon N. Ray provides a fairly depressing account of the down-side for Rebecca:

> From the beginning, indeed, their 'great adventure' had its sordid side for her. While Wells led an exciting if hectic double life, Rebecca led a boring and difficult single life. The truth of the old cliché, that it is the woman who pays, impressed itself upon her. She found herself confined to a back street, hole-and-corner existence, in which she played a succession of parts that might have been invented by Wilkie Collins for the heroines of his 'sensation' novels. For a time she was Mrs.

11 Anthony West, *H.G. Wells*, p.25

West with Wells as Mr. West and Anthony as their son. Then she became Miss West with Wells as a friend of the family and Anthony as her adopted son or nephew. Even the role of 'widow West' was once considered. On trips abroad she was Wells's secretary, Miss West. Each of these roles presented its particular problems.[12]

Rebecca was also very isolated, cut off from her family – her mother strongly disapproved of the liaison (according to Wells, it was the disapproval of her family which forced all these subterfuges upon her) – and from her friends, who found it difficult to visit her in the remote hideaways Wells procured. And then there was her work: 'Most devastating of all to Rebecca was the interruption to her career. The immense promise of her journalistic debut in 1912–1913 was hardly borne out in the ten years that followed. Under the conditions that her life with Wells imposed upon her, she could work only halfheartedly and irregularly.'[13] This at least was the impression she gave to Gordon N. Ray. It seems Rebecca suspected herself at this period of a self-undermining tendency, a part of her working to thwart her true aims, by preventing herself from obtaining the peace she needed in order to work. This can be a common characteristic of the mistress-type and again, as in the case of the superiority/ inferiority polarity noted particularly in George Eliot and Charlotte Brontë, contradictory forces are at play, sometimes within one woman. Thus the conflicts involved in being a mistress can be used both as a stimulus to creative work and an excuse for not doing it, a source of energy and inspiration and a drain on that energy. In Rebecca's case there are yet more contradictions and variant interpretations, for what she *saw* as a drain on her creative resources may, to judge from what she did ultimately achieve, have been after all a source of energy.

According to Ray, Rebecca's intense antagonism towards Jane centred on what she perceived as the lack of honesty in

12 Gordon N. Ray, *H.G. Wells & Rebecca West*, pp.xx–xxi
13 Ibid., pp.xxi–xxii

this wife – that she pretended to be a victim in Wells's affairs whereas she was really a colluder. Her clinging to the victim role made it impossible to work out any third way, so that Rebecca felt forced into the traditional mistress role, with all its secrecy and pretence. 'It was not that Rebecca wanted to replace Jane. "There would have been an honorable way of dealing with the situation," she wrote in 1944, "we could have lived side by side, H.G. was worth that." '[14] But what Rebecca wrote in 1944 cannot be taken necessarily to represent her real feelings more than twenty years previously.

Rebecca had some kind of psychic collapse in 1920 (after falling into an open cistern while staying in Cornwall), and during her convalescence Wells met and became involved with Margaret Sanger, the American birth control pioneer. Sanger and Wells were active in the same areas, and both seemed able to become emotionally and sexually involved with one another while maintaining other relationships and getting on with the rest of their lives. Sanger spent a year in England, where she and H.G., as well as she and Havelock Ellis, could meet to make love and talk. Whenever Wells went to the States he and Sanger usually managed to find time to see one another, either just before or after a conference. Wells congratulated her when she married J.N.H. Slee in 1922, but this did not seem to make any difference to their relationship, their correspondence suggesting that they continued to meet and make love whenever it could be arranged. Sanger sounds a fulfilled, non-possessive, busy, and well-balanced woman, who did not try to impose anything on H.G. They could talk about one another's other loves, as well as loving one another. She sounds an ideal occasional mistress. Such a relationship was possible partly because she was committed to her own work, was unplagued by self-doubt and had no time for fantasising.

A few months later, on a visit to Russia, Wells had a sexual encounter with Moura von Benckendorff (later Budberg),

14 Ibid., p.xxiii

Maxim Gorky's 27-year-old secretary. A decade later she was to become the most important woman in his life. On his return from this trip he told Rebecca about Moura, which strengthened her resolve to put some distance between herself and H.G. But as soon as she exhibited an increased independence – which Wells had appeared to want – he would attempt to reclaim her. In the autumn of 1921 he went to the United States to report on the Washington Peace Conference, from where he wrote devotedly to Rebecca, while planning to see as much as possible of Margaret Sanger. Then early in 1922 he travelled to Spain where Rebecca had agreed to meet him. After being fêted and exhausted in the States, he arrived in Spain expecting to continue to be treated as a great man, with his mistress attending to his every need. This did not go down too well with Rebecca who, despite H.G.'s expectations of his mistress as expressed in the epigraph of this chapter, was never prepared to play humble servant and muse to her man.

Some of the problems of the relationship came to focus on what Wells referred to as Rebecca's 'little friends'. The term demonstrates several things: Wells's tendency to patronise Rebecca, unsurprising given the age difference, and the fact of his fame; his dislike of the fact she had a separate social life from him, even though he had a separate domestic life from her and needed her to maintain some independence from him if the relationship was to work at all; and the different kinds of things they liked to do socially, partly again because of their ages. The balancing of that see-saw between independence and dependence can be very hard for the mistress: she has to be strong and independent in order to survive the times – often considerable – when her lover is with his wife or away elsewhere; then she has to drop that independence and try to accommodate to being part of a couple as soon as he returns. Eventually these two aspects of a woman may become wider and wider apart, until they can no longer be held in balance – and something has to give way. It also becomes harder when a mistress is increasingly successful in her own right. During the time of her affair with Wells and despite the interruptions and difficulties which made her feel she did not achieve as much as she might have done, Rebecca grew from a very intelligent and able young woman on the threshold of her career into an established writer, able to stand on her own feet economically; that change in her status was bound to affect the relationship. At the outset she would have been flattered by the attentions of a famous writer; by the end she didn't need them any more. Nor did she need to carry on fighting the losing battle with Jane.

Rebecca's psyche eventually found a way out of the Wells affair – in the way it usually does. She became interested in another man. And here we have another fascinating example of her ability to rewrite her life. Victoria Glendinning and Carl Rollyson both identify the man as William Maxwell Aitken, otherwise known by this stage in his life as Lord Beaverbrook. He also was married, with a wife who played a similar role to that of Jane Wells. Rebecca had first met him in 1918 when he was the wartime Minister of Information. They had had some kind of encounter in London and when Rebecca was in the United States on a lecture tour in 1923, Beaverbrook looked her up. He traced her to the Town House Hotel in New York and they spent Christmas together. Rebecca, who had been falling in love with Beaverbrook for months, imagined this was the beginning of a permanent relationship, but she was mistaken. It seems likely that Beaverbrook, a man of many mistresses, had been looking for company over Christmas and probably a casual affair. He was seeing more than one other woman at this time, and had a roster of ex-mistresses to whom he sent $50 at Christmas and on his birthday. Rebecca never made it on to that list. As well as the difference in their expectations – exacerbated by Rebecca's inexperience (Wells was her only previous lover, she had never gone in for 'flings') and by her not unnatural assumption that the effort he expended, or got his secretary to expend, in tracking her down in New York meant he was serious about her – the sex, it seems, was no good. Maybe the difference in expectation was a contributory factor to the failure. Victoria Glendinning also suggests that Beaverbrook couldn't get on with Rebecca because she was mature and not malleable, and he was the kind of man who liked to be able to 'make' and mould his young mistresses. Nevertheless the affair with Beaverbrook helped her get over Wells – which may have been unconsciously the whole point of it – and she remained obsessed with Beaverbrook for years. After he left New York following their unsuccessful Christmas together, Rebecca became ill with distress and the rest of her lecture tour had to be delayed. She carried on with it after her recovery, and was mildly consoled by the attentions of other men.

This episode, distressing to Rebecca at the time and in recollection, appears in an entirely different version in Gordon N. Ray's book. There is no mention of the man being Lord Beaverbrook, and the lovers' romantic idyll is interrupted by external events. Ray's source, presumably, was Rebecca herself:

It was with relief that Rebecca returned to New York for Christmas. There she encountered another complication. Before her departure from England, a couple she had known well for years reached an amicable parting of the ways. The wife called on Rebecca to tell her the news and startled her by suddenly saying that of course Rebecca must have known that her husband was in love with her and would certainly ask her to marry him when the final arrangements for separation were completed. During her lecture tour Rebecca received kind and solicitous letters from him, and on reaching New York she found him waiting for her. They were happy together for two weeks, and then there was a tragic interruption, which meant that he returned to England, though they were still in love, and for some years afterwards he made agonizing reappearances in her life.[15]

15 Ibid., p.154

Wells's wife Jane and Beaverbrook's wife Gladys died within two months of one another in late 1927. Rebecca was never able to feel any sympathy for Jane Wells, resenting her for holding the powerful position of wife and for the use she made of that position. And in 1944, more than twenty years after the end of the affair, these are the charges Rebecca laid against H.G.: ' "that he treated me with the sharpest cruelty imaginable for those horrible years, that he humiliated me . . . that he overworked me and refused to allow me to rest when I was ill, that he has cheated me of all but one child, that his perpetual irascibility ruined my nerves, that he isolated me and drove away my friends." '[16] That does seem to be rather overdoing it.

Rebecca West married Henry Andrews, a 35-year-old banker and a long-time admirer of her work, in 1930 and, again in a way reminiscent of George Eliot, she attached great importance to her married name. She was very happy for the first five years of her married life, but in the mid-1930s Henry stopped making love to her, which hurt her deeply. For a while she feared she had made him impotent – this had been one of her diagnoses of the abortive affair with Beaverbrook – but eventually she decided that her husband considered sex to be no part of marriage after the first few years. She did notice that he had a tendency to develop crushes on young women, but Rebecca's skills in only seeing what she wanted to see were by now very advanced.

Rebecca herself did little straying during her married life. She had a brief fling with Francis Biddle, the American Chief Prosecutor at the trial of Nazi war criminals, when she was in Nuremberg to report the closing sessions in the summer of 1946. He was sixty, some six years older than her, and was also married; there was no question on either side of a change of marital partner. Otherwise, her only extra-marital affair was with a plastic surgeon, Thomas Pomfret Kilner. After Henry's death she discovered the nature and extent of his extra-marital

16 Ibid., p.120

activities which were considerable and necessitated some rewriting of her marriage.

Rebecca had felt a strong compulsion to marry, and not to be a woman on her own. Looking back, she didn't really know why. ' "I would have been better off if I had not married him or anybody else. Men are not good companions or allies on a long haul. They always bring trouble. There is no real reason why any woman who can keep herself should marry." '[17]

Coincidentally with the ending of the relationship between Rebecca and Wells, the latter was seduced by an extraordinary woman, Odette Keun, and this resulted in a stormy, passionate and eventually bitter ten-year affair. While this was going on, he also maintained his long and fairly passionate long-distance friendship with Margaret Sanger. Odette entered Wells's life as an interviewer for a newspaper; she stayed overnight and entered his bed to 'fill out her impressions', as she was supposed to have said. She came from somewhere in the Levant (she was the daughter of Dutch and Italian parents), and was extremely pretty in an exotic kind of way. Wells fell completely in love with her. He kept her though for the warm climates of the Riviera or for Paris; he didn't appear publicly with her in London. After a year or two of leasing fairly primitive lodgings, they built a house (called Lou Pidou) in Grasse, very remote from everywhere. Here they spent part of each year and entertained friends, until their final falling-out in 1933.

While the house was being built, Wells took Odette on a tour of Spain and Portugal, where he is said to have first discovered her violent temper, her jealousy, and the vulgarity and bitterness of her speech. She seems to have enjoyed shocking prestigious visitors. 'She apparently delighted in using street and sewer words to describe their love life, which she was apt to do at table or at dull moments at tea.'[18] Wells

---

17 Victoria Glendinning, *Rebecca West*, p.235
18 David C. Smith, *H.G. Wells: Desperately Mortal*, Yale University Press, New Haven & London, 1986, p.409

was apparently upset and shocked by Odette's language, manners and demeanour, and attempted to re-educate her. She also importuned him to marry her: at first she wanted him to divorce Jane, and later, after Jane's death, she continued to demand marriage, threatening to publish their correspondence and generally provoke adverse publicity. Wells was unmoved, however, and told her to go ahead and do what she liked. Eventually Wells decided he had had enough; but Odette continued to attack him once he had left her for good. In 1934, she published a small book entitled *I Discover the English*, which, though mainly a collection of amusing and sometimes percipient generalisations about, for instance, the 'politeness' of the English, also contains some strong criticism of the attitudes to sex and morals displayed by certain English people abroad where 'Husbands, wives, lovers, mistresses, rubbed shoulders, mixed, dined, played, and expatiated on their relations publicly. The jumble was that of a troop of monkeys mating in a cage. Everybody knew everything – chief of all, the interested parties themselves. They called this brothelism "experimenting" and "being civilized".'[19] She does not criticise Wells by name, but his inclusion in the 'brothelism' could be, and was, inferred.

Yet again, however, we are faced with variant – at times completely opposing – versions. The version I have just summarised – of Odette as a loud-mouthed, vulgar, possessive woman whom Wells eventually tired of and dumped – is the story told in most of the biographies of Wells and is clearly the version he and his followers approved. Wells sounds both vituperative and bewildered when he tries to explain Odette: 'She was indeed not sane; she was crazy with vanity, with the cruellest vindictiveness if ever her vanity were bruised. Periodically she was mad, I think; certifiably mad.'[20] But then one finds references to Odette in other places, such as in the letters of Winifred Holtby to Vera Brittain, which make one suspect she may not have been an arch-cow after all, but an

19 Odette Keun, *I Discover the English*, John Lane, London, 1934, p.195
20 *H.G. Wells in Love*, p.117

intelligent, dynamic (if also bombastic and flamboyant) woman, moving in literary circles in her own right. Then
Anthony West tells an entirely different, and very believable,
version of the ending of the relationship. According to him,
on the death of Jane Wells in 1927 – which came as a great
shock to H.G. – Wells attempted to recast Odette in the role
his wife had played in his life, that is, as the woman who
would always be there to receive him with open arms and a
comfortable house in the intervals between his other affairs. As
Odette had (again according to Anthony) been able to cope
with Wells's returning to Jane whenever it suited him, he
imagined she would also raise no objections to his going off
with other women when he felt like it. Odette, however, had
been prepared to accept the existence of Jane as someone who
had a prior claim on Wells, both in terms of having been there
first and because she cared for him and looked after him well;
but to be expected after Jane's death to remain lovingly in the
background while Wells became passionately involved with
other women was something else altogether and completely
unacceptable. And so, according to this version, when H.G.
happily told Odette that he was about to go on holiday with
Moura Budberg, she threw him out. This is so utterly at
variance with Wells's own version of events ('At the end of
May I said goodbye to her for the last time, and behind her
farewells it was evident that she thought it was all just another
quarrel in an endless succession of quarrels and that I should
come back – not so much to her as to our life at Lou Pidou.'[21])
that I can only suggest the reader take his or her pick.

Wells's final long-term liaison was with Moura. Born in
1892, the daughter of a Russian landowner, she had married
H. Von Benckendorff in 1911, who was then the Russian
ambassador to England; he was later shot by the Bolsheviks.
She then married Baron Budberg, whose name she kept,
though she later divorced him because of his addiction to
gambling. She was briefly imprisoned in Moscow in 1918, but

21 Ibid., p.154

released into the custody of the British agent Bruce Lockhart, with whom she lived for a time and with whom she remained friendly throughout his life. When Lockhart returned to England, Moura took up with Maxim Gorky. She was also friendly with Alexander Korda, the great film-maker. It seems more than likely that Moura was a Soviet agent of some variety, and that her various liaisons were initiated on the orders of others. That merely makes her yet another of the extraordinary women surrounding H.G. Wells whose life stories are open to endless interpretation. She made her living as a translator, speaking five languages well. She had first met Wells when he visited Russia in 1914, but only at a brief social occasion. On another visit in 1920, when Wells had stayed with Gorky, they seduced one another.

Moura later made her way to Berlin, staying there when Gorky returned to Russia, and subsequently shuttling back and forth to Vienna and Florence. Wells may have met her again in 1924, but in 1930 she began to spend part of each year in London, and it was from around this date that she became his mistress and companion until his death. She lived on for nearly thirty years after his death, increasingly isolated as her old friends died off.

At the time of Albert Camus's death, in a car crash in 1960 at the age of forty-six, he was married with two children and three mistresses. Of these the actress Maria Casarès was the most long-standing. They had first had an affair in 1944, broken off by her when Albert's wife Francine, with whom he had claimed to be having only 'sisterly' relations, became pregnant; it was resumed, never to be broken off again, in 1948. (In her autobiography, *Résidente Privilégiée*, Maria does not mention Francine's pregnancy as a reason for the break, but that they had decided anyway to separate at the end of the war, though Camus also used to talk about them emigrating together to Mexico. Maria relates that at this point she was not prepared to give up everything, so that when Camus offered her 'all or nothing', she chose nothing.) Maria remained for him 'the Unique One', despite the many flings and more serious affairs he had in tandem. Olivier Todd reports in his biography of Camus that 'Maria felt no guilt, saying "I didn't take anything from anyone, because in this domain, one can only take what is already available or made available" '.[22] This situation did not alter even during Francine's most serious bouts of depression, in which she was hospitalised, sometimes suicidal, and subjected to many forms of treatment including electro-convulsive therapy; part of the cause for her depression was certainly her husband's relationship with Maria (she talked about it obsessively).

Camus's second mistress at the time of his death was another actress, Catherine Sellers, and the third was a young artist called Mi. He loved them all, as is evident from the letters he wrote to each of them a few days before his death. To Maria he wrote: ' "See you soon, my superb one, I'm so happy at the idea of seeing you again that I'm laughing as I write it . . . I have no more reason to deprive myself of your laugh and our evenings together, nor of my homeland. I kiss you and hug you tightly until Tuesday, when I can start all over again." '[23] His letter to Catherine Sellers says almost the same thing: ' ". . . now I am returning and glad about it, so see you Tuesday, my dear, I'm kissing you already and bless you from the bottom of my heart." '[24] He is even more ardent when he writes to Mi, but then she is his most recent love: ' "This frightful separation will at least have made us feel more than ever the constant need we have for each other. I knew it before, and I know it even better now. I bless my need and I await you, full of force and passion, yes, I await you, my beloved and ardent one, my little girl, dear lover!" '[25]

Each of the three women seemed able to accept her limited

22 Olivier Todd, *Albert Camus: A Life*, tr. Benjamin Ivry, Chatto & Windus, London, 1997, p.262
23 Ibid., p.412
24 Ibid.
25 Ibid., p.411

role in the writer's life; it is probably significant that each of them had a profession and a life to live in her own right (unlike Francine who, though a talented musician and a teacher, seems never to have acquired a sense of independence and self-fulfilment).

Maria Casarès writes very movingly of the effect on her and others of Camus's death:

> Of this death – a conjuring trick – the last which touched me so closely, I know nothing and I have never known anything – Perhaps a photograph leaping out from a newspaper which I didn't want to see. A face congealed behind a car windscreen, open-mouthed, the bright eyes wide open – astonished. But I am not even sure whether I really saw this – document or whether I dreamt it. It is the only one of my deaths – as people say in their desperate need to possess – which I was not allowed to see. – To make up for it I have been able to see the hole which his death hollowed out. For days and days I received his friends and mine who were also his as well as unknown or barely known people, who, here as there, came to see if real life was still going on somewhere.
>
> But it's still too soon and perhaps it will always be too soon for me to speak of all that.[26]

Are there any reasons to be discovered for this ability evinced in so many writers, artists and musicians to surround themselves with numbers of mistresses, either serially or simultaneously? Perhaps these men, likewise politicians and princes, find it easy to acquire mistresses because of the fascination of fame and being out of the ordinary. Perhaps also their wives are more tolerant – as is society in general – than the wives of 'ordinary' men, because of the belief that 'genius' excuses what in other people is viewed as bad behaviour. Similarly the

26 Maria Casarès, *Résidente Privilégiée*, Paris, Fayard 1980, p.393 [Author's own translation]

mistress may be prepared to tolerate being only one among many, accepting that the man's creative and sexual energy is such that it leaps out in several directions at once. Or perhaps – and probably – they recognise that there is nothing they can do about it, and their addiction to their lover means they would rather have a bit of him than none at all. Or else, as Camus himself suggested, they each believe that they can succeed where all others have failed and come to be every-thing for their Don Juan of a man: 'Camus wrote that each woman hoped to give Don Juan what no one had ever given him before, and in this, each one is deeply wrong, and only makes him feel the need for repetition.'[27]

Another writer with a long line-up of mistresses, including a further two experts in the art of rewriting their lives, was Ford Madox Ford (1873–1939). 'Janice Biala once estimated that there had been eighteen women in Ford's life, including one of considerable importance of whom nothing is known except her first name, which was Elizabeth.'[28] Those of his women about whom we do know a fair amount present a spectrum of mistress-types – one could write a book on them alone. There are three principal ones in addition to his legal wife, Elsie Martindale. His first significant mistress, Violet Hunt, was set on becoming a wife, and was thereby doomed to permanent frustration and anger. His second, Stella Bowen, was far better at being a mistress, but had that tendency, dangerous if not fatal to her own creativity, to put her man first above all else, until in the end she felt resentful at what she had brought about herself. Then finally Janice Biala, the best mistress of all, who seemed equal to her lover and in whose arms he died. There were others along the way, including Jean Rhys, and there may also have been an affair with his wife's elder sister, Mary.

Violet Hunt came from an artistic, pre-Raphaelite, milieu. Her father was an Oxford don who had been persuaded by

27 Olivier Todd, *Albert Camus*, pp.96–7
28 Alan Judd, *Ford Madox Ford*, Collins, London, 1990, p.365

Ruskin to become a watercolourist. She also mixed regularly in high society, as well as being a writer herself and a suffragette. She began taking arsenic in her youth – a common practice at the time – in order to preserve her youthful looks. She was in general reluctant to grow up, and by the time she was in her late twenties had little to show for her life, beyond a string of affairs. She knew many people in the literary world, she wrote poems and occasional reviews, but had produced nothing substantial, and still lived with her parents on whom she was financially dependent. In her youth she apparently charmed Oscar Wilde, but her first serious affair was with the painter George Boughton; this began in 1884 when she was twenty-two and he fifty-one. The affair continued after he married (someone else). Violet was later pursued by an older man called Walter Pollock, and received several offers of marriage, in particular from a Dr Cholmeley. But it seems that the only men she wanted to marry were the unobtainable ones.

The great love of her thirties was one Oswald Crawfurd, the British consul at Oporto who spent six months of each year in London. Again there was a significant age gap: when he first showed interest in her during the summer of 1890 he was fifty-six and she twenty-eight. He was handsome and married to an invalid. He had had many mistresses, was very interested in the arts, wrote novels and edited *The Novel Magazine* and a review called *Black and White*. 'Violet found him a fascinating and dangerous character. He talked to her of "free love" and "exceedingly delicate matters". For a while she tried to keep the relationship on the basis of an intense flirtation. She wrote in her diary of this time that she felt "there would be something very ridiculous in my being engaged for the second time in an intrigue with a married man." '[29] But Crawfurd, who did not want a mere flirtation, was not to be resisted. They became lovers in 1892, the affair lasting until 1898.

29 Joan Hardwick, *An Immodest Violet: The Life of Violet Hunt*, Deutsch, London, 1990, pp.37–8

Crawfurd's wife was not expected to outlive him, so Violet may have anticipated that he would eventually be all hers. Yet the relationship between them was never happy, no matter how much Violet tried to deceive herself about it. By the end of the affair, according to Alan Judd, Crawfurd was tired of her possessiveness and her lack of discretion. She was in love with him both during the affair and after it ended. A year after the end, his wife died, but if Violet expected this to lead to a resumption of the affair and even marriage, then she was disappointed: Crawfurd first had an affair with one of her friends and then married another. Yet Violet cherished the memory of this relationship for many years, building it up in her mind as a grand passion – or, in a word, rewriting.

Between 1898 and 1907 Violet wrote six books, including a novel about her affair with Crawfurd called *Sooner or Later*, and she also acquired a reputation as a literary journalist and an energetic hostess. She lived with her mother at South Lodge in Campden Hill Road in London (where later she invited Rebecca West to take refuge with her baby), not far from where Ford had rooms in Holland Park Avenue. In 1906 the lesbian novelist Radclyffe Hall fell in love with her. She also had a brief affair with Somerset Maugham and a flirtation with H.G. Wells which did not develop into anything more: 'she was one of the few women who did not succeed in becoming Wells's mistress'.[30] (At least so says Joan Hardwick. Barbara Belford, on the other hand, says Violet had a year-long affair with H.G. in 1906–7 while he was also having an affair with Dorothy Richardson.[31] And indeed H.G. says so himself; at least he uses words such as 'understanding', 'mysteries of Soho and Pimlico' and 'found great satisfaction in each other's embraces',[32] so I can only surmise that Hardwick and Belford have drawn differing conclusions from these words.)

In 1905 Violet had been told she had syphilis. For some years she persuaded herself that there was nothing seriously

30 Ibid., p.54
31 Barbara Belford, *Violet*, Simon & Schuster, New York, 1990
32 *H.G. Wells in Love*, p.63

wrong with her, and it was not until she began to suffer from serious nose bleeds that she was forced to acknowledge the true nature of the disease. She carried her talent for self-deception into her relationship with Ford (whose full name at this time was Ford Madox Hueffer). Since he too was blessed with the ability to bring his imagination into play in his life, theirs was a powerful combination when it came to make-believe. Their relationship began in 1907, though they did not become lovers until 1909. In May of that year Ford asked her if she would marry him if he ever obtained a divorce (perhaps intuiting that such a dream was the way to her heart – and bed). She pretended not to take him seriously while at the same time being indiscreet about their relationship to most of their mutual acquaintances in London.

'When at the age of forty-five [Violet] established relations with Ford her driving ambition was social: she wanted to be a married lady. What had complicated previous attempts was that she had also wanted to be wildly in love. She still did.'[33] Judd here makes the assumption – was it also Violet's? – that marriage and 'wild love' are mutually exclusive. Certainly they work on different time spans, and maybe women who want one are best advised not to be desperate to have the other. This is the old courtly love, the old Tristan and Isolde theme – the woman who loves and is loved wildly is not 'the woman one marries'. It seems to have been at her father's funeral in 1896 that Violet, then aged thirty-four and still in the throes of her affair with Oswald Crawfurd, became convinced of the advantages of marriage; she saw that her sisters were accompanied and supported by their husbands while she was alone (according to Barbara Belford, Crawfurd attended the funeral but 'Propriety prevented his taking her arm'[34]), and she realised how strong the love between her parents had been. Then later, when marriage continued to elude her, she bent all her forces to gain the semblance of marriage – rewriting her life not only in her imagination and

33 Alan Judd, *Ford Madox Ford*, p.171
34 Barbara Belford, *Violet*, p.106

her novels, but attempting to do it in reality. Yet Violet was full of ambiguities, and it was not (I would say it never is) entirely by accident that she did not succeed in marrying. She was at best ambivalent about the whole idea, aware of the potential loss of freedom; she didn't quite know, though, how to exercise the freedom she did have, wasn't quite able to let go of the idea of 'respectability'. And – as for so many of these women – the grass is always greener on the other side. 'While she is prepared to condemn marriage as "a tyranny tempered by divorce", as long as Ford still acknowledges that he is married to Elsie, she is anxious to assume the yoke of that tyranny herself.'[35]

Ford, it seems, did his best to obtain the divorce which never came. Elsie, influenced both by her brother and by the Catholic Hüffers in Münster, never liked the idea of a divorce and worried about the status of their two daughters and whether Ford would automatically gain custody of them. At one point he and Violet tried to anger Elsie into initiating divorce proceedings, alleging as the third party one Gertrud Schlabowsky, who was possibly a prostitute. This rather strange plan, like all their other strange plans, did not work. At least, Elsie did start proceedings but then dropped them, and subsequently went to court with a successful petition for the 'restitution of conjugal rights'. Possession of Ford had become a matter of pride to her.

The next mad plan, in the face of Elsie's obduracy, was to abandon English matrimonial law and turn to Germany instead. Violet and Ford talked to a German lawyer who expressed the opinion that it would be fairly easy for Ford to obtain German citizenship and then a German divorce. The couple seemed to think this would sort everything out. Violet left Ford behind in Germany, with the intention that he should get his citizenship and divorce finalised, but the proceedings seemed to drag on and on, until Ford suddenly grew tired of waiting. On 22 October 1911 a piece appeared

35 Joan Hardwick, *An Immodest Violet*, p.170

in the *Daily Mirror*, after Ford had given an interview to a persistent reporter in Germany, claiming that he was divorced and now married to Violet. She was appalled when she found out what Ford had done, being able to envision the consequences in a way that he apparently could not. For the sake of convenience she now decided to accept, without seeing any official documents, that Ford had indeed obtained German citizenship and a divorce. It was difficult to go through a marriage ceremony in Germany, after it had been announced that they were already married, but it seems that some kind of religious ceremony took place on 5 November which Violet later described as their marriage. 'The power of mutual illusion must have been very great since it enabled them to overlook Ford's never having appeared before a divorce court, his having no evidence of German nationality and the absence of a marriage certificate.'[36]

Returning to England, the couple began a busy social life, Violet being determined to establish herself in what she saw as her new status, even having new stationery printed for herself and her 'husband'. Friends tried to warn them that fantasy could not so easily be converted into reality, but they took no heed. During 1912 the real Mrs Hueffer brought a court case against a literary journal for referring to Violet by that name. Violet and Ford assured the journal's proprietor of her right to be called Mrs Hueffer and so he refused to back down, and the case came to court in February 1913. And of course Elsie Hueffer won – apparently to the astonishment of both Ford and Violet who had managed so firmly to convince themselves that they were married in Germany. The repercussions of the verdict came quickly. Some old friends commiserated with Violet, but her clubs asked her to resign, her sisters – who had long been hostile towards her – felt their attitude was vindicated, and her clergyman godfather cut her out of his will. Concealed adultery could be tolerated, while the scandal of being involved in a court case could not.

36 Alan Judd, *Ford Madox Ford*, p.204

Both Violet and Elsie spent the rest of their lives insisting on the right to be called 'Mrs Hueffer'. Alan Judd points up the irony: 'The two women continued their fight over the name long after its original owner had abandoned it and them'[37] for in 1919 Ford changed his surname by deed poll from Hueffer to Ford.

In July 1915 Ford took a commission in the army. He was already forty-one years old. 'There is little doubt that Ford, like many who enlist in mature years, was taking the opportunity to escape from a domestic situation. There is even less doubt that Violet took it as desertion.'[38] She was lonely and upset. Many of her friends saw clearly that it was now only a question of time before Ford left her for someone else, and they urged her to take the initiative and make a break. But she found she could not bear to maintain merely friendly relations with him during his leaves, and was incapable of breaking with him herself. She admitted that by now she had neither love nor respect left for him, but she was still in the sway of a 'passion'. Ford was posted back to Britain in 1917, where he continued to see Violet though the situation between them was clearly very unhappy. Most of his mail was directed to South Lodge where Violet got the maid to open it. At one point she humiliated him by drawing out all the money in his bank account (on forged cheques) so that his own cheques were dishonoured.

Then in the spring of 1918 Ford met Stella Bowen (ironically through Violet, who had already befriended her). 'She was twenty-three, attractive, enthusiastic, unattached, an Australian studying art in London and relishing the cosmopolitan intellectual world into which she had fallen. He was forty-four, married, involved in a dying and joyless affair, shell-shocked, unsure that he could write again and very hard up.'[39] Violet had feared the possibility of being left for a younger woman for some years and she couldn't bear the

37 Ibid., p.208
38 Ibid., p.254
39 Ibid., p.313

reality of it – particularly after having fought so hard to establish her 'marriage'. She was never completely reconciled to losing him, always retaining her hope that eventually he would see the error of his ways and come back to her.

Stella came from Adelaide. She was the daughter of an estate agent who died when she was three, and she had come to England in 1914, after the death of her mother, in order to develop her artistic talents. She and Ford were corresponding by June 1918 and it is usually assumed that they became lovers during that summer. As had been the case in the early days of the affair with Violet, it was hard for the couple to find somewhere where they could be alone together for any length of time. After leaving the army Ford rented a room containing his camp-bed and kit, and Stella lived in a shared flat with a young actress friend. Violet continued to want to see Ford, but when she did she was generally horrible to him. Eventually Ford and Stella found a dilapidated cottage in West Sussex, where they moved in 1919, while attempting to keep it – and particularly its address – a secret from Violet. When she was eventually told what was going on – but still not where they were – she was furious, took to her bed and summoned Ford, who spent a morning by her bedside as they argued. It was at Stella's suggestion that he continued to appear at Violet's parties so that it wouldn't look as though she had been officially deserted; clearly at this stage Violet 'would have preferred to have him and hate him than to see him disappear'.[40]

In September 1920 Stella and Ford moved to a slightly less uncomfortable cottage (though Ford never really minded primitive conditions – he seems, in fact, to have enjoyed them) in Bedham. And now Violet somehow found out where they were, and proved they were right to have been wary. Not only did she occasionally turn up to keep watch on them herself, but she also paid a local woman to spy on them.

In late 1922 (by which time they had a daughter, Julia)

---

40 Ibid., p.325

Stella and Ford were offered the loan of a small house in Cap Ferrat in the South of France, so off they went, and though they continued to move around, they stayed in France, hoping to sell the cottage in Bedham for enough money to buy an apartment in Paris and a small house elsewhere in France. They never managed to attain this degree of security. Yet the nine years of their affair represented, on the whole, a rich and fulfilling time for them both and they managed the ending – which came about partly through the agency of Jean Rhys – well. 'Even when we were on the brink of separating, we could still go out to dine together and have a grand argument about Lost Causes, or the Theory of the Infallibility of the Pope, or some such theme. But by that time our real relationship had become quite a different thing from what it had once been, and my education had received a big shove forward.'[41]

When Ford became involved with Jean Rhys, she was not yet a writer and had been living in Paris in a fairly desperate situation. At sixteen she had left the West Indies where she was brought up to go to drama school in England but she had had to leave when her father died. She then became a chorus girl and model. Her first serious lover was a man considerably older than herself, but that did not work out, and she subsequently met and married a Dutch poet. They lived in Paris, where she had a baby who died, and their lives began to drift without much direction or hope of income. Ford and Stella took her up and let her live with them while her husband was in prison for a currency offence. Ford fell in love with her and encouraged her to write, while Stella undertook to increase her wardrobe.

Jean Rhys was another rewriter. Her short novel, *Quartet*, first published in 1928 under the title *Postures*, is a thinly disguised account of her affair with Ford in which she attacks – particularly – Stella, portraying her as the rather loud, un-gainly, insensitive, outwardly caring but inwardly vindictive

---

41 Stella Bowen, *Drawn from Life*, Collins, London, 1941, pp.165–6

wife, Lois. She further portrays both Stella and Ford as horribly concerned with 'keeping up appearances' and 'playing the game', and herself as victim of them both. It's a sad little book in its unresolved anger and yet it is also a brilliant vindication of Ford's conviction that Rhys could write. It's succinct, vivid and stylish, and contains a very good depiction of certain aspects of being a mistress. Here, for instance, is the married lover taking his leave in the way they so often do:

> '. . . You pretty thing – you pretty, pretty thing. Oh, you darling. I say, did you notice what I did with my wristwatch? Lois has got hold of two Czecho-Slovakians and that young American chap – you know – what's-his-name? – the sculptor – for tonight and I promised I'd turn up. Are you all right for money? I'd better leave some money, hadn't I?'
>
> The endless repetition of that sort of thing became a torture. She would wait for him to say, 'Look here, I must go now. Because Lois . . .'[42]

The affair Ford had with Jean, whatever importance it may or may not have had in itself, signified the beginning of the end of his 'marriage' with Stella. It took another three years for the end actually to arrive, and their friendship continued beyond it, but Stella knew the affair with Jean was an important marker.

> The obvious and banal business of remaining in love with someone who has fallen for someone else is anybody's experience and no one will deny that it hurts, or that it creates an essential change in the original relationship, however well it may afterwards appear to have been mended. And to be suddenly called upon to change one kind of relationship into another is rather like changing boats in midstream – a difficult operation, though not necessarily impossible.

42 Jean Rhys, *Quartet*, Penguin, Harmondsworth, 1973, pp.92–3

To realise that there can be no such thing as 'belonging' to another person (for in the last resort you must be responsible for yourself, just as you must prepare to die alone), is surely a necessary part of an adult's education! How trite it sounds, how not worth mentioning. But what a discovery it makes!

After being quite excruciatingly unhappy for some weeks, I found on a certain day, at a certain hour, that for the first time, I was very tired – not to say bored – with personal emotions, my own no less than Ford's. This feeling recurred with greater and greater frequency, until it became perpetual.

I think that the exhilaration of falling out of love is not sufficiently extolled. The escape from the atmosphere of a stuffy room into the fresh night air, with the sky as the limit.[43]

Once the entanglement with Jean Rhys was over, it seemed Ford imagined they could carry on much as before. But Stella had tasted freedom and was ready to move on. In 1927 Ford was in New York, where his books were finding success, and from there he corresponded regularly with Stella. The change in their relationship was mirrored in the changes in the tone of their letters, as love was gradually transformed into friendship. By the end of the year he was able to ask her to rent a small flat on his behalf near to the one in which she and Julia were living. Stella comes out as the best kind of mistress – Circe-like – in the way she handled this change in their relations.

Though such an ability to cope with change would suggest Stella's possession of a basic self-confidence, belief in her artistic ability seems to have been altogether more fragile. Consequently she let her own creativity be blocked by being mistress and muse to a man. That is a simplistic way of putting it, but it nevertheless contains some truth and is a common enough phenomenon. Throughout her time with Ford, Stella

43 Stella Bowen, *Drawn from Life*, pp.167–8

let the creative-artist side of herself be overrun and take second place to the woman who nurtures the male artist. This was always a source of conflict for her – she knew she was sacrificing the full development of her talent – but there was no real struggle. Her love for Ford, her understanding of how that relationship worked and how it would cease to work if its terms were significantly altered, dictated that she place his needs as an artist above her own. She viewed the work of her man as of far greater importance than her own anyway. Ford knew what he was doing – albeit unconsciously – when he picked Stella as his unofficial wife. From this description of their life together, it's clear why Stella couldn't get on with her painting:

> But if we managed to achieve beauty in our surroundings at Bedham, and in our subsequent wanderings, there was another commodity which was much less easily attained, the provision of which, both there and afterwards, became one of my chiefest difficulties. This was called 'working conditions', and it meant seeing that Ford had somewhere to write, and unmolested quiet whilst he was doing it. It meant, of course, putting off meals until all hours, and acting as a shock-absorber when problems and interruptions occurred during working hours, and not only during working hours. Ford would put it to me that he could not finish his book if his mind was upset, and that I must manage to keep all worries from him, which was difficult.[44]

Yet Stella still thought, on one level at least, of art as the mainspring of her existence, her real joy. She talks about going up the stairs to the art classes she attended after leaving school as the happiest moments of her life. What she lacked was ruthlessness. And Ford was very hard to resist. 'When Ford wanted anything, he filled the sky with an immense ache

---

44 Ibid., p.78

that had the awful simplicity of a child's grief, and appeared to hold the same possibilities of assuagement.'[45]

Part of the reason women get themselves into this situation is that they are flattered to be loved (or what they interpret as being loved) by 'genius'. Stella describes that unfailing recipe by which 'great' men get women to love them – the revelation of vulnerability:

> The stiff, rather alarming exterior, and the conventional, omniscient manner, concealed a highly complicated emotional machinery. It produced an effect of tragic vulnerability; tragic because the scope of his understanding and the breadth of his imagination had produced a great edifice which was plainly in need of more support than was inherent in the structure itself. A walking temptation to any woman, had I but known it![46]

Stella had a gift for loving non-possessively, teaching herself to do this because of her underlying belief that one must let people go their own way. She is impressive in her willingness to change and develop, meeting the varied situations in her life as they arose, allowing her behaviour to be influenced by her reason, despite the accompanying pain. 'Her daughter, Julia Loewe, wrote that Stella's favourite proverb was the Spanish one that was also Ford's favourite: "Take what you want," said God, "take it, and pay for it." '[47] Stella's generosity was such that not only did she pay for her relationship with Ford, but she also never ceased to give thanks for it. 'But to have a mind of that calibre, with all its inconsistencies, its generosity, its blind spots, its spaciousness, and vision, and its great sense of form and style, was a privilege for which I am still trying to say "thank you".'[48]

In May 1930, Ford met Janice Biala, a young and attractive

45 Ibid., p.63
46 Ibid., pp.62–3
47 Alan Judd, *Ford Madox Ford*, p.315
48 Stella Bowen, *Drawn from Life*, p.64

painter with, as Judd puts it, the same sort of fearless honesty as Stella. She was Polish-American-Jewish and aged twenty-six; Ford was fifty-five. Their love lasted until his death. Janice was as devoted to the arts as was Ford and 'fought his corner in a way he never could, taking on publishers, landlords, editors, bank managers, relatives, friends and enemies, excelling in exactly the sort of confrontation he could never really cope with. She was also the only one of the women he lived with whose lack of interest in domestic comforts matched his own; she didn't care about curtains.'[49] Early on in their relationship, Ford sent Janice to meet Stella and Julia, whose approval was important to him both because he didn't want to lose contact with his third daughter as he had with his first two and because he trusted and respected Stella's judgement. They both liked Janice, Stella later writing of her: 'Janice was with [Ford] at the end and did everything that it is possible for one human soul to do for another, to comfort his last days.'[50]

After Ford's death, Stella lived the remaining twenty years of her life as a painter. She spent most of the war in London and Essex (her memoirs end in July 1940, with Stella and Julia awaiting a German invasion at any minute), having been appointed an official war artist by the Australian government. She died of cancer in 1947, at the age of fifty-two. And when dying, she sent for Janice Biala as the only person she could talk to about her 'real' life.

Violet Hunt died in 1942 during a London bombing raid which she mistook for thunder in the Welsh mountains.

Judd recorded in 1989 that Janice was living and painting in Paris with her husband, the painter Daniel Brustlein, better known as the *New Yorker* cartoonist Alain.

More than anything else one is left with a sense of ambiguity after considering these mistresses, nearly all creative themselves, clustered around these male writers. (And I have only included three male writers here – one could go on for ever.)

49 Alan Judd, *Ford Madox Ford*, p.395
50 Stella Bowen, *Drawn from Life*, p.244

The ambiguity resides in what these women really want – part of the time at least they appear to want to be wives, but one is not entirely convinced – and is demonstrated in the tendency of many of them to present variant versions of their lives to themselves and others, and in the very fact that variant interpretations are possible. There is also the sense that these women hope that attaching themselves to a male literary figure will provide an entrée into the world of art; what it actually provides an entrée into is more likely to be part-time artistic housekeeping. Wells and Ford (like Rodin and Augustus John) provide telling examples of the way creative men can use up the energies of the women around them – if the women allow or even encourage it – so that the women's own work is adversely affected. Women with a tendency to undermine themselves, through fear of failure or more particularly, I would suggest, fear of success (for success in a male world could destroy the very foundation of how these women were brought up to be), may be particularly drawn to the kind of man who will drain their energies in this way. Yet conversely – for these things are never simple and there is always an 'and yet' – they may also be drawn to set up complex and, to some degree, unsatisfactory lives and relationships as a spur to creativity and to provide the raw material for their own art. They may also, in their deepest selves, fear that to be the wife would both drain them totally of their creative energies and provide them with less material to draw upon. Yet such unconscious fears do little to lessen conscious jealousy and resentment. In short, the writer's mistress, as witnessed here, particularly the writer's mistress who writes herself (in all senses of that phrase) is at war with herself, quite as much as she is at war with the wife.

A CONTEMPORARY WRITER'S MISTRESS

*You know how much I esteem and adore
you, my darling – but I really can't do
anything about it.*

W hat about the present day? Do many writers still have
mistresses? And how do contemporary writers' mistresses differ from or resemble their predecessors? I have
interviewed and had access to the correspondence of Vanessa,
a woman who had an affair with a novelist for about four years
in the early 1990s. A close friend, Vanessa entrusted to me the
letters she'd received from her ex–lover – he used to write to
her nearly every day, and she's kept them in case they ever
turn out to be useful to some poor thesis-writer or biographer.
So, using this material, I'll try to piece together the story of the
affair, and show how this particular mistress handled her
situation. I'll begin with an edited version of something
Vanessa wrote – but didn't publish – after a profile of her
lover (as he then was) appeared in a national newspaper.

My lover is a well-known novelist. He's considerably
older than me, and is married – has been for well over
thirty years (to the same person). I met him through his
wife, and he initiated our relationship. Such a possibility
had never entered my head when he rang me one
Sunday morning and invited himself for coffee. He
declared he was in love with me, and I didn't send
him away.

That was over four years ago. He has written to me
nearly every day of those four years. I see him for a few
hours most weeks, and occasionally we go away somewhere for a couple of nights. He usually phones me from

public call boxes as he won't phone from home when his wife's there – as she nearly always is – and I don't phone him, as it would probably be she who would answer the phone. He tells me I am vital to his life, but I'm obviously not vital enough for him to want to change it by leaving her. Some of the time I wouldn't want him to anyway: I fear I might find him irritating to live with, and I value my independence and solitude. Some of the time I long to be with him, and be officially recognised as his partner. Most of the time I'm not sure what I want. I try to feel sympathetically towards his wife – she was my friend and I betrayed her in the worst way imaginable – but it's not my strong point.

He told his wife about our affair over three years ago now. I think he hoped she would get used to the idea and would allow him more freedom as a result. This was a major misjudgment. At the time of revelation, he told me she was 'surprised'. Years later, and with no sign of acceptance on her part, he has amended this to 'shocked'. In general, he tells me as little as possible. I surmise that she is using the same tactics which have operated in their relationship for about forty years – silence, denial, and manipulation of his passivity. I'm sure there's more to it than that, but nobody understands someone else's marriage – least of all, probably, the 'other woman'.

Recently an article about my lover appeared in a newspaper, featuring a cosy scene over supper with the journalist, my lover and his wife. The journalist painted a picture of complete and intuitive understanding between my lover and his wife, even claiming they looked 'twenty years younger' when together. No mention, of course, of anything to mar this scene of tranquil, domestic bliss.

'Well,' said my sister comfortingly, 'we know it's not really like that,' but I can't dismiss the picture so easily. For one thing, in the earlier part of the piece, the journalist had caught various aspects of my lover fairly accurately, though at times the portrait verged on caricature. But it meant I couldn't dismiss everything she claimed to have seen. And then he and his wife have been married for a very long time – they're bound to have some ability to communicate intuitively, and to enjoy a kind of literary camaraderie. These things don't not exist, just because I don't want to see them.

I find Vanessa's approach, at least as it is evinced here, reasonably unblinkered and honest. Her lover, Brian – maybe partly because of his age, partly also because of his temperament – never brought the same clarity to the relationship. The letters she received from her lover, with the evasions, the unkeepable promises, the sense of not knowing what he really wants, the refusal to face reality or to admit how important a continued relationship with his wife really is to him, bear comparison to those sent by Philip Noel-Baker to Megan Lloyd George, and will probably sound familiar to many mistresses. But I must let Brian speak for himself.

Vanessa has lost the first card she received from him – from Paris – a few days after he turned up on her doorstep in September 1991 and told her he loved her. (Her immediate thought was that he had gone mad, her second that she felt flattered, her third the knowledge that she was incapable of resisting adventure, particularly if it was illicit. Her first action was to go to a bookshop and look up his age, her second to check how old T.S. Eliot was when he married his second wife, reassuring herself that wide age-gaps in literary liaisons were not abnormal.) She does still have his second card, which in a way sets the tone for the entire correspondence (at least on his side – I do not have access to Vanessa's letters to Brian; she doesn't even know whether he kept them on receipt or destroyed them straightaway): there is some mundane information about what he is doing and a rather extravagant claim – considering he hardly knew Vanessa at this point – about his feelings for her. By the end of October, another characteristic of Brian's letters has manifested itself – the ability to use a lot of words to weave a kind of emotional spell which, when analysed, contains little of real substance: 'Anyway, words being the next best thing to actions, just to let you know – though don't be alarmed, free spirit – that I think of you as well as think much of you, which makes it inconceivable not to write when I can sit down with a glass of beer at my elbow in this quiet club.'

In November Vanessa and Brian spent their first night together, in a hotel in the Malvern Hills. Brian's first written communication after this event contains a sentiment which, in those early days of the affair, may have sounded merely romantic but which later on Vanessa came to resent and be irritated by, because it suggests Brian doesn't really need her actual presence – what he is in love with is her image: 'You're always with me and I like it that way.' In 'real' life, she wasn't 'always with him' at all, and the two principal obstacles to her 'always' being with him were his wife and his work.

Very early on a pattern was established – of Brian coming to see Vanessa most Saturday afternoons, of writing to her every day, and of calling her most days, always from a callbox and usually on his way to buy milk, bread or the newspapers. To begin with, Vanessa would write to Brian at his club; then he said she could write to him at home, provided she type the envelopes; eventually she got tired of typing envelopes and took the risk of his wife recognising her handwriting, which occasionally happened. The worst Brian's wife could do, as far as Vanessa could see, was create a difficult atmosphere, which really didn't seem worth worrying about.

Throughout the course of these letters Brian had a tendency to apostrophise various parts of Vanessa's body, another habit which at first didn't seem to bother her – maybe she even liked it – but well before the end it had become an irritation, and looking back now she finds it demeaning. The irritation had to do with a feeling of not really existing for Brian as a whole person in her own right, but as being some kind of treat for him to 'feast' on. Here is an early example by which Vanessa, in re-reading the letter, feels reduced to a 'delectable mouth': 'What a treat for the heart (mine) to come here and get your letter this morning, such a wonderful lot of it that my eyes can feast on with perhaps even more avidity than your delectable mouth feasted on your coffee and cakes!'

The letters continue their theme of presence in absence, over and over. November 1991: 'Sorry to leave you today, an awful pull. I can only read tonight, fitfully, because thankfully you are here, I'm seeing and hearing you.' Later the same month: 'I don't want to be out of touch with you for a second, but of course I'm not; even when I'm not writing to you I feel your presence – and that is golden to me.' Brian's idea of Vanessa as two people, one somewhere else and one with him, is made explicit in a letter of April 1992: 'I walked here across the park, thinking of you. No – thinking won't do. Conjuring maybe – I'm glad at times there seem to be two of you, one of yourself at [the place where Vanessa worked] (or wherever) and then that fairly tangible *other* who, by my warlockery, I call to my side and imagine I'm conversing with.'

Also, almost from the start, Brian continually stresses how important Vanessa is to his life, in such extravagant terms that it is no wonder she found his determination to maintain the *status quo* of his married life hard to understand. November 1991: 'I can't tell you how good it is to be out of the valley of the shadow.' December 1991: 'I live to see you, and see you in order to live.' January 1992: 'I love you and live always, every minute, in hope of seeing you. Nothing else.' Later the same month: 'It's impossible to tell you my love how much you mean to me. My life has changed so much for the better, and I can't think of what it was like before.'

In April there is the first mention of Brian's wife, Fiona, by name; at this stage Vanessa is still in touch with her and has deliberately phoned her at a time when she knew Brian would be out. He writes:

Fiona said you phoned her this afternoon, but nothing else. We must talk more about that, my love. I'm still not sure what's the best thing to do, though if you think I should tell her I will. During our time together the policy has evolved that even though we know we neither of us say anything. But I don't feel convinced at all that that is right in our case, and as I say I'm willing to tell her. But I want to talk more to you about it first.

He also seems anxious to tell her he doesn't sleep with his wife, as a rule: 'I'll slowly get ready for bed – a single one, in my own room.' In the same month he refers to the first time he saw Vanessa, underlining the cataclysmic nature of the experience for him. It is no wonder if, after receiving letters like this, Vanessa expected their relationship to develop into something more than weekly sex, occasional lunches and doing his VAT return:

> I see in my old diary that in the space for 26th November 1990 it says: 'Vanessa X . . . for supper.' That's when I first saw you, and from then on only wanted to get to know you, because I had become utterly fascinated by you and was in love. It finally took ten months, until 21st September of the following year, for me to phone and hope you would allow me to see you . . . But in those ten months I thought about you a lot, saw your face before me, and knew finally that I had no option but to see you and let you know how I felt . . . There were many times during that waiting period when I was in anguish at wondering what to do, or when in fact I would do it – make that call – for I never lost the feeling of inevitability about it.

Generally, when Brian relates something involving his wife, he tends to use the passive mode, as though to distance himself as well as to avoid naming her. Perhaps he fears that to do so would hurt Vanessa, though it is also a way of avoiding the issues. February 1992: 'there's a film on the TV which might be watched later tonight.' This way of talking also underlines another aspect of Brian's handling of the relationship, as indeed of life in general – a belief that his life is controlled by 'fate', that there's really nothing much he can do about what happens to him. This sense surfaces the first time he mentions something Vanessa always finds difficult – the long stays Brian and his wife make at their other house, in the South of France: 'The time may well be coming, and believe me sweetheart, I dread to think of it, when we'll have to be parted a few weeks. There's talk of going to France, about the middle of January.' The resignation to fate is reiterated before they set off: 'I dread the separation of France, but alas! it must be gone through and endured.'

The first clear indication of Brian's work as a reason for his not seeing more of Vanessa comes in March 1992: 'The terrible fact is, darling, that this bloody stint of toilsome writing is our enemy in that perhaps it's keeping me from you more than it should, and certainly more than I desire. I hope you don't mind too much, and that you'll forgive it as I am forced to forgive it and just plough on with the task.' He doesn't seem to be aware – or, at best, is only half-aware – that he's made a choice: 'What a price one has to pay for such deadly dedication. I love you, sweetheart, and know I'll see you again soon, but how anguishing it is to have to wait.' One cannot help but be reminded here of H.G. Wells writing to Rebecca West in March 1923: ' "I want to say plainly to you that I will not accept any imputation that I have treated you badly or broken any promise to you . . . I have done my utmost to love you and I would have come to you and lived with you under any circumstances that would not have wrecked my work." '[1]

In June 1992 Vanessa and Brian managed to have a few days together near Calais and Brian decided, quite suddenly, that he would tell Fiona about the affair on his return. He did so, but the references in his letters to this presumably momentous event are minimal, giving Vanessa very little clue as to what

---

1 Gordon N. Ray, *H.G. Wells & Rebecca West*, p.131

was actually going on: 'Things are a little frosty here from time to time, but generally all right.' From then on the sense of Brian being 'stuck', unable to act, intensifies. By mid-August Vanessa has clearly decided it's about time Brian told her something about the reality of his domestic situation, as he writes: 'You ask about Fiona. Well, I had thought that telling her could be no bad thing and that it might be possible for friendship [i.e. between Fiona and Vanessa] to go on, but up to now at least it begins to seem a possible mistake on my part, though who knows what the future will bring? There's nothing we ought (you and I) not to be able to talk about, and will do so. But it's an up and down situation here.' Since Brian told Fiona of the affair, there has been no communication of any sort between the two women.

In October 1992 comes the first intimation that Brian is beginning to think of selling the house in France, at least partly in order not to have to spend so much time away from Vanessa: 'Property is a curse. It wouldn't hurt me not to have this place – though at the same time I am fond of it. Yet I would gladly give it up to be with you. It was bought four years ago, at a time when one could not see into the future and know that such a wonderful person as you would come into my life. So the place has to be lived with and looked after, but it's a vile situation, all the same.' At times Brian launches into strangely archaic language, which seems to underline the stylised nature of his devotion – the fact it is more an image than a person he relates to: 'I'm longing for Sunday to come, when I hope to – nay, will! – see thee.' In November 1992 there is another letter protesting his inability to do anything to change the situation, and by this time – it is now more than a year into the relationship – one is starting to wonder what the word 'love' means in this context:

I'm devastated, because I seemed to leave you in a not very good state, and, God help me, I feel it is all my fault . . . I know I should have stayed longer, indeed all night and even more than that, but I could not, because I'm

fearful of psychic devastation – a coward, perhaps, meaning that I would like to alter my nature – even to the
extent of being someone else who is able to handle his
life better and thus make you happier. But this is my life
at the moment, and I don't seem capable of doing more
than going from day to day and getting as much work
done as I can, and seeing you as often as possible, which
isn't often enough for either of us. I love you, as you
know, and always will, and that is all I can do at the
moment. I feel rung [sic] out with sorrow and anxiety,
but please believe how much I love you my darling.

It is also quite clear by now that for Brian the act of writing
letters to Vanessa is a ritualistic solace in itself – he does it more
for his own sake than out of a desire to communicate anything
to her (they are for the most part by now very repetitive):
'You have to put up with so much from these missives –
meagre or not – but they are my delight of the day, say what I
will, because I am with you intensely (though not ideally, I
know). They save my life, as you do my dearest heart by
existing.'

At the very end of 1992, Brian is no nearer to a clear answer
about anything and has presumably managed to resist actually
talking about the situation, as he keeps promising that they
will talk some time in the future:

I know I have to give you answers, and that it's only
justice that I do, but I don't have answers, and if I force
myself to make them I may not be giving a truthful
interpretation of my own mind, supposing I can ever
know what my own mind is. You are so vital to me,
that's all I know; but at what cost to you? This of course
is what we must talk about but hardly seem to have the
length of time in which the unrolling of such talk would
be possible, though I will try to make it – unless that it's
only in letters that it can be done. But no, it's only face to
face that we can really talk, and must . . . Unhappily I'm

under the ocean most of the time – practically all the time – with the work I am doing, and it's often a wrench to come out of it to the surface and get back to real life . . . I am as I have always been, in that I know what I want but have never been able in any clear way to see a way of getting it, that I have avoided all vital decisions because my work has pulled me in with a force I couldn't break free from to do something about my unsatisfactory life. And there it still is for the moment.

The correspondence continued unabated for another three years, Brian continuing to tell Vanessa she was the most important woman in his life, 'the one person in the world I feel at ease with'. 1993 began exactly as 1992 ended, with Brian's brain 'a quagmire from which I can't get anything clear', yet with him seeming to promise something: 'You must believe me darling when I say we shall see more and more of each other and go out together.' A couple of weeks later he actually admits that his 'Saturday absences make things fraught here [i.e. at home]. But what the hell. I love you too much to let it bother me. Life must go one [sic], and you are my life.'

In June 1993 Brian and Fiona took off again for France, his apologies for this reinforcing Vanessa's impression that his marriage left a lot to be desired: 'I wish to God the house in France had never been bought, but at the time I only saw it as a place to escape to and possibly be alone in, away from my intolerable life in London.' It is clear from his letter of 1 July – from France – that there is really no room for negotiation with him; he still protests his love, but instructs Vanessa on what 'has to be':

Dearest, I wish I could live with you too, and in my most warming fantasies that is exactly what is happening. I agree that we spend far too much time apart, but it's absolutely essential that I stay down here for a while to get the house in order, and also to work in a way at my

raw material that isn't always possible in London . . .
Remember that I love you with my most profound
heart, and also that you are my mainstay in life.

In late July he makes the clearest statement yet about what he
would like to happen, though it still remains in the arena of
fantasy: 'If I had the money (and who knows, maybe one day
I'll be able to get it) I'd like to get hold of a small house in
Matlock where we could be together whenever we liked.
That is my dream, ambition, object, desire or what you will.'
On 5 August – still in France – he writes as though there is
hope of change:

> What I always thought, and still think, is that by the
> passage of time (and not too much time, either) I would
> detach myself from this web of steel which I have been in
> for so long. It seems as if this is not happening, but in fact
> it is, and I shall spend more time with you than has been
> possible in the past. My whole heart has always wanted
> this, and will go on wanting it for not too much longer
> when it will become a fact. I feel that really we must talk.
> There are difficulties here with me because my psyche
> even at the best of times is a Gordian knot, and I have
> never found it easy to talk of what is most essential. I long
> for that kind of ease and freedom, and loving you as I do I
> want to do it most with you – that is to say: talk openly
> and honestly. When I am with you this seems to be
> taking place within the context of our meeting, but you
> are right when you say that these meetings are so
> infrequent or of such short duration that it doesn't really
> get done as it should. I want it to, with all my heart,
> because I love you and you mean so much to me. If there
> are any difficulties – and there are – they are mine, and I
> have to resolve them; and I will. This devastatingly long
> period away from you has shown me that I can, and that
> things will be different from now on, because I can't go
> on like this either. As I say, it is a matter of talk between

us, but also, as you say, it is for me to act also. I must go
more my separate way from this situation – towards you,
my heart's desire – and this I will make plain. In any case I
shall *never* spend so much time away from you again –
that I can promise with absolute conviction.

The practical difficulties are underscored a week later: 'Your
letter of the 8th was put onto my table this morning. The
handwriting was recognised, and a hard day ensued.' And by
the end of August, back in London, the sense that Brian might
ever act has already evaporated: 'I feel your problems deeply,
and wish I could eliminate or at least ameliorate them – do
something about them anyway. I know it's just not enough for
me to exist and love you, but I do think about it and wonder
what I might be able to do.'

It will by now be amply clear to any dispassionate reader
that for Brian the weekly lovemaking sessions, the almost
weekly lunches, the other occasional brief meetings at Vanessa's place of work, the almost daily phone calls and the
daily letters, and the thoughts of his 'love', are the backdrop
which make the rest of his life liveable. Things are pretty
much as he wants them to be:

No work is onerous, or waiting without its acceptable
anguish, and loving anticipation, now that I know you.
Tomorrow is Saturday, the consummate day of the week
which is always looked forward to more than the tomorrow of any other day because we've settled on it for our
ultimate meeting time. Since it can't always be *that*
tomorrow we have the pleasure not only of waiting for
it, but living it once a week! By the time you get this it will
have passed, but at least another will be on its way. I give
God a silent thank you every morning – and more often,
indeed – for my good fortune in being associated with you.

Any idea of him changing his *modus vivendi* seems to have
vanished. Mid-October he writes:

Regarding next week, my love, I shan't be able to make Saturday, which galls me, and which I regret very much, because I must take Fiona to Bath for the weekend. I'm so sorry about this, because I would much rather be with you on Saturday . . .

You know how much I esteem and adore you, my darling – but I really can't do anything about it.

1994 saw significant changes in Vanessa's life. She had a new job – at a place less convenient for Brian to drop in to – and her father was diagnosed with cancer. Nothing changes, however, in Brian's litany of love mingled with excuses. This is from a letter dated 7 February:

I'm just in from having 'phoned you, and know that something is wrong – I'm so sorry about your father's illness. And at not being with you at this time. I'm still in the immovable block of having come back from France, so forgive me. Ever since my return I have had hardly a moment free – in any case it was only forty eight hours ago. I've had a great deal to do . . .

Darling, you are the precious person of my life, my loving mainstay, the one I care for most of all. Any thoughts I have of you make me happy, and I'm happiest of all when I'm with you. I'll try to see you as soon as I can, of course, but as I say I'm locked in with work and things to do.

Brian and Fiona then spent about three weeks in Israel, returning to London only days before the death of Vanessa's father. Brian never managed to phone from Israel, but he wrote his usual letters, describing how he felt Vanessa to be with him all the time. She appears to have taken him to task over this, as he responds:

I know that when I think of you as if you are with me you at the same time are where you are, on your chaise

longe [sic], being your separate and alone self, but I feel
you nevertheless and love you all the same because I have
no alternative in being as I am . . . All I mean when I say
you are with me is that I'm thinking/imagining intensely
about you, which obviously brings you close, while not
violating *you* at all in where you are.

At the end of March he is once more as explicit as he ever
manages to be about his marriage, prompted to these thoughts
partly by Vanessa having just attended her sister's wedding
(three weeks after her father's funeral, a busy time for her).

Marriage I suppose is all right providing the two people
are made for each other to the extent that they are not
mutually discontented enough to turn the union into a
hell that neither can get out of. Perhaps most people can
do it without any (or not too much) mental suffering.
They must be the simple ones, or the blessèd of the earth.
   Your letter from Malvern came today. I'm afraid Fiona
would see anyone else I'm connected to as a practical
threat. It's all or nothing with her, and as a consequence
my mind is constantly on getting out as the only tolerable
solution, to live somewhere and somehow on my own –
as I know a writer finally should. I want to do this yet am
locked in a horrible kind of glue which has taken so long
to get thicker and thicker. I've tried to loosen the ties
many times, and will go on trying – or suddenly break. It
certainly gets worse instead of better, but this is all my
problem which I have to resolve, and certainly nothing
to agonise you with because I love you too much to
impose any of it on you. So please, my love, bear with
me. I shan't despair. I do want to be with you more, and
will try to see that I do.

Events conspired to increase Vanessa's disillusionment in the
latter part of 1994 and the beginning of 1995. The house in
France did get sold, but the timing of this meant that a

projected week away in Cornwall, to which the lovers had been looking forward for months, had to be cancelled. As Brian put it: 'I hate it when Fate takes such a hand, but there's nothing to be done. At least the house will be gone and there'll be no more long times apart while I'm in France.' What then came as a considerable shock to Vanessa was Brian's sudden announcement, and in tones that anticipated no need for or expectation of discussion, that he and Fiona were now looking for another house in England to replace the one sold in France (in addition to keeping on the flat in London). After all his declarations of wanting to change his life, to loosen his ties with Fiona, he proposed to act instead, without any consultation with Vanessa, in a way that would only strengthen those ties. Vanessa could see, if Brian could not, that buying another house together was an expression of the continued commitment between husband and wife. Brian as usual talked as though there were no alternative: 'I got rid of the house in France for the reasons you know about, and now another has to be got. Acquiring it is a laborious task, and I don't like it, but a house seems not to be as much of a symbol to me as it does with you . . .'

One of the more galling aspects of the situation for Vanessa was that, from her point of view, there could now have been room for more flexibility than ever before: not only had Brian made a change which could have been handled differently (selling a house), but she had inherited some money after her father's death and perhaps they could – if they had actually talked about it (and Vanessa admits that she had discussed all this no more than Brian, having waited to see how things worked out rather than doing anything about it) – have bought a property together where he could have lived at least part of the time with her, while also maintaining his London base with Fiona. When she finally got around to mentioning this idea to him (too late for anything to be done about it, a fact whose significance is not lost on her now) Brian chose to interpret this as the possibility of a *third* property for him to be involved in and said it was currently 'impossible', but maybe some time in the future . . . He had always held up economic considerations as part of the reason for being unable to change his domestic arrangements – how could he afford to live separately from Fiona, where would he go, etc.? When, from the detailed account of negotiations Brian (disingenuously?) included in his letters, Vanessa learnt he had bought the new house for a six-figure sum in cash, she finally realised he had far more practical options at his disposal than he ever cared to admit, either to himself or to her. He clearly still *perceived* himself as hemmed in, unable to move – but this was only a perception and was indicative of his refusal to admit that he had made, and continued to make, choices about his life.

Brian had asserted, in his defence, that the acquisition of a second property in England would free things up for him, making it possible for him to spend more time – including nights – with Vanessa. The reality, as might have been – and indeed, by Vanessa, was – anticipated, turned out somewhat differently. In June, a few months after the new house had been acquired and while work was still being done on it, Fiona fell over and cut her leg badly. This incapacitated her sufficiently to make it harder than ever for Brian to get away on his own, though he and Vanessa did manage to fit in a few days together at the end of that month. It seemed to Vanessa, however, that Fiona's falling over had put paid to any idea of the new house leading to greater independence of either spouse, and even that any future sign of Brian trying to get free would result in another 'accident' or illness. Not that she considered Fiona had fallen over deliberately, or that she wished her ill, but the unconscious knows how to arrange things. The next month was full of publicity for Brian's latest book, including the newspaper profile with which we came into this story.

Eventually the situation was resolved in the way unsatisfactory affairs usually are – by one of the partners finding somebody else. In this case, hardly surprisingly, it was Vanessa who found someone better able to maintain a full relationship with her. She tried over several months to let Brian down lightly, by hints and by gradually changing the nature of their meetings, and for a time she tried to 'manage' two men in tandem. But as the letters kept coming, she eventually wrote to him informing him she had another lover and asking him to leave her alone for a while. He continued to write to her from time to time, only breaking off when she moved house (she imagines Brian assumes she is now living with someone).

Why did this affair go on as long as it did, when it had so clearly become unsatisfactory? Part of the reason is that Vanessa still kept expecting something to 'happen'. She admits that one reason she got involved in the relationship in the first place, and at first found the *idea* of it exciting, was that she likes drama and being at the centre of it. She thinks part of her motivation was that she wanted to have some kind of effect on Fiona, by whom she has always been fascinated. She allowed herself, at least part of the time, to think in stereotypic terms of 'wife v. mistress', and she saw the wife winning this battle by digging her heels in, presumably understanding her husband quite well enough to know that if she gave no quarter he would be quite incapable of bringing about change. When Vanessa eventually realised nothing was ever going to 'happen', that the pattern of the relationship was firmly set and that, if continued, it would just go on and on with no variation, she became bored. Yet for a long time Vanessa must have actually enjoyed having the affair. When she reads back over those early letters, she sees images of autumn, soft light and warm teashops, an aura of a rather stylised melancholy which she felt at the time suited her and to which she became addicted, a sense of romance heightened by the inevitable partings and the web of loving words Brian wrapped around her. The sex, though, was never entirely satisfactory – though it contained glimpses of something good, some 'might have been' – she says she used to think 'he must have been a wonderful lover twenty years ago'.

One thing Vanessa discovered in this relationship was that, after the initial flattery has worn off, it's no fun being someone's muse. A muse is some kind of a goddess and it's all very well – and at first very pleasant – to be worshipped, placed on a pedestal and apostrophised – but lovers need to be human. Ultimately, no matter how much a muse is adored, she exists for a specific purpose – to inspire the musee, to amuse, bemuse and, in the case of Brian, to enliven and keep him feeling youthful – but not to enter into a fully mutual relationship, in which the muse can be seen for what she actually is: a woman. The muse, being conjured largely out of the bemused's imagination, begins to exist independently of the person on whom the image has been projected, so that the person playing the role of muse can start to feel invisible. Vanessa felt Brian could have gone on writing letters to 'my darling Vanessa' even if she ceased to exist. This in itself was probably an overreaction – Brian might not recognise himself in the image Vanessa has built up of *him* – but she nevertheless experienced a sense of becoming something other than herself in Brian's eyes, as not really existing for him as a flesh and blood person.

Connected to the unreality of the muse relationship is the use – indeed overuse – of that difficult little word: 'love'. It is a particular hazard of the illicit relationship that the very word upon which the relationship appears to be founded becomes gradually drained of content. Love, to be love, needs to be expressed in more ways than the verbal, or even the sexual; it can benefit from a social context; love is demonstrated in what the lover *does* for the beloved, and the nature of illicit relationships means they very often exist in no social context at all, in a vacuum, where it is not always easy for love to be lived. This is not to say – far from it – that love cannot exist within a purely private relationship, known only to the two participants, but it needs more working at and more acknowl-edgement of the limitations implicit in the illicit relationship than is necessarily encompassed in endless repetitions of 'I love you'. That phrase can begin to contain, or conceal, other meanings, such as 'I love you, so stop complaining', 'I love you, so the problems which seem real to you must be only imaginary', 'I love you, so stop upsetting me', 'I love you, so nothing needs to change'. To Vanessa it felt that Brian's abundant use of the language of love was one of the techniques he used to slide away from confronting the real issues in their relationship.

And what were those issues? First, and mainly, it was that the expectations set up at the outset of the relationship were not realised, that the hopes Brian himself raised of an increased practical involvement with Vanessa, connected with a change in his relationship with his wife, slipped into silence – or would have done if Vanessa had allowed it. She felt indignant precisely because she was not the prime mover in creating these expectations. When she looked at Brian, she saw a man who had turned up on her doorstep one Sunday morning, completely out of the blue, and declared he was in love with her and needed her for his soul. This sounded like a major statement, and likely to have greater repercussions than the almost routine affair it developed into. The background was that Vanessa had been a friend of Brian's wife for the previous couple of years, she had hardly seen him other than to say hello to, apart from one occasion when they had all three had dinner together at Brian and Fiona's flat. She had noted that Brian and Fiona *seemed* to lead fairly separate lives; they each got on with their writing in their separate rooms and did not appear to go out together much. Vanessa was therefore surprised to discover how little flexibility there really was in the marital relationship. She had imagined that there really might not have been much problem with a writer having a mistress; it was not as though it was likely to damage his reputation – probably the reverse – and she couldn't see how an affair with her would *practically* alter the relationship between Brian and Fiona (though here she admits that she may have been being naïve and unimaginative). She says she never intended that Brian should leave his wife; rather, she could imagine a kind of arrangement in which he spent part of his time with each woman – particularly as he was already dividing his life between two houses. In the early days, she was bolstered in this fantasy by Brian appearing, by the intensity of his language, to place his love for her at the highest value in his life. Only gradually did she realise how much this was a question of language alone, or, if it was indeed 'true', how it related to only one aspect of his life. Maybe he did indeed want her supremely for his 'soul', but he didn't want his *modus vivendi* to be disrupted, particularly those aspects of it which he had set up to be conducive to his writing. When Vanessa stopped to think about it – that is, about two years into the relationship – it irritated her enormously that Brian was often unable to leave his desk even to phone her while he appeared to think nothing of regularly disrupting her working time, both at the office where she worked during the early years of their relationship and, more importantly – given the order of his priorities and the value he said he placed on her own work as a poet – on her Saturday afternoons when she would otherwise have been writing.

The fact Vanessa was also a writer goes some way to explaining why she became enmeshed in this affair in the first place and, to some extent, why she stuck with it as long as she did, and in this she displays certain typical mistress characteristics. In the beginning she did have some idea that Brian might be able to help her advance her career – though sensible friends warned her Fiona would have been more likely to do that – but, more important, a part-time relationship by and large suited her, as we have seen it suit other 'creative' mistresses. Just because I have been concentrating here on the relationship with Brian, one should not assume that Vanessa was doing nothing else with her life for its duration. On the contrary, she had a busy and fulfilling existence, with an interesting and demanding job, some very good – largely woman – friends and, above all, her own developing work as a poet. And Brian was very encouraging to her about her writing, at a time when editors turned her down more often than not. But also, however much she may have fussed at Brian to give her more of his time, she was never sure in her inmost self that she really wanted it.

Domesticity would have driven her mad, as would living with someone prone to absent-mindedness and sometimes slow on the uptake. Vanessa's main gripe against Brian was his lack of honesty, his talking about her and the relationship in different terms from what he *really* wanted. I think, if she will forgive my saying so, Vanessa might have done well to remove the plank from her own eye before blaming Brian for the mote in his.

Vanessa has been, as you will have gathered, very open in her willingness to discuss her experience as a mistress with me. The one area which she shows a marked disinclination to discuss relates to that pattern I have noticed of mistress-types often having strong, frequently unresolved, relationships with their father. She clearly hates to think of Brian as having been anything of a father-figure to her, though I can't help being struck by two factors: first, Brian was indisputably old enough to be Vanessa's father; secondly, her actual father became ill and died during the course of the relationship and almost from that point the affair began to sprout its seeds of destruction. This may be no more than coincidence, connected to Vanessa's greater financial independence and ability to get on with what she wanted after her father's death, or it could arguably be that some part of her psyche said 'I no longer need a father of any sort now'. Or again, relationships with parents have a tendency to continue *after* parental death; maybe Vanessa in some way resolved the relationship with her father, and so no longer needed a substitute. These are only hypotheses, but are none the less worth reflecting on.

Vanessa has now, as far as I know, given up being a mistress, but I think that, if she were to give it a second go at some point, she would have learnt from her experience with Brian and might do rather better in the role. She would need to relish her independent lifestyle rather more, concentrate on her work, enjoy the times with her lover but not seek to demand more from the relationship than it can realistically afford, try to be more aware of the potential feelings of the wife and, by achieving greater understanding of the role of the mistress, view the affair as less of a battle between two women. Yet also she might think more than twice before becoming anyone's muse, be cautious of flattery, and keep practising the virtue of honesty – principally in relation to herself. And she is at least now in possession of much potential raw material for her creative endeavours, as well as of a large cache of letters likely to prove invaluable to future biographers and scholars of mid- to late-twentieth-century English literature.

A REPENTANT MISTRESS

Not all the long years of happiness together,
of love and friendship and almost perfect
companionship (in spite of its background),
was worthwhile, it cost too much, to us and
to other people.[1]

S omeone with the independence, breadth and depth of
interests, and ready affection of the novelist and journalist
Rose Macaulay (1881–1958) could not be expected to love
conventionally or not to love where it might be undesirable.
Rose, however, was at war with herself throughout her life.
From all descriptions of her, she *sounds* so fearless; 'intrepid'
seems to be the adjective that best describes her, whether she
was cycling round London, pursuing foreign travels and
experiences to write up, accompanying her godchildren to
a Butlin's holiday camp, or leaning out into space from a
'tangle of girders'[2] to rescue books from a bomb-damaged
London Library during the Blitz. And yet she also appears to
have been inwardly terrified and to have capitulated to that
fear. The story of Rose's life is surely more complicated, more
compromised and compromising, than is suggested by the
following statement made by her biographer, Jane Emery:
'Her own active, autonomous existence is a model of independence and individualism for women.'[3] Rose never
succeeded in freeing herself from her parents, their values,
and her perceived sense of their judgement of her; even after

1 Rose Macaulay, *Letters to a Friend, 1950–1952*, ed. Constance Babington Smith,
   Collins, London, 1961, p.62
2 A.N. Wilson, 'Rose Macaulay' in *Founders & Followers*, Sinclair Stevenson,
   London, 1992, p.130
3 Jane Emery, *Rose Macaulay: A Writer's Life*, Murray, London, 1991, p.3

they had died, they – and particularly her father – were a strong internal presence. And all her adult life she sought out older male mentors, with whom she developed deep emotional bonds.

For the first six years of her life, she lived at Rugby School where her father was a master. Then the family moved to Italy, where until she was thirteen she lived much of the time out of doors. Here she developed her love of landscape, her tomboyish qualities and her lack of respect for time-wasting social conventions. Back in England, she found the restricted life of a schoolgirl hard to bear, and hated being at home, particularly as her father had become largely inaccessible to her, being immersed in scholarship in the Bodleian. She perceived her non-intellectual mother as 'unreasonable', in every sense of the word, and found her very difficult to live with. She was eventually rescued by an uncle who realised her need for escape from the family and paid for her to study Modern History at Somerville.

After three happy and stimulating years, Rose sat for her final exams in June 1903. At that time women could still not take degrees, but they could nevertheless be classed in their finals (as was Amber Reeves). Unfortunately 'sit' was all she did, and she didn't do that for long. She was still recovering from a bout of influenza and, after having read the questions, she gave up and left. Her father pleaded her ill health with the examiners, who awarded her an aegrotat – which signified that the candidate, judging from her record over the three years, would have received at least a good Second had she not been prevented by illness. This termination to Rose's Somerville career was a bitter disappointment to her; it induced a sense of failure which stayed with her for the rest of her life. But was it perhaps an unconscious fear of success rather than of failure which prompted her to walk out? George Macaulay, her greatly admired father, had not succeeded in his first attempt to gain a Cambridge Fellowship in 1877, and it is clear that his sense of disappointment and failure had permeated the family.

Ever since she could understand such things, she had known that her father's 'disgraceful' results (as he described them) on his first Fellowship examinations had been a shadow on the family life and fortunes. The posts he had applied for had fallen to others with higher credentials; despite admirable accomplishments he saw himself as a failure in academia. When the time came, could it have been possible that the unsatisfactory first Fellowship results of her father, a scholar she admired, discouraged her? Or that subconsciously the opportunity to surpass the father she so respected was not an appealing one?[4]

Whatever the underlying causes, this represents a failure of nerve at a crucial point, a failure to be repeated later in Rose's life.

So after Somerville, Rose had no choice but to return to the bosom of her family. After her three years of academic discipline, she found her mother's dependence on emotion rather than logic even harder to bear than previously. Two of her chief targets in her later work as a critic were muddled thinking and imprecision of language, both defects which she identified in her mother.

George Macaulay died in 1915 (by which time Rose was setting up on her own in London, helped by opportunities for war-work) and three years later, at the age of thirty-six, she met for the first time the man who was to become the most important person in her life. Early in 1918 she was transferred from the War Office to the new Ministry of Information, where the head of the Italian section was Gerald O'Donovan. Ten years older than Rose, he was the son of a Supervisor of Public Works from the west of Ireland; he nevertheless had an upper-class British accent and the manners to go with it. For a brief time his wife Beryl was also an employee of the Ministry; she was fluent in Italian and acted as her husband's translator

4 Ibid., pp.82–3

on an official trip to Rome. Gerald was an able administrator and an excellent speaker. He had a quick mind, a forceful presence and, like Rose, he was skilled in repartee.

At the turn of the century Gerald had been Father Jeremiah O'Donovan, a young Roman Catholic priest well known in Ireland for his involvement with not only the spiritual, but also the cultural, social and political aspects of Irish life. But he was to be thwarted in his local reform projects by his bishop, and reprimanded and suspended for engaging in social and political activism at the expense of his parish duties. Disheartened, he eventually left the priesthood altogether. (And he changed his Christian name – now how could poor Rose conceivably resist a man whose initials were GO'D and who had officially been a 'Father'?) In April 1910 Gerald was appointed sub warden of Toynbee Hall, a large residential hall and night school in the East End of London, and in the summer of the same year, at the age of thirty-eight, he met the 24-year-old Beryl Verschoyle at a house party in County Donegal. With the unwise speed of an ex-celibate, Gerald proposed to her five days later; they were married in the autumn.

Beryl was the younger daughter of an army colonel from an Anglo-Irish Protestant family and an English mother. The conventional and superficial education which had been provided for her by tutors, governesses and a year at a private school in Brussels had not been designed to stimulate intellectual curiosity. It also sounds as though she didn't like sex much: 'Beryl's sexual instruction to her older daughter in her adolescence was a brief and frigid description of resigned wifely passivity.'[5] In her memoirs Beryl describes dinner parties of the 1920s at which Shaw, Wells (a family friend), Arnold Bennett and Maynard Keynes held forth, and where she felt left out. She was always admiring of Gerald's intellectual abilities but disgruntled that he did not like to go out visiting with her – they clearly did not share many mutual

5 Ibid., p.169

friends – preferring instead to stay at home and let her go alone. Just the kind of wife an intellectual woman like Rose Macaulay might rather look down on, and where the gaps a mistress could fill in the life of the husband are all too clear and tempting.

Beryl spent most of her time in the family home in Norfolk with the children, and Rose and Gerald, as colleagues, were often invited together to various London gatherings. Their regular companionship was publicly acknowledged at this time, and Gerald also began to make visits with Rose to meet her mother and sisters. Her mother was charmed by him, unlike her two sisters who attempted to persuade Rose to give him up. But she was not to be persuaded and eventually they agreed not to discuss the subject further.

It would have suited none of the parties for Gerald to divorce Beryl and marry Rose. Beryl wanted to keep the respectable position of wife, whatever her private suspicions may have been. She and Gerald had worked out a tolerable *modus vivendi* and he was a devoted father (another reason for Rose to love him). 'More to the point, however enchanted she was with Gerald's company, Rose had always been and was at the time opposed to marriage for herself. Her parents' marriage and Gerald's were examples for her of the hampering bonds of wedlock.'[6] Then there is that 'choice' the artist often makes, or which seems to be made for him or her, to live with complicated situations and emotional tensions – which become the seedbed of creativity. Some time in late 1921 or early 1922 Rose and Gerald became secretly committed to one another for life. After 1922 Rose gave up her membership of the Anglican Church, which had previously been important to her.

Even before meeting Gerald, Rose had been very opposed to publicity about her private life – and presumably about anyone else's – on principle. During the latter part of the 1920s, to most of her friends as well as to her family, she

6 Ibid., pp.179–80

became intensely secretive about Gerald. By this time they were quite often spending discreet holidays abroad together, Gerald ostensibly going to study church architecture. It seems to have been accepted that Beryl, with or without children, would not accompany him on these trips. 'When Rose and Gerald went together secretly, they seemed to believe they were injuring no one.'[7] There was also always Rose's flat for the lovers to escape to; she made it clear both to her friends and to the public (in her essays) that she did not welcome unannounced visitors. And on the other side, so to speak, Rose became an honorary aunt in the O'Donovan family. She was a fortnightly guest at Sunday lunch, and in later years was godmother to Gerald's first granddaughter.

It is clear that this part-time yet emotionally fulfilling relationship suited Rose very well, giving her ample time for her work, sparing her from the demands of domesticity (her housekeeping skills didn't extend much beyond making pots of tea) while also allowing full scope to her need to love and be loved. 'In almost every way this agreement seemed to work for Rose; she was not a back-street wife waiting for the telephone to ring, but a very busy author, a friend to many and a public figure.'[8] Yet one should not forget the less visible down-side; it is hard to imagine, for instance, that Rose never suddenly dropped other commitments in order to see Gerald, or that there were no times when she wanted or needed him and he couldn't be there. Or that she was never tempted to stay in 'waiting for the telephone to ring'.

Rose's story illustrates the ambivalent relationship between mistresses and feminism, in that while the mistress appears to enjoy freedom and independence, this so-called freedom is bought at the expense of another woman, the wife. And the freedom and independence are themselves, to a greater or lesser extent, illusory. Rose may have had no legal ties but she was certainly bound in very tight illicit ones, ties which affected her relationships with everyone else in her world,

7 Ibid., p.194
8 Ibid., p.138

if only because of the amount of personal information she had to withhold. How many times – again, we can have no idea – did she feel ungenerous because someone was unburdening themselves to her, and she couldn't reciprocate? (Though maybe that's an anachronistic, late-twentieth-century way of looking at it; people didn't talk so freely of their loves then anyway, or at least most of them didn't. Some of Rose's acquaintances, and certainly her family background, were still firmly 'Victorian'.)

Being far away and out of contact when something happens to a member of your family or a friend, and having to live with the subsequent guilt, is the kind of risk you run when you have a secret life. Rose was in Europe with Gerald in April 1925 when her mother, who had had a heart attack the previous year, was again taken gravely ill. Her sisters tried to reach Rose via a poste restante, but she did not call for her post. By the time she finally received the news of her mother's critical condition and rushed back, Grace Macaulay was unconscious and remained so until her death on 5 May.

And so the affair went on. Its ending, brought about by death, was prolonged and painful. In June 1939 Gerald, who was not a driver, asked his daughter Brigid to drive him through the Lake District for a holiday. She had apparently done this before, but for some reason declined this time, and Rose – with the full knowledge of the family – was asked to take him instead. There seems to have been no question of Beryl's joining the expedition or of her expressing any desire to do so. Bookings were discreetly made at separate hotels. But it was not to be a happy trip. On the way to Hadrian's Wall, Rose was driving up a very steep road where approaching cars could not be seen until the top of the hill. Always known for her erratic driving, it seems that at some point she swerved to the middle of the road and hit an oncoming car. The other driver was unhurt, but Gerald was concussed. Rose climbed out of the wreckage, blaming herself aloud, and fainted. Gerald, who was sixty-eight, was in a grave condition after the accident; he was unconscious for some time, and six months later he had a stroke. Meanwhile Rose had been charged with careless driving and had her licence endorsed. She never forgave herself for this accident (she was never good at forgiving herself for anything) and its effect on her lover. But then the Second World War began and there was work to be done. Rose reported for ambulance training in London and was also contracted to write a novel on the Spanish Civil War.

Early in 1942 Gerald was diagnosed with cancer. From January to June Rose was in the anguished position of being unable to visit him as often as she would have liked because of petrol-rationing, and of rarely being able to see him alone when she did. She had to let him go, not only to death but into the embraces of his family, so suffering one of the worst nightmares of the committed, but secret, mistress. She did what she could to say goodbye to him. During the last month of his life, she put aside all her other responsibilities, somehow managed to arrange transport, and visited him two or three times a week.

Rose's novel, *The Towers of Trebizond*, in many respects autobiographical, tells us much about the author's state of mind as she struggled to reconcile the long history of her love of this married man with her love of God and of the Church.

> And then I thought how odd it was, all that love and joy and peace that flooded over me when I thought about Vere [the heroine's married lover], and how it all came from what was a deep meanness in our lives, for that is what adultery is, a meanness and a stealing, a taking away from someone what should be theirs, a great selfishness, and surrounded and guarded by lies lest it should be found out. And out of this meanness and this selfishness and this lying flow love and joy and peace, beyond anything that can be imagined. And this makes a discord in the mind, the happiness and the guilt and the remorse pulling in opposite ways so that the mind and soul are

torn in two, and if it goes on for years and years the discord becomes permanent, so that it will never stop, and even if one goes on living after death, as some people think, there will still be this deep discord that nothing can heal, because of the great meanness and selfishness that caused such a deep joy. And there is no way out of this dilemma that I know.[9]

Laurie, the heroine of *The Towers of Trebizond*, despite her awareness of the 'discord' of happiness and remorse and despite her residual attachment to the Church, does not take that final step of true repentance, of wishing the affair had never happened. She feels that to do so would represent an even more complete severance from her lover than that already achieved by death, that such a turning-back to the Church would constitute 'a gesture against the past that we had shared, and in whose bonds I was still held'.[10] Rose, however, did eventually take that final step. I think part of the reason for this capitulation was that the fear she here ascribes to Laurie was her own fear, inculcated in her conventionally religious younger days, and that it became overwhelming: 'when the years have all passed, there will gape the uncomfortable and unpredictable dark void of death, and into this I shall at last fall headlong, down and down and down, and the prospect of that fall, that uprooting, that rending apart of body and spirit, that taking off into so blank an unknown, drowns me in mortal fear and mortal grief'.[11] Also playing a part in Rose's reconversion was her habitual desire for fatherly approval. The father-shaped hole in her psyche created by the death of George Macaulay in 1915 had been plugged three years later and for the next twenty-four years by her relationship with Gerald (the ex-Father Jeremiah). Following his death, the hole was first partially filled by Professor Gilbert Murray, Regius Professor of Greek at Oxford, and Chairman

9 Rose Macaulay, *The Towers of Trebizond*, Collins, London, 1956, p.226
10 Ibid., p.286
11 Ibid., p.287

of the Executive of the League of Nations Union. He was fifteen years older than the sixty-year-old Rose, and the sort of man who had always enjoyed having female acolytes around him. He and Rose engaged in a close epistolary friendship until his death. Finally the hole was filled by another Father, the Reverend John Hamilton Cooper Johnson. Thus the 'bonds' she had felt herself to be held in were loosened, and the stage was set for her renunciation of Gerald and her re-entry into the fold of Anglicanism.

Father Johnson, a Cowley Father based in America, first wrote to Rose in 1950 after reading the American edition of her novel *They Were Defeated*. They began to correspond regularly, Rose poured out her heart to him, and four and a half months after receiving his first letter, she made her first confession in thirty years and re-established herself as a communicant member of the Church of England (her ex-communication having been entirely self-imposed). Now Rose finally betrays her love. 'I told you once that I couldn't really *regret* the past. But now I do regret it, very much. It's as if absolution and communion and prayer let us through into a place where we get a horribly clear view – a new view – so that we see all the waste, and the cost of it, and how its roots struck deep down into the earth, poisoning the springs of our own lives and other people's. Such waste, such cost in human and spiritual values.'[12]

It is not easy to understand exactly what it was that Rose wished to have been different in her past. She clearly wished that she had not 'sinned', but does that also mean she wished she had never met Gerald, or that he was happily married, or that she had not fallen in love with him? She writes: 'If only I had refused, and gone on refusing. It's not a question of forgiveness, but of irrevocable damage done.'[13] What exactly should she, in her view, have refused? Sex, certainly, but I doubt that was really the central issue for Rose. Should she have refused to love Gerald, or to have acted in any way out of

12 Rose Macaulay, *Letters to a Friend, 1950–1952*, pp.61–2
13 Ibid., p.62

that love? Would even friendship be too much for a single woman to offer an unhappily married man, because it might be too dangerous, too much of an incitement to sin? More- over, Rose knew very well that had she gone on 'refusing', Gerald would have found somebody else, maybe several somebody elses. So the 'irrevocable damage' would have been done anyway – to Beryl, presumably, perhaps to Gerald as well – only not to Rose. Her letters to Father Johnson reveal that at least part of her concern was indeed the damage inflicted on herself by the affair, that it had prevented her becoming the self she believed God wanted her to be. Such an attitude betrays a concern with self, a kind of moral fastidious- ness – 'I mustn't be contaminated, however much my beloved needs me' – which is inimical to love, and to the self-giving courage involved in loving. Or maybe my adverse reaction to Rose's repentance merely demonstrates how benighted I am.

Poor Rose has even managed to poison her memories, so that she has lost Gerald twice over. She is such a self-punisher: 'Sometimes one is jerked back into the past by some thought or memory, and it all comes back, the happiness that isn't happiness any more to think of because of the wrong, and the whole awful mess it made of life, and yet it should have been so good. Forgive this maudlin whimpering.'[14] She comes down firmly now on the side of conventional morality, and does not see 'standards of right and wrong' as drawn up by human beings, to make society work. Instead she believes that human mores reflect 'eternal laws' in which she seems to include faithful monogamy. Furthermore, she wants to turn her art into propaganda. 'Human passions against eternal laws – that is the everlasting conflict. And human passions use every device to get the best of it, and set themselves above the laws. All very tragic and pitiful; but writers about it should be on the right side – if they can.'[15]

Perhaps I am rather hard on Rose, but her rejection of Gerald after his death, her wishing this affair, central to both

14 Ibid., p.116
15 Ibid., p.172

their lives, had never happened, does seem to me ungenerous, pusillanimous and a betrayal of love. If it had been possible to rewrite these lives, it might have been better had Gerald never married Beryl, had he been forced to delay marriage to anyone for some years after he left the priesthood. Given that he did marry her, that it was an unsatisfactory marriage yet that Beryl did not wish him to leave and that there were children to be cared for, Rose could be viewed as the family's saviour. She made his family life bearable for Gerald, and provided him with long-term stability in a way few other women could have done. And the lifestyle suited her too. But Rose could not maintain this interpretation of the story and simultaneously win approval from Father Johnson and Mother Church.

I am comforted though by a letter Rose wrote to Rosamond Lehmann on 11 September 1956 which suggests her repentance may not have taken quite such a firm hold of her after all, that she too, along with that other repenter Abelard, brought 'even to the altar' the memory of her guilty love: ' "Looking back now I am getting old, I can't not be glad of the past, in spite of knowing I behaved dishonestly and selfishly for so long. Love is so odd. It can't help being everything at the time." '[16]

16 Jane Emery, *Rose Macaulay*, p.317, (the original of this letter is held in the Archive Center at King's College Library, Cambridge)

17 Throughout this chapter I am indebted to the work of Jane Emery, and would like to make clear that the quotations I have used from her book represent only a fraction of what she has to say about the complex character of Rose Macaulay. I recommend her book to any interested reader.

A CONVERSATION

*The premise of this fictional conversation is
that these three women – Lara from Boris
Pasternak's Dr Zhivago,* Dinah from
Rosamond Lehmann's The Echoing Grove
and O from Pauline Réage's Story of O
– have all (despite the chronological
impossibility) read one another's stories.
And now, in some limbo of the
imagination, where characters brought to
life by their creators can never die, they
compare notes.

*I was born to make life simple and to look
for sensible solutions, she – to complicate it
and confuse the way.*[1]

Lara: That was what Tonya, my Yury's wife, said. And she was
right, don't you think? She was sensible, and a good person.
My husband Pasha was good too, far better than me or Yury.
We never pretended to virtue, or stopped feeling remorse
that we had hurt those good people so much. Though to hear
Yury talk, you'd think I was life itself – something elemental –
or representing life to him. I kept trying to live simply and well,
just working, doing what had to be done. But things got
complicated, even before I was grown up, something in me
invited the complications. I didn't do anything to attract
them – at least I never felt as though I did. It all got messed
up, I couldn't do the right, the normal thing, and when I tried
to – in marrying Pasha – it somehow got spoilt, I drew him into

1 Boris Pasternak, *Doctor Zhivago*, tr. Max Hayward & Manya Harari, Fontana,
London, 1961, p.408

the complications instead of getting myself out of them. Whereas Tonya, as she says, was born for the simple things – to grow up, get married to the suitable, obvious man, have children. Poor Tonya. If it wasn't revolution, it was me. In a way I was the revolution.

Dinah: Lara, what you say reminds me so much of the difference between me and my sister Madeleine. And between Olivia, my predecessor in *The Weather in the Streets*, and her sister Kate. The sensible sisters, living cut-and-dried, respectable lives, doing what's expected of them, which just seems to come naturally. Whereas *we* are on the outside, always different, looking in, excluded – and, as you say, when we try to imitate our sisters, the Tonyas, Madeleines and Kates, by behaving in the way we imagine is expected of us, by acting a role which isn't really ours – it all goes wrong. It *is* wrong, even before we start. Yet we think we're making ourselves do the right thing. Olivia married young, but it was a disaster. I was engaged to a barrister for a bit – a good prospect, respectable – but I broke it off. I did marry in the end, and it might have worked, but he was killed in Spain, in the Civil War. Our creator, Rosamond, didn't fare any better. Both her marriages went wrong.

O: Part of it – forgive me if I talk more bluntly than you're used to – must be to do with sex. I mean you, Larissa Fyodorovna, and you, Dinah, and Olivia – all liked sex. In fact, 'liked' is probably too trivial a word; you were connected with sex, on some deep level, you embodied the sexual part of femininity, in a way your 'respectable' sisters didn't. That's why I think you're rather like me.

Dinah: You wouldn't catch me in a castle, chained to the wall, and being whipped.

Lara: Nor me.

O: Why are you so sure? I can believe you wouldn't ever get Tonya in such a situation, Tonya who lives by rules and reason and who has talked sex into a safe place. But you, Lara – for you sex is right at the front, you respond to it completely, it guides you, and it's one of the things that

makes you dangerous to society. You can't be contained by
structures, especially not totalitarian ones.

Lara: I can agree with that. But I don't see how that leads
you to the conclusion that I might end up in your place.

O: What about Komarovsky? Didn't he have the same kind
of power over you Sir Stephen had over me? And wasn't
that to do with sex?

Lara: I don't talk about him.

O: No. I'd noticed. But there are many ways of being
whipped. You never got free of Komarovsky, that man
who ruined you – but also awakened you to your own
sensuality – when you were still almost a child. It's Komarovsky, not Tonya or Pasha, who finally separates you
from Zhivago; you even somehow let him lead you to
whatever action it is that results in your losing your
daughter, the one you had by Zhivago . . .

Lara: Stop it! You're right, O – there are many ways of
being beaten, and you're doing it to me.

Dinah: Don't be upset, Lara. Whether O is right or not
about our sexual responses, your creator paints you with
such wonderful physicality. There are images of you I'll
always remember – sitting over your books in the library at
Yuryatin, ironing in the hospital, the first glimpse Yury ever
has of you sitting despairingly in a chair after your mother's
suicide attempt. And the images that go with you – iced
rowanberries, crisp fresh linen, strong white arms – there's
always a sense of cleanliness, of being just right, every action
a perfect expression of your essence, the essence of femininity. You do have an elemental quality; you never
attempt to be something you aren't.

Lara: Oh, I do. All the time I attempt to be a good person . . .

Dinah: But people love you, they go to you for help.

O: Good . . . bad . . . we're talking beyond those categories. And Dinah's right, there is something elemental,
something inevitable about you, Lara. Yury couldn't have
not loved you, or you him, however much he also loved
Tonya, and you Pasha (or Strelnikov . . . now there's a

name to conjure with . . . you know it's connected with the words for arrows and shooting . . . I can just imagine him at Roissy . . .).

Dinah: O, must you always bring things back to the awful fantasies your creator indulged herself with? We were just getting to something important, and now you're imagining Strelnikov sticking arrows in you!

O: Well, what of it? At least I'm honest about being a masochist. You two make life just as uncomfortable for yourselves. You can't tell me you don't get any satisfaction from being miserable.

Dinah: I know something of inviting violence, of the kind of women who become 'murderees', who give off some kind of subliminal odour and, as I've described it, I was fairly 'rank' myself at one time. I suppose that can be just as true of invisible, psychological violence as the more obvious sort. One must give off messages – 'I am the kind of woman you can treat this way', 'I expect you to hurt me'.

Lara: But also, Dinah – perhaps because of the life you've lived, the experiences you've had – despite the vulnerability implicit in your unsettled lifestyle and unsuitable loving, you have a certain hard quality often found in people capable of living outside the prescribed norm. *With what cold certainty she burned; with what contempt for weakness.*[2]

Dinah: Yes, that was said of me, certainly. But if I'm so hard, why have I spent so much of my life feeling anguished? My story is desperate at times, hopeless and horribly lonely. And all that waiting . . . Just like Olivia . . . Waiting, letting go, then waiting again. And pretending you're not waiting at all, allowing the lover to imagine he's only a part of your life, not almost the whole of it. *Ten. Ten-past-ten. Ten-fifteen. Twenty-past ten, and a car came round into the street and stopped, and next moment the bell rang. Starting up weak in the bowels from waiting, starting downstairs in a flurry, then making myself go slow, in a calm way, opening – and there he was on the doorstep.*[3]

2 Rosamond Lehmann, *The Echoing Grove*, Penguin, Harmondsworth, 1983, p.102
3 Rosamond Lehmann, *The Weather in the Streets*, Collins, London, 1968, p.148

Lara: I believed in keeping busy, never sat around waiting for Zhivago, or even for my husband Antipov – to turn up. That's not to say I didn't long for him – well, for both of them, at different times, sometimes at the same time – and I worried, constantly, desperately, but couldn't allow myself to stop, I had to keep working, caring for my daughter, just going on. Those were terrible years, of course – war, revolution, civil war, oppression – the authorities tried to stamp out personal life altogether. It couldn't be done – not to people like me and Yury, they had to stamp us out in the end – but it did mean there was never any time to sit and mope. Things changed too fast; you had to keep going just to survive.

Dinah: There was war in my life too, and in Rickie's. First, we grew up after a war; we were all scarred by it, those of us who came after that lost generation. Maybe that was part of the dislocation, why we never seemed to belong, never felt solid like our parents seemed to. Then the next war . . . we were all in that in some way or another.

O: War never touched me. Nothing outside could touch me.

Lara: And what of your creators? I don't particularly want to talk about mine, Boris Pasternak. I can't identify myself with a man, and I've never had very much sympathy for the woman who claims she was me, Olga Ivinskaya. She wrote a book, *A Captive of Time*, but she was far too self-dramatising ever to have been me, in my opinion. Of course, she had a hard enough time – labour camps and all that – but who didn't in those days?

Dinah: Mine married her first husband a year or so after coming down from Cambridge – his sister had been one of her friends at Girton. Shortly after the wedding they went to live in Newcastle-upon-Tyne where he worked in his father's shipping business. It was there she wrote her first novel, *Dusty Answer*. By the time she wrote Olivia's novel, she was on her second marriage, to Wogan Phillips, and she had two children. Wogan had abandoned his job in order

to live in the country and paint, but this marriage was also
having problems, and by the end of the 1930s he had gone
off to fight in the Spanish Civil War. And he transferred his
affections to a woman more active in politics than Rosamond was.

O: Maybe like the one your sister Madeleine loses her lover
to.

Dinah: Maybe. Anyway, after that Rosamond lived part of
the time in the country with her children. And when they
were away at boarding school she would be with Cecil Day
Lewis, the poet, who was married. His wife Mary lived in
another village, also with children. Rosamond's relationship with him, during which she seemed to put up with his
being married, lasted nine years. Then in 1950 he abandoned her to marry a much younger woman.

Lara: Tell me, Dinah, what do you think of what the critic
Judy Simons said about *The Weather in the Streets*?

Dinah: Remind me . . .

Lara: (reading) 'In its analysis of the relationship between
Olivia and Rollo Spencer, *The Weather in the Streets* depicts
the suffering that is seen to be the inevitable accompani-
ment to romantic love and shows how twentieth-century
women, despite their veneer of emancipation, are still
victims of a cultural heritage that is powerfully weighted
against them. The book's sexual politics are far more overt
than in Lehmann's earlier works and the text comprises a
savage attack on the patriarchal establishment, complacent
and hierarchical, that conspires against vulnerable women.'[4]

Dinah: I think she's rather wide of the mark. She seems to
be trying to inject Rosamond – who was primarily interested in the personal, not the political – with her own
agenda. Olivia doesn't suffer because of the 'patriarchal
establishment', but because she's a particular sort of woman
having an affair with a married man. It may be true that the
women's roles are more circumscribed than the men's –

4 Judy Simons, *Rosamond Lehmann*, Macmillan, London, 1992, p.78

except in the case of the artists, like Anna – but it's the way they love that Rosamond is concentrating on, not whether they have enough power in the social sphere, earn large enough salaries, all that sort of stuff. Still, what can you expect from critics? Tell us something about your creator, O.

O: Well, it's rather hard to. I'm not even sure what to call her. She wrote as Pauline Réage, and was eventually 'unmasked' in a *New Yorker* article in 1994 as Dominique Aury – but it turns out that even that was a pseudonym. It seems she was born as Anne Desclos. She wrote my story as a bait to keep her married lover, Jean Paulhan, interested in her. They were both literary figures, working for Gallimard at the same time as Albert Camus and others. Paulhan's wife was an invalid. Dominique (I'll call her that for ease) and Paulhan's affair lasted for three decades. She wrote my story when she was in her mid-forties and was afraid Paulhan, then almost seventy, was going to abandon her. The book had the desired effect, Paulhan loving it from the begin-ning, arranging for its publication, and continuing to be the lover of its author. It came out in the summer of 1954.

Dinah: A year after *The Echoing Grove* was published.

Lara: And about four years before *Dr Zhivago* appeared in the West.

O: When Paulhan was dying, in 1968, amidst all the ferment in Paris at that time, Dominique sat in the hospital with him and wrote a disguised account of her original writing of the story. This account – which she called *A Girl in Love* – came out the following year, again under the name of 'Pauline Réage', along with a sequel called *Return to Roissy*. There are some very poignant descriptions of her life with Paulhan – the homelessness of it, the usual difficulties of an affair as well as its very literary nature – in *A Girl in Love*.

Books were their only complete freedom, their common country, their true travels. Together they dwelt in the books they loved as others in their family home; in books they had their compatriots and their brothers; poets had written for them, the letters of lovers from times past came down to them through the obscurity of ancient languages, of modes and mores long since come and gone – all of which was read in a toneless voice in an unknown room, the sordid and miraculous dungeon against which the crowd outside, for a few short hours, beat in vain. They did not have a full night together. All of a sudden, at such and such an hour agreed upon ahead of time – the watch always remained on the wrist – they had to leave. Each had to regain his street, his house, his room, his daily bed, return to those to whom he was joined by another kind of inexpiable love, those whom fate, youth, or you yourself had given you once and for all, those whom you can neither leave nor hurt when you're involved in their lives. He, in his room, was not alone. She was alone in hers.[5]

O: And she realises, this intelligent and sensitive narrator, that to 'win' against the wife, for the affair to turn into a regularised relationship by the married man escaping from his marriage, would bring them no more real freedom than they already have.

They both used a vocabulary of prisoners whose prison does not revolt them, and perhaps they realized that if they found it hard to endure they would have found it just as hard to be freed from it, since they would then have felt guilty. The idea that they would have to return home gave a special meaning to that stolen time, which came to exist outside the pale of real time, in a sort of strange and eternal present.[6]

Dinah: The main question about the *Story* itself seems to be whether masochist fantasies are really central to women's sexuality – as Paulhan claims in his epilogue – or foreword, I'm not sure which – or whether 'Pauline Réage' wrote as she did because that's what men want to believe about women.

5 Pauline Réage, *Story of O Part Two*, Corgi, London, 1997, pp.8–9
6 Ibid., pp.11–12

Lara: That's what Joan Smith thinks in *Different for Girls*[7] – that it's just what men want women to be like.

O: You're quite the intellectual, Larissa Fyodorovna, aren't you? Always quoting this and that.

Lara: Well, I've always read a lot.

Dinah: We're all fairly intellectual, O, even you.

O: I suppose so. And to prove it, I'll say I'm sure Freud would agree with my opinion that I'm far from unusual in my sexual fantasies always having been masochistic. Sado-masochistic, in fact. Anyway, to return to Dominique or Pauline or whoever she was – she never sought publicity, and if anyone ever asked if she was the author of my story she would say that it was a question to which she never replied.

Dinah: What struck me most about your story, O, was the sense you could have ended your servitude, to René and then particularly to Sir Stephen, whenever you wanted. Certainly in the second half of your story, the bit your creator describes as a 'degeneration' – the 'return to Roissy' seemed to bring you very little satisfaction, almost entirely misery. Yet you stayed.

O: And how, in that, do I differ from you, Dinah? Or Olivia? Or even you, Larissa Fyodorovna? You didn't have to get involved with married men, and you certainly didn't have to stay involved with them, and they hardly brought you unalloyed joy.

Dinah: Somehow it didn't feel as though there could be an escape. As though in loving you give up your freedom, in hopeless loving perhaps most of all. For one thing, you don't want to lose what little you have. For another . . . well, I don't know. Perhaps you always think it's going to get better, or – and this is an important point – you don't want to hurt your lover, and you fear that if you try to claim your freedom you'll hurt him irreparably. And you're all he's got – which sounds ridiculous, when the whole point

---

7 Joan Smith, *Different for Girls: How Culture Creates Women*, Chatto & Windus, London, 1997

is, as you know perfectly well, that he's already got at least a wife and often enough a family – but the way he tells you about it, the way you see it, the way you *want* to see it, that makes him more lonely, not less, so he needs you, and you have to be available. And then you find you need him too.

O: I never found out whether my master, the one who branded me and put his irons on me, had a wife. I knew very little about his outward circumstances. But my creator, Pauline, Dominique, Anne, I think she knew what she was about. She touched on a deep, dark and generally secret aspect of the sexuality of at least some women – the desire for submission, for a complete abandonment of self, the desire to prove one belongs to a man, the desire for punishment, to be recognised and treated as worthless – and in that recognition and treatment to find one's true worth.

Lara: These are hard things to say, O, hard even to think.

O: I know. But the finding of oneself through the loss of self is an understanding which has long been known to spiritual teachers – the New Testament is full of it – and self-abandonment is always a feature of the best sex.

Dinah: That's true, but what makes *Story of O* different from simple self-abandonment is the addition of pain, your finding of pleasure in torture, not to put too fine a point on it, and not only in your own pain but, by the end of your story – whatever that end is – in the same pleasure/pain being inflicted on your friends. My question is whether this dark aspect of female sexuality, portrayed by your creator in such a way that it holds the imagination, is to be found – hidden, of course – in the type of woman likely to become a mistress, our type of woman in fact.

Lara: I think, however much I don't want to think it, that it may be.

Dinah: It certainly fits in with that superiority/inferiority thing, the sense of innate worthlessness living in some strange symbiosis with a sense of being able to endure more than one's fellows —

O: The paradoxical exultation, the perverse pride, in being found worthy to be treated with exquisite cruelty —

Lara: The awareness of being different, set apart from the conventional run of women —

Dinah: Women who 'get married and have children', and hardly exist for their husbands.

O: Réage/Aury carries all this to its absolute extreme in my story, but I believe that story resonates in the lives of women who share some of my deepest, most shameful, feelings, who may find themselves acting out of buried impulses brought to light by me, who might even fantasise about being taken to Roissy by their lovers —

Lara: Provided it stays in the realm of fantasy.

O: I imagine that a woman who finds no fascination at all in my story, who sees it only as pornography and refuses to read beyond the first few pages, is unlikely ever to become a mistress.

'Who am I, finally,' said Pauline Réage, 'if not the long silent part of someone, the secret and nocturnal part which has never betrayed itself in public by any thought, word, or deed, but communicates through the subterranean depths of the imaginary with dreams as old as the world itself?'[8]

Lara: A friend of ours turns up in Paulhan's essay in the book — and it's no surprise to find her there — *It may be that in writing to Abelard: 'I shall be thy whore' Heloise did not simply wish to turn a pretty phrase.*[9]

The women pause for a while. Then:

Dinah: I wonder what our respectable sisters, the wives, would make of our conversation. In the end, after all the disasters of our lives, I did find Madeleine and I had more to say to one another than I'd previously imagined. We seemed to achieve some kind of equilibrium, an understanding between us, a basic sympathy despite, maybe even

8 Pauline Réage, *Story of O Part Two*, p.14
9 Pauline Réage, *Story of O*, Corgi, London, 1998, pp.281–2

partly because of, all the pain we'd caused one another. And you, Lara, when Yury was in captivity with the forest brotherhood, you went to see Tonya, didn't you? Even helped her with the delivery of her baby?

Lara: Perhaps. I don't talk about that much. I think I was able to help her a little. But it was after we met, and when they were about to leave for Paris that Tonya wrote to Yury, addressing the letter to my house, knowing he would be there or that I would find him, and where she wrote of me the words I told you at the start. She also called me – wrongly – a 'good person', but said I was the opposite of herself.

Dinah: Madeleine was 'good' I suppose. Both before she was married and throughout her married life she never did anything the conventionally minded could disapprove of.

O: The way I read Madeleine she was beautiful, kind – yet somehow limited. Whereas you, Dinah, are mysterious, difficult, not quite respectable, and you exert a fascination, both sexual and emotional, over Madeleine's husband, Rickie. You don't seem made for happiness; something in the intensity of your living anticipates tragedy. Madeleine, on the other hand, like Tonya, was not made for drama; her life ought to run along a smooth, even track. She is forced off that track, partly because of you, forced to feel more than she might have liked, forced to accept and live with the complexity of life when she was really designed for simplicity. You are never simple; complicated yourself, you complicate the lives of those you become involved with.

Dinah: The crazy thing is . . . I think I made Madeleine feel just as inadequate as she did me. We were both envious of, or perhaps more bewildered by, the qualities each possessed which the other didn't share.

O: Yes. I think the different types of women are very often bewildered by one another, and jealous – in both directions. Madeleine saw you – and perhaps this is how your creator deliberately made you – as *outside* of 'normal' life, a threat to stable society and conventions because you appear to offer another way, you have other values. This is what makes you dangerous in Madeleine's eyes – and here your sister represents the whole of conventional society, stable marriages, what politicians and popular moralists term 'family values' – for you are like a siren or a mermaid, luring a man out to the beauty of the limitless sea, where sensible Madeleine knows he may drown.

Lara: That's beautifully put, O. And I'm sure that's how Tonya felt about me.

Dinah: If your circumstances had been different, Lara, if Yury and you hadn't already been married to other people, if your lives hadn't been lived against the backdrop of revolution and turmoil, do you think you would just have 'settled down', been a normal family together?

Lara: I don't know. I don't know whether our kind of intensity can be translated to 'normal' family life.

O: I doubt it, I must say. For all your domesticity together – in those few months in Yuryatin and those last days in Varykino – there is some kind of play-acting about it, as though you knew it couldn't last . . .

Lara: We did know that. It certainly couldn't last, they would have come for us if we hadn't left when we did. We knew we were doomed.

O: So for that short time you built a sort of cocoon around yourselves. But your life together was always unreal . . .

Dinah: Or more real than anything else. That's what I think. What Lara and Yury had together was life – real life – it was everything else that was pretend.

O: But a real life that was unliveable – or that could only be lived in the short term, under conditions of crisis and social upheaval. Don't forget Zhivago had just given up Lara, to return properly to his family, when he was intercepted by the forest brotherhood and so couldn't go to either of them.

Dinah: He hadn't really given her up – he couldn't – he had already decided to go back for 'one last time'. But it is hard to imagine that kind of love – rarefied, intense, elemental, like Lara herself – being put into the straitjacket of marriage, the day-to-dayness of marriage, the long drawn-out years, the habits of years and years spent with the same person. Though their parting is tragic, it is also fitting. It keeps their love at that high level, there is no chance of it descending to the ordinary, of growing stale.

Lara: And yet, we – Yury and I – had no greater desire than for the day-to-dayness, as you put it.

O: You, again like me, Larissa Fyodorovna, seem to have been very passive in your loving. You never attempted, never would attempt, to hold on to Zhivago, to make him stay if he didn't want to, or to try to force him to leave with you when you knew – did you? . . . one of the great unanswered questions – he wouldn't come. Yet you respond completely to him when he's there.

Dinah: Isn't that what all mistresses have to do?

O: Perhaps.

Lara: I certainly couldn't have acted in any other way. I understood and sympathised with Yury's divided loyalties – indeed I had them myself. And though I depended on him when he was there, I could cope when he wasn't. I had to, you see, we all did then, especially for the sake of our children – of those children we hadn't lost . . .

Dinah: And yet for all your so-called passivity, you were Yury's strength, and he gradually falls to pieces once he has let you go (though the woman he takes up with in Moscow, Marina, is also good and kind to him). I suppose your ultimate failure – the failure your creator wrote for you – is that you lost the child of your love. It's the kind of thing my creator would have devised as well, making it impossible for the mistress, the other woman, to be a successful mother, to keep – even, in our case, to give birth to – her children. And of course you mustn't forget that the whole story – yours and Yury's and Tonya's and Antipov's – all took place against a backdrop of such ferment, when the rules for institutions such as marriage were in a state of flux, when the word 'wife' could be used of women other than those a man was joined to in a formal ceremony. People became husbands and wives simply by virtue of setting up house together – so, for instance, Pasternak can refer to Marina as Yury's third 'wife', even though he was only ever legally and officially married to Tonya.

Lara: So that makes me his second wife, you mean?

Dinah: Exactly.

Lara: Yes. I don't know that I ever felt like his wife. And, anyway, I was too conscious of being Pasha's wife, as long as he was alive, and I was convinced that he still was. But Tonya . . . she deserved to be a happy, contented wife. That's what she was designed to be.

Dinah: Yes, like Madeleine, and Kate, as I said before. They're designed for a more stable kind of love, none of these peaks and troughs we go in for.

O: Or is it just that their sensuality has never been really touched, they've never been awoken to passion?

Dinah: Lara, whatever the 'rights and wrongs', whether or not Tonya was the more 'deserving' woman, you are the one who lives on in the imagination. And you are the one who kept Yury *alive*. Not only in a poetic sense. After all, you gave him the impetus – when he 'saw' you in the rowan tree – to escape from the partisans.

It was covered half in snow, half in frozen leaves and berries and it held out two white branches welcomingly. He remembered Lara's strong white arms and seized the branches and pulled them to him. As if in answer, the tree shook snow all over him. He muttered senselessly: 'I'll find you, my beauty, my love, my rowan tree, my own flesh and blood.'[10]

Another pause. Then:

Dinah: Have you ever just wished you could cut out the

10 Boris Pasternak, *Doctor Zhivago*, p.368

feeling part of yourself, be done with all this pain? Once, oh, more than once, I expect, it's just this one sticks in my memory, after one of those conversations so well known to illicit lovers (*I must go – yes, I suppose you must – I'll telephone – when? – I don't know, it depends . . .*[11]), I had that fleeting desire to withdraw, just run away, become fully autonomous, separate as I was before. *Pull up the anchor, set forth once more, transparent yet solid, to the ocean. It was best so. Put away those wretched years: nothing but wear and tear, concealment, lies, suspicion; only half a person. Now I can be true only to myself again. Leave them to clean up the mess – or not: I wash my hands of it.*[12] And yet a few days later, when Rickie attempts to end the relationship, I felt quite differently – largely because I objected to what often seems to happen to the third party in a triangle, that is, I felt left out of all the decision-making. I was not to be given a choice; after having been invited into the situation, I was also to be thrown out of it.

'*I didn't dream you would leave me like this in outer darkness. I'm in this too, aren't I? – up to the neck. You can't just – go to earth as if I didn't exist. Or present me, some time or other, at your own discretion, with a* fait accompli. *What's to happen must be my choice, my responsibility as well as yours. And Madeleine's,*' she added.

He said obstinately, sweeping breadcrumbs off the table into his hand and pouring them on to a plate: '*I don't see it like that.*'

'*If you deny me my share of responsibility you deny me the basis of my life.*'

'*I don't follow,*' he said. '*However . . . I'll come.*' *It was not, he knew, said graciously.*

'*What time?*'

'*As soon as I can get away. Six at the latest. I'm afraid I shan't be able to stay long.*'

Her face contracted; she said quickly: '*I haven't asked you to.*'[13]

11 Rosamond Lehmann, *The Echoing Grove*, pp.103–4
12 Ibid., p.104
13 Ibid., p.109

O: All the pain of a difficult affair is in that exchange – the inevitability of ending and the attempt to pretend it isn't inevitable at all . . .

Lara: The continual presence of the absent wife —

Dinah: The fear the mistress has of appearing to ask for what she knows she can't have—

O: Which is also the fear she will drive her lover away —

Lara: The guilt of the man towards both women.

Dinah: And all that is left unsaid. Of which there is a lot. Olivia's Rollo, for instance, rarely mentions his wife Nicola, and Olivia copes with the idea of her – both the perceived threat Nicola represents and her own sense of guilt – by imagining her in a state of permanent invalidism, unable to be a proper wife so not really deserving of much consideration – hardly there at all, in fact. Olivia thinks of Nicola as 'she', a remote, unreal figure, untouched by her own developing relationship with Rollo, and not touching it herself apart from being an inconvenience to the lovers. Of course, Olivia can only see what Rollo is prepared to reveal.

O: Then contradicting the apparent unimportance of Nicola to Rollo is his absolute insistence on caution, that he and Olivia must not be 'found out'. As Olivia puts it, it 'dashes her a bit at first', this inexplicable caution. Inexplicable, because it is not in line with what he has intimated – that he doesn't really care about his wife. The mistress knows, though will rarely admit it to herself, that it doesn't make sense. She also knows that discovery would mean the end of the affair.

Dinah: Then there is that awful fear, which every 'other woman' knows, of the lover meeting with an accident, or illness, or even death – and of being kept apart from him, of no one knowing about the terrible grief, having to bear it alone, not being there to comfort him, to say goodbye. And because in many of us there still lurks that almost atavistic sense – which at other times can be sensually exciting – of doing 'wrong', there is also the half-hidden irrational fear that eventually 'God', or whatever it is that orders the world and likes people to be married, will strike in punishment and vengeance.

O: As I see it, and as we've already said, Dinah, both you and Olivia are quintessential outsiders, and you tried to use your affairs with married men to break – desperately – into the charmed circle, both to damage it and to be embraced by it. You see yourselves as both superior and inferior to your rivals – superior in a sort of refined sensibility, a fragility of feeling, as well as a certain Bohemianism, and inferior in the usual way of not deserving a whole man to yourselves, and in not knowing how to conduct your lives in the conventional, but also secure and tidy, way. Then, despite this sense of inferiority, you feel you can exercise the right to take away – or at least attempt to take away – a man from another woman. Because you're different you're fascinating, but you're ultimately not the kind of women men marry, or leave their wives for. You aren't safe enough for that. You promise excitement, emotional and sexual highs the wives can never attain to, but – almost because of this – you can't be envisaged in the context of domesticity, kitchens, drawing rooms and dinner parties. You're too volatile, too unstable. Yet through women like you, if only the men were themselves sufficiently imaginative, brave enough, to discover how, a man might reach new heights himself, be made a fuller, deeper human being.

My idea being we were too fine for the world, our love should have no dealings whatsoever with its coarseness, I'd spurn the least foothold . . . What was my idea, what was it really?[14]

O: That last question of Olivia's is a good one, and I'm not sure it's ever fully answered, that even she has a complete answer. There are of course very limited options as to what she could legitimately want – there's no point having an

14 Rosamond Lehmann, *The Weather in the Streets*, p.165

'idea' that can never be realised – and so she allows herself, and the relationship, to remain in a state of dream.

Dinah: I've often wondered about how we get into these things in the first place. When Olivia is dancing with Rollo, really early on, before anything has actually happened between them, there is already a sense of the inevitable. Maybe another sort of person, recognising the signs, could back away at this point, make sure she didn't meet the man again – but not our sort. The thrill of recognition, the anticipation, the sense of being swept along in a current, are all too strong. So Olivia gives in to Rollo's suggestion he drive her home – and in that surrender she gives in to everything, as though there were no choice.

O: The way it ends, or doesn't end, for Olivia is particularly depressing. She's been changed irreparably by the affair, she's had an abortion for one thing, jeopardised relation-ships with friends and family, neglected her writing, ne-glected her whole life for her love – while for Rollo it's clear that nothing much has happened at all.

'Do you remember our drives in the mountains?' he was saying. 'And the heavenly places where we stayed? The little inns? Do you remember that queer one under the chestnut trees? – with the funny little band? . . . It was fun, wasn't it, darling?'[15]

Dinah: You can hardly talk about depressing endings, O. You were completely dehumanised or . . .

There existed another ending to the story of O. Seeing herself about to be left by Sir Stephen, she preferred to die. To which he gave his consent.[16]

O: Oh, no one knows what really happened to me. You shouldn't believe everything you read.

Dinah: No. Lara's end is the really sad one.

15 Ibid., p.383
16 Pauline Réage, *Story of O*, p.263

One day Lara went out and did not come back. She must have been arrested in the street, as so often happened in those days, and she died or vanished somewhere, forgotten as a nameless number on a list which was afterwards mislaid, in one of the innumerable mixed or women's concentration camps in the north.[17]

17 Boris Pasternak, *Doctor Zhivago*, p.491

A BALANCING ACT

She who longs to strengthen her spirit
must go beyond obedience and respect.
She will continue to honour some laws
but she will mostly violate
both law and custom, and live beyond
the established and deficient norm.
Pleasure will have much to teach her.
She will not be afraid of the destructive act;
one half of the house must be pulled down.
This way she will grow virtuously into
knowledge.[1]

The above is a version of a poem by Cavafy, 'Strengthening the Spirit', changing the male pronoun he uses to the female. It strikes me as saying some of the things I want to claim about living the life of a mistress. Certainly one is living 'beyond the norm', 'beyond obedience and respect'; what is interesting is the unexpected use of the word 'virtuously', as such a life would appear to be the opposite of virtuous. It has something to do with being brave, by living – and loving – according to one's own inner truth, and not by a code imposed from outside by conventional morality. Once you've come out of the Garden of Eden, out of the state of innocence and being prepared to live by imposed rules, you can't possibly go back.

I've called this final chapter 'A Balancing Act' because that is what it is – an attempt to balance what may seem to be opposing conclusions, thinking one thing one moment, something else the next, sometimes two or more things at

1 Cf. C.P. Cavafy, *Passions & Ancient Days: 21 New Poems*, tr. Edmund Keeley & George Savidis, Hogarth Press, London, 1972

once. I didn't want to call it 'Conclusions', as any conclusions I may reach are tentative, and the stories of mistresses I have included and the inferences I have drawn from them are intended as starting-points for the imagination rather than recipes for living. A balancing act is also what a mistress is called upon to perform, balancing her own needs and desires with those of the other 'members' of the triangle, balancing her independence and her dependence, her need to be loved with the strength of a self-giving love, and so on – keeping her balance in a situation in which it would be so easy to fall and wreck everything. It is also an 'act'; disguise is necessary a great deal of the time.

I said in the Introduction that my primary reason for writing this book was self-examination. So have I succeeded in understanding myself better as a result? I think so. At least I am more conscious of certain aspects of myself of which I had previously been only half aware. I am more firmly convinced than ever that little, if anything, is accidental in human behaviour and that my recurrent pattern of being a mistress is a matter of choice. The role suits me, or at least it has so far, partly for what can be termed, from my point of view, positive reasons (the desire to avoid marriage but not to avoid intimacy, the involvement in difficult loving as an aspect of fully becoming myself) and partly for negative reasons (the sense of not deserving a complete relationship of unconditional love, the desire to compete with and outdo the wife). Whether the role will continue to suit me, or whether it is transitional and I will eventually become either celibate or a wife – or at least the one woman of a man – I do not know. But I think it unlikely somehow. I'm too fond of complications and of living my life as though it were a novel.

I wonder whether, as so many of my examples come from around the turn of the last century, I am just about a hundred years behind the times in my practice of how I conduct love relationships, whether I suffer from a failure of nerve quite as much as Rose Macaulay did, but in a different way. My failure of nerve would be, if this is right, that of a weak-willed feminist, unable really to grasp the issues of living equally with men, escaping into a pretence at independence – after all, I *look* independent, I *appear* to live without a man – while really hiding behind a mask of deceit the fact that I am, emotionally and in some ways even practically, still dependent on my male, married lover. Do I reside in some halfway house, a tenant in my life as much as in my flat (for confirmed mistresses can be as averse to mortgages as they are to husbands)?

The truth the lover tells his mistress bears the same relation to the truth he tells his wife as the truth of poetry to the truth of prose. The successful mistress knows how not to confuse the two.

I have been reminded again and again of how difficult, if not impossible, it is to consider objectively anything to do with relationships – not only, but perhaps particularly, with relationships between the sexes. Memory is inconstant: what we remember today about yesterday will not be what we remember in a fortnight about the same day, let alone what we will remember in a year, a decade, half a century. Then there is the human tendency, probably at its strongest in novelists and poets, to rewrite our own experience, to find patterns, explanations, make sense of it all – quite apart from the desire to present the version we most desire posterity to inherit. There is our inability to understand our own motivation, let alone anyone else's, and the tendency to ascribe significances to other people's words or actions which may never have been intended. In reading our own stories and those of other people, we trust to our intuition and hope for the best.

The type of woman likely to become a mistress is attracted to what is illicit and frowned upon by society; she has a streak of exhibitionism while at the same time she does not really want to be found out and takes pride in her ability to play a part. She tends not to worry too much about the consequences of her actions, to love for love's sake, and let tomorrow take care of itself. She may dislike the very idea of marriage, with its legal and social ramifications, the domestication and making ordinary of love.

Partly why mistresses become serial mistresses is that the first affair, involving the first breaking of the taboo, the first transgression (literally a 'stepping across' the boundary) is the hardest. Once you realise you have survived the first affair without being struck by lightning, the second is easier to embark upon. The third feels like habit; by the fourth it's become an addiction.

I also said in the Introduction that I hoped what I had to say would make some wives less anxious. I think it rather unlikely I have succeeded in that particular aim, having told them rather firmly that mistresses are not going to go away. I have stressed that the best sort of mistress will not attempt to take on the wife and that, if a mistress is foolish enough to be drawn into a contest of ownership of a man, the wife usually wins. So perhaps I have been a little reassuring after all. And in my view it's no more sensible for a wife to be completely dependent – emotionally or practically – on a husband than it is for a mistress to be dependent on her lover. It is possible for wives and mistresses to get on well together, but when they do they are probably either ganging up on the man or guarding vast areas of silence.

The mistress likely to succeed in her role – that is, not to wreck a family and not to be exceedingly miserable herself, but to play a positive part in the life of her lover and to enjoy a fulfilling relationship with him – will understand the importance of the core relationship between husband and wife and will do her best (given the limits of human fallibility) not to undermine it. Penelope Orth offers some good advice: 'Sympathy should be all a mistress offers when her lover complains about his wife; to join in and take the wife apart would be in appalling taste. Impolitic, too, because the lover may suddenly about-face, spring to his wife's defence, and pounce on his mistress with full force. If she is really smart, the mistress will defend the wife and come out clean.'[2]

Wendy James and Susan Jane Kedgley, in their book *The mistress*, define the type of mistress most likely to succeed as a 'free agent'; they also indicate how in this role, as in any other, practice makes perfect:

> Out of the thirty-five mistresses interviewed, the free agents were the only ones thoroughly reconciled to their roles and the only ones who continually derived great pleasure from their affairs.
>
> Previous less satisfactory, even traumatic, encounters with married men had taught them a lot. They had learnt not to expect too much, and they had certainly learnt not to let their lovers expect too much from them.
>
> By not shaping their lives around their lovers, they don't become inextricably involved. They are sceptical rather than naïve, and are self-interested rather than masochistic. They are determined to remain as independent as possible, and to avoid a situation that might lead them to collapse into dependence and submissiveness.[3]

But relationships are fluid, ever-changing things, and once you become involved with another person your 'freedom' is unlikely to remain absolute:

> Only in one area is the free agent as susceptible as any other mistress – when the affair escalates into deep involvement on her own as well as her lover's part. Several mistresses who had started off with rational

2 Penelope Orth, *An Enviable Position*, p.196
3 Wendy James & Susan Jane Kedgley, *The mistress*, pp.41–2

independent attitudes, had gradually found themselves succumbing to irrational behaviour and expectations as their emotional involvement intensified.

Despite their intellectual commitment to independence and personal responsibility, they found themselves wanting to be dependent and possessed. It takes an unusual woman to win against those feelings . . .[4]

A saving grace for a mistress is a genuine commitment to her own work, whatever it may be, the work always being there to fall back on in the absence of the lover or when the affair goes wrong. Writers and artists in particular can find the life of a mistress suits them very well; as Erica Jong puts it: 'With married men, you have weekends, holidays, New Year's Eve to write. When the whole world is pretending to be delirious, you can be really delirious, writing. It may not be for everyone, but for writers in mid-career, it's perfect.'[5]

The other side to this is that it may be very difficult for a mistress to be committed to her work, when she simultaneously wants always to be available to her lover.

A particular aspect of the mistress-figure is the enjoyment of playing with disguise, with masks, and especially a tendency to experiment with naming themselves. So, most famously, we have George Eliot – or Mary Ann, Mary Anne or Marian Evans, Mrs Lewes or Mary Ann Cross. Charlotte Brontë writes as Currer Bell, and then disappears in the guise of Mrs Nicholls. Dorelia, Augustus John's mistress, was known variously as Relia, Ardor, Dorelia or Dodo – while her 'real' name, which nobody called her, was Dorothy. Augustus's wife Ida also played with names, one of the symptoms perhaps of her desire to be a mistress rather than a wife: for a while she called herself Anne, or Ann, the third of her Christian names; then she signed some letters Susan. She had also wanted to call her sister-in-law Gwen by the name 'Anne'; meanwhile

4 Ibid., pp.42–3
5 Erica Jong, *Fear of Fifty*, pp.258–9

Gwen addressed herself to her lover Auguste Rodin as Marie. Then there is 'Rebecca West', born Cicely shortened to Cissie Fairfield, marrying to become Cicely Andrews, later choosing for particular occasions whether to be Dame Cicely or Dame Rebecca. There are plenty of others. The mistress becomes accustomed to being several selves, and to wearing the appropriate mask for each occasion.

I began by thinking there are definite roles to be played by the wife and the mistress, that they can comfortably complement one another, and that trouble only begins when either actress tries to step out of her role and into the other one. I think I still think so, though I am also more aware than previously of how such an arrangement may have been drawn up by men for men, and of how I may be colluding in an ancient system which has never accorded women their full worth and in which the male has always felt threatened by the idea of a *complete* female.

It helps enormously if the mistress not only does not have, but also does not want, children. And effective contraception – along with mobile phones and pagers – is one of the ad- vantages the modern mistress has over her historical counter- parts. The childless mistress can afford to devote all her emotional and caring energies towards her lover, while the wife may be too tired and busy to do so and may think the husband – compared with the children – ought to be able to look after himself. This gives the mistress an unfair advantage.

Relationships don't have to last for ever to be valuable.

Am I really trying to uphold the contention that being a mistress, and the kind of loving that involves – that is, at its best, loving without the desire to possess, retaining some independence and a sense of separateness, being at ease with one's solitude as well as with one's lover – is, or can be used as, a pathway to what Jung calls 'individuation'? Well, yes, but in much the same way as anything can be, if one uses one's life

experiences as material for the attaining of greater consciousness. Maybe this has something to do with the acceptance of
limitation – that in human life one can't have everything one
wants all of the time; the mistress will never succeed as the
mistress if she takes no account of the wife and of her
legitimate demands, and accepting this may help to create
a greater sense of reality than human beings generally seem
able to accept. On the other hand, I may be completely
wrong; one thing that has been underlined for me time and
again in the course of my reading and thinking for this book is
that human beings are infinitely gifted in self-deception and
that I am no exception. We all look for gilded reasons to cover
over the tarnished material of our base motives; we want what
we can get for nothing, we like to win and see others lose, and
we like to be able to congratulate ourselves and admire our
own reflection, no matter what distorting mirrors we need in
order to create an acceptable image to gaze upon. Yet I still
think being a mistress can give greater opportunities for facing
the reality of the world and of the self than being a wife may
do, partly because playing a socially unacceptable role forces a
greater degree of self-reflexiveness, self-questioning, than does
playing a conventional role viewed by society as the 'right
thing' and not open to challenge.

Connected with the search for becoming my full self, as far
as I am concerned, is a rejection of the family. One sees this
also in several of the women I have considered, from Heloise
with her view of family life as inimical to the pursuit of
philosophy, to Rose Macaulay and her sense of being stifled
by life at 'home' and her determination to set up on her own.
There is some part of me which strongly wants to be alone,
separate from the compromises and the eclipsing of individuality entailed in being a member of a family. I, or at least a
part of me, always desired a kind of apartness from my birth-
family (now attained through parental death – another part of
me, of course, misses my parents every day), and I am strongly
resistant to the notion of becoming part of any other family,
sensing that any such 'belonging' would threaten my individ-

uality, my belonging to myself. So it is no surprise to me that I should choose for my lover a man I cannot marry – there is no danger of my ever becoming related to his mother, no threat of absorption into some clan who might think they had the right to exert demands on me or, even worse, seek to define me as part of itself. And for such a fierce desire to remain separate one can expect little understanding or sympathy from the majority. As the Jungian analyst Aldo Carotenuto puts it: 'The art of becoming ourselves is not looked upon positively by the collective mind because, as the collective mind is intent on perpetuating uniformity, it will inevitably see diversity and differentiation as a threat.'[6]

One needs to be brave consciously and deliberately to live and love at odds with society, in a way open to censure by the respectable and even – at times and in some aspects – by oneself. I don't expect to be congratulated for what I have revealed of myself in this book, and this is partly because people like me frighten those who live by conventional codes of behaviour. 'Anyone in open conflict with the prevailing code of conduct will inevitably be condemned by the average person. The reason for this is the danger implicit in shedding light on the insubstantial quality of the average individual, who lives only to embrace current values uncritically, without ever examining his own morality or conscience on the basis of his interior experience – that is, by listening to his inner voices.'[7]

A striving after individuality may be viewed as the light side of my motivation in choosing to be a mistress; the dark side may have something to do with responses left over from childhood, the deep-seated belief that love has to be earned by good behaviour, can never be guaranteed or expected through some kind of contract or by the simple fact of 'belonging' to someone. The role of the mistress suits this belief, whereas the role of the wife would seem to assume too

---

6 Aldo Carotenuto, *To Love To Betray: Life as Betrayal*, tr. Joan Tambureno, Chiron Publications, Wilmette Illinois, 1996, p.16
7 Ibid., pp.16–17

much. And it's something to do with how I perceived the love I had from my parents. Possibly.

I seem to go on fighting a battle – with shadows – which I won long ago, that of escaping from 'the family'. Perhaps I'm wrong, and I have never really escaped at all, despite almost half a lifetime of living on my own and appearing to make unconstrained choices. Actually my current choices aren't unconstrained at all, but revolve around the needs and desires of my (married) partner.

I suspect that my hatred of the very words 'marriage' and 'the family' has its roots in my early childhood, that one or other or both of my parents must have been unconsciously ambivalent – to say the least – about the lives they led as mother or father, wife or husband. It was so unconscious that I have no idea which of them it was who suffered from such ambivalence; all I know is that something in me resonates to these words of C.G. Jung: 'Generally speaking, all the life which the parents could have lived, but of which they thwarted themselves for artificial motives, is passed on to the children in substitute form. That is to say, the children are driven unconsciously in a direction that is intended to compensate for everything that was left unfulfilled in the lives of their parents.'[8]

Yet I also recognise that my fearlessness in examining my own motivation as well as my ability to live in a way which is morally unacceptable to the majority, without needing the props of societal approval, have their basis in the interior confidence fostered by my mother's unconditional love of me as a small child. I have always had this sense that, no matter what life events assail me, there is a psychic level below which I will not fall, a foundation holding me up, steadying me, and I have always put this down to that early experience of maternal, totally accepting, love.

8 C.G. Jung, *Aspects of the Feminine*, p.43

Aldo Carotenuto holds that 'it takes more courage to maintain a relationship than to live alone, for the life of a couple is constantly exposed to the possibility of betrayal'.[9] I would suggest that it takes even more courage to maintain a relationship *and* to live alone.

Guilt is not an emotion I have any time for. It is only useful if it prompts a person to change his or her way of life. As I do not intend to stop being a mistress, it would be an emotional indulgence to feel guilty about being one.

What are my doubts, if any, about the way I conduct my life? Principally they are that I give too much time to my lover, I put my own interests second to his. Instead of using my much-trumpeted independence to my own benefit, I play a role in his life far more like that of the traditional supportive wife than his actual wife does. Indeed, that may be partly why he experiences the need for a mistress in the first place (though it's also because he likes women, is easily bored, has a self-destructive rebellious streak, and so on . . .). I am like Rebecca West in relation to H.G. Wells, Stella Bowen in relation to Ford Madox Ford, Camille Claudel in relation to Rodin. I don't even give as much time to writing this book as I think I ought to, because I exhaust myself fulfilling his professional and personal demands first. And then I turn in fury on myself for allowing – indeed being unable to prevent – this sort of behaviour. I don't know why I do it; I seem unable to stop. I suppose knowing these other brilliant women were as fatally flawed is some sort of comfort. And I'm probably exaggerating anyway.

Being a mistress is the outward sign of a conflict within myself – between the desire to achieve in my own right and enjoy total independence, and the desire to give myself completely to a man and care for him to the exclusion, or at least detriment, of all my own ambitions. To have a husband

9 Aldo Carotenuto, *To Love To Betray: Life as Betrayal*, p.89

would be to give in totally to the second compulsion; to be celibate would be totally to obey the first. Having a married lover is the uneasy compromise, the attempt to hold both compulsions in balance.

I think as a society we probably make far too much fuss about these things. Monogamy isn't an eternal law. It's just how we tend to arrange things, but we don't have to.

The mistress must always think before she speaks. She must never make demands and never criticise – or she'll be told she's behaving like a wife – which is a coded warning that the relationship will end if she doesn't keep to the terms of being the mistress, whose job it is to be endlessly, uncritically supportive, the warm (unreal?) refuge from the harder (real?) relationship with the wife.

So would I like to marry my lover? We have discussed this recently and we concluded that if his marriage were to end – which is not something I would ever press for – I would marry him. This is partly because he is not in a position to be seen to be living with someone he isn't married to. But he has also said to me 'I don't want you to be my wife, I want you to be my mistress' and, on the whole, that's what I want too. I don't want us ever to be bored with one another, take one another for granted, lie in the same bed and not want to make love – and all these things are more likely to happen if we were married, living under the same roof, as guaranteed to be there as a piece of furniture. Also and I've told him this, if we married, I would expect him to have affairs – he would still be *him* – and I wouldn't much like it. I would be unlikely to have them myself. And yet . . . I do wish I could be with him more of the time, I do wish we could spend most nights together, I wish we didn't have to pretend not to be intimately con-nected. And yet . . . I also enjoy our role-playing, and how good we are (or do I deceive myself?) at donning our masks.

It is, I suppose, possible that a life of constant disguise and dissembling rots the soul, until one can't distinguish truth from falsehood, and one takes pride in the ability to live a lie, to play one's role with such skill that 'reality' becomes invisible, as well to oneself as to others. On the other hand, maybe everyone is in disguise all – or most – of the time, and at least the mistress knows she is.

It does worry me that so many of the mistresses I've written about have a tendency to self-denigration, do not fully believe in themselves, and I recognise exactly this tendency in myself: on the one hand, the belief I am special, *above* convention, don't need to worry about rules made for the masses; on the other, that I haven't quite grown up yet, have to earn love, wouldn't be any good at doing the domestic things wives are supposed to do.

A fundamental question for the mistress must be: if a man can betray his wife, how can I ever be sure he won't betray me? Or, to put it another way, if you get involved with a polygamist, you mustn't be surprised when he practises polygamy.

Films, television programmes, women's magazines are so quick to fall back on the clichéd responses of 'If you're having an affair, that's the end of our marriage', 'You have to choose – me or her', 'You can't love two people at once' and 'You don't have affairs if you're happy'. I don't know that any of these responses are 'true'. They're just the stock, unimaginative things to say, as if life were a pantomime, not an exceedingly rich experiencing of raw material, out of which we are free to fashion the art work of our individual lives. You need courage, and principally you need imagination, to transcend the clichés, to experience what you really feel instead of what other people and the propaganda industry of press and popular entertainment tell you you're supposed to feel, and to make your life into your own art work. But to do so – even to try to do so – is infinitely more rewarding than to sink into soap opera cliché, other people's scripts.

Alexandre Dumas is reputed to have said: 'So heavy is the chain of wedlock that it needs two to carry it, and sometimes three.'[10] Certainly in the case of my lover I have noticed the need for the maintenance of the triangle; not only does he need affairs to make the marriage work, but the marital needs to be functioning reasonably well for the extra-marital to flourish.

Concerning triangles, it may be worth noting that Hecate, goddess of witches, was the original triple-goddess before being transformed into the power of destruction and black magic. Her triple nature was retained as the witch-goddess in that she was invoked at places where three roads met, and she had the three heads of lion, dog and mare. Perhaps the goddess of witches is the goddess of the eternal triangle.

What is vital in the maintenance of a triangle – which can be both stable and dynamic – is that the three do not constantly try to become a two. That is, if the mistress accepts the wife, and the wife has some degree of confidence that the husband will not leave her (and if he's happy with his mistress that may be *more* likely rather than less), then the triangle can flourish. This, I would argue, can be the case whether or not the wife knows about the mistress.

What happens when the wife does find out about the mistress? In most cases that's the end of that particular affair, as husbands tend to be cowardly creatures. But the affair may resume once the wife has become less vigilant – or he'll just go on to someone else. Occasionally the marriage will break up, in which case the mistress may or may not 'get' the man – and may or may not want him.

10 *Vice: An Anthology*, compiled by Richard Davenport-Hines, p.10

Mistresses are wrong if they denigrate, or make little of, their lover's relationship with his wife. There's generally far more to it than he is prepared to admit to a mistress – unless the mistress fulfils her role so perfectly that she really does understand and accept, and he tells her (nearly) everything. And when there's a contest between wives and mistresses for 'possession' of the man, wives usually win, but then – one of the most galling aspects for the mistress – wives frequently don't seem to appreciate what they've got. Security breeds carelessness, in the literal sense of lack of care, a form of taking for granted.

I am not sure now whether what the psychotherapist Thomas Moore writes, in his best-selling book *Care of the Soul*, about the attaining of consciousness, isn't a trifle optimistic:

> We are condemned to live out what we cannot imagine. We can be caught in myth, not knowing that we are acting as a character in a drama. Soul work involves an effort toward increasing awareness of these myths that form the foundation of our lives, for if we become familiar with the characters and themes that are central to our myths, we can be free from our compulsions and the blindness that comes upon us when we are caught up in them.[11]

I think he is right that we are condemned to live out what we cannot imagine, but I wonder whether, having attained an awareness of our compulsions – why we act the way we do – we may continue to be subject to them. We go on doing the things we do; we just notice more that we're doing them. Jung is another optimist; he holds out enormous hope for integration – indeed, salvation would not be too strong a word – when he writes of the positive aspects of some of the types he has identified. He has the following to say in the case

11 Thomas Moore, *Care of the Soul*, HarperPerennial, New York, 1994, pp.223–4

of the 'overdeveloped Eros' which, in its negative aspect, may lead a woman to want to smash up marriages: 'The woman whose fate it is to be a disturbing element is not solely destructive, except in pathological cases. Normally the disturber is herself caught in the disturbance; the worker of change is herself changed, and the glare of the fire she ignites both illuminates and enlightens all the victims of the entanglement.'[12] And again: 'If a woman of this type remains unconscious of the meaning of her function, if she does not know that she is "Part of that power which would/Ever work evil but engenders good" (*Faust*, Part I, Act 1), she will herself perish by the sword she brings. But consciousness transforms her into a deliverer and redeemer.'[13] I can only hope he is right.

Jung's own long-term mistress, Toni Wolff, seems to have played the part of 'deliverer and redeemer' for him, in particular helping him survive, and attain greater consciousness through, a major psychic breakdown. She had a difficult time herself, having to put up with Jung's other affairs as well as maintain a sometimes uneasy relationship with his wife Emma. Eventually she found herself being ignored by Jung as she grew old and lost her beauty.

My basic position is that I stand alone and find security only in myself. This is actually true for *everyone*, but is not generally recognised; the popular conception of marriage deliberately blinds people to it, with the erroneous idea that security can be found in another person and be guaranteed by legal and/or sacred contract. For one thing, everybody dies, no matter how firmly they cling to their marriage vows.

Though I find Heloise and her way of loving an inspiration, I cannot allow myself to believe she would have approved of me – especially regarding my attitude and behaviour towards

12 C.G. Jung, *The Archetypes & the Collective Unconscious*, p.96
13 Ibid., p.97

women who happen to be wives – but I think she would recognise some of my arguments and perhaps applaud my attempt to examine myself truthfully, at least to ask difficult questions.

Is mine an escapist love, not grounded in day-to-day realities of work, illness, sharing the bathroom as well as the bed, meals as chores rather than treats, bad temper, or just run-of-the-mill monotony of life? Not to mention children. Perhaps it is. As Erica Jong says: 'As a mistress, I am my best self: charming, tender, funny. When you live apart from a man, it's easy to be nice to him.'[14] But why shouldn't I escape if I want to? Does getting married, having children and 'settling down' really have so much to recommend it?

One aspect of love without a contract or certificate is that whenever my lover's a bit 'off' with me, I start to worry that the relationship may be in decline. I doubt most wives are so receptive to the slightest change of mood.

I have several times inveighed against the too easy use of that slippery little word: love. Yet I have also used it, in much the same way that I have criticised others for using it. I think I need to look at what I actually mean by it, particularly what I think I mean when I say to my lover, as I frequently do, 'I love you'.

So what do I mean? Many things. Part of what I mean is suggested by *when* I say it – when I'm happy in the company of my lover, when I couldn't conceivably want to be anywhere else or with anyone else. I mean that my relating to him makes me feel more myself, more fully alive, than I would feel if I didn't have him to relate to. Yet I also mean that I respect him as an autonomous individual, that I grant him freedom to be himself, which can include not having to be with me. 'I love you' means I rejoice in his idiosyncrasies, I take him as he

14 Erica Jong, *Fear of Fifty*, p.259

is, accepting his weaknesses as well as his strengths, because they are all part of him. I mean 'I want you to be all right', 'I want you to be happy', as well as the wholly irrational 'I want you never to suffer', 'I want you never to die'. And because he is married, and because I want him to be all right, 'I love you' must include 'I want your family to be all right', 'I want you to rejoice in your children' – even 'I love your family, because they are part of you'. And the logical conclusion of that must be: 'if our relationship threatens your well-being, if it threatens your family, I am prepared to let you go'. Easier said than done, that bit; of course one convinces oneself the relationship is good for the lover, and consequently for his family.

'I love you' is a phrase one says while knowing its truth and its untruth simultaneously. One believes this feeling will last for ever, while knowing it never has before. Like sex, it feels constantly new and endlessly repetitive. 'I love you' can imply – and usually does – 'I need you', but to love properly also includes an obligation to be as fulfilled and independent a person as one can be; one wants to give to the lover, not deplete his energy out of need.

And I insist that 'I love you' must predominantly mean 'I want you to be yourself, to be the fullest expression of yourself you can possibly be *whether or not that has anything to do with me*. I do not want to possess you, and will try to ensure that I never do.'

And when my lover replies 'I love you, too', I must not imagine that means he loves me only, and that we're about to run off into some magical land where past actions have no consequences, wives evaporate and children bring themselves up. And when he doesn't reply at all, I mustn't force him, as real loving implies freedom to respond or not.

No easy thing – I love you – but being a mistress, as Heloise knew well, provides good training in learning how to love.

I think in the end I arrive at only one absolutely firm conclusion: as long as there is Marriage, there will also be the Mistress.

BIBLIOGRAPHY

T hese are most of the books which have fed into my thinking during the writing of *The Mistress*. The interested reader will also find here stories of other mistresses which I have either not had space to include or which I have felt do not add anything to an analysis of the mistress-type.

Abelard, P., *Historia Calamitatum*, tr. J.T. Muckle, Pontifical Institute of Medieval Studies, Toronto, 1954

Ackroyd, P., *Dickens*, Sinclair Stevenson, London, 1990

Anthony, M., *The Valkyries: The Women Around Jung*, Element, Shaftesbury, 1990

Ariès, P. & Béjun, A., *Western Sexuality: Practice & Precept in Past & Present Times*, Blackwell, Oxford, 1985

Armstrong, K., *The Gospel According to Woman*, Elm Tree Books, London, 1986

Asquith, H.H., *Letters to Venetia Stanley*, eds. Michael & Eleanor Brock, OUP, Oxford & New York, 1985

Auerbach, N., *Woman & the Demon: The Life of a Victorian Myth*, Harvard University Press, Cambridge Mass. & London, 1982

Babington Smith, C., *Rose Macaulay*, Collins, London, 1972

Baker, D., *In Extremis: The Life of Laura Riding*, Hamish Hamilton, London, 1993

Balsdon, J.P.V.D., *Roman Women: Their History & Habits*, Bodley Head, London, 1974

Baring, A. & Cashford, J., *The Myth of the Goddess*, Penguin/Arkana, London, 1991

Barker, J., *The Brontës*, Weidenfeld & Nicolson, London, 1994

Baruch, E.H., *Women, Love, & Power: Literary & Psychoanalytic Perspectives*, New York University Press, New York & London, 1991

Basch, F., *Relative Creatures: Victorian Women in Society & the Novel 1937–67*, tr. Anthony Rudolf, Allen Lane, Harmondsworth, 1974

Beauvoir, S. de, *The Second Sex*, Picador, London, 1988

Beckett, L., *Richard Wagner: 'Parsifal'*, Cambridge University Press, Cambridge, 1981

Bedell Smith, S., *Reflected Glory: The Life of Pamela Churchill Harriman*, Touchstone, New York, 1997

Belford, B., *Violet*, Simon & Schuster, New York, 1990

Benjamin, J., *The Bonds of Love: Psychoanalysis, Feminism & the Problem of Domination*, Virago, London, 1993

Benson, R., *Charles: The Untold Story*, Gollancz, London, 1993

Bergan, R., *An Independent Woman: Katharine Hepburn*, Bloomsbury, London, 1996

Beroul, *The Romance of Tristan*, tr. Alan S. Fedrick, Penguin, Harmondsworth, 1970

Block, J.D., *The Other Man, The Other Woman: Understanding & coping with extramarital affairs*, Grosset & Dunlap, New York, 1978

Bowen, S., *Drawn from Life*, Collins, London, 1941

Bridenthal, R., Koonz, C., Stuard, S. (eds.), *Becoming Visible: Women in European History*, Houghton Mifflin, Boston, 1987

Briffault, R., *Sin & Sex*, Allen & Unwin, London, 1931

Brook, S. (ed.), *The Penguin Book of Infidelities*, Penguin, Harmondsworth, 1995

Brooke, C.N.L., *The Medieval Idea of Marriage*, OUP, Oxford & New York, 1989

Brownmiller, S., *Femininity*, Paladin, London, 1986

Brundage, J.A., *Law, Sex, & Christian Society in Medieval Europe*, University of Chicago Press, Chicago & London, 1988

Burns, E.J., *Bodytalk: When Women Speak in Old French*

Literature, University of Pennsylvania Press, Philadelphia, 1993

Butler, R., *Rodin: The Shape of Genius*, Yale University Press, New Haven & London, 1993

Calder, J., *Women & Marriage in Victorian Fiction*, Thames & Hudson, London, 1976

Campbell, J., *The Masks of God: Creative Mythology*, Penguin, Harmondsworth, 1976

Capellanus, A., *The Art of Courtly Love*, tr. John Jay Parry, Columbia University Press, New York, 1941

Carlton, C., *Royal Mistresses*, Routledge, London & New York, 1990

Carotenuto, A., *To Love To Betray: Life as Betrayal*, Chiron Publications, Wilmette Illinois, 1996

Carrington, D., *Letters & Extracts from her Diaries*, ed. David Garnett, Cape, London, 1970

Carter, A., *The Sadeian Woman: An Exercise in Cultural History*, Virago, London, 1979

Casarès, M., *Résidente Privilégiée*, Fayard, Paris, 1980

Chitty, S., *Gwen John: 1876–1939*, Hodder & Stoughton, London, 1981

Clarke, W.M., *The Secret Life of Wilkie Collins*, Allison & Busby, London, 1988

Cobb, N., *Archetypal Imagination: Glimpses of the Gods in Life & Art*, Lindisfarne Press, Hudson NY, 1992

Cole, W.G., *Sex & Love in the Bible*, Hodder & Stoughton, London, 1959

Coren, M., *The Invisible Man: The Life & Liberties of H.G. Wells*, Bloomsbury, London, 1993

Cunningham, P., *The Story of Nell Gwyn*, ed. Gordon Goodwin, Edinburgh, 1908

Davenport-Hines, R. (ed.), *Vice: An Anthology*, Hamish Hamilton, London, 1993

De St Jorre, J., *The Good Ship Venus: The Erotic Voyages of the Olympia Press*, Pimlico, London, 1995

Doyle, C., *Richard Aldington: A Biography*, Macmillan, London, 1989

Edel, L., *Bloomsbury: A House of Lions*, Penguin, Harmondsworth, 1981

Eliade, M., *A History of Religious Ideas*, Vol. 3, University of Chicago Press, Chicago & London, 1985

Eliot, G., *Selected Essays, Poems & Other Writings*, eds. A.S. Byatt & Nicholas Warren, Penguin, Harmondsworth, 1990

Ellman, R., *Yeats: The Man & the Masks*, Penguin, Harmondsworth, 1987

Emery, J., *Rose Macaulay: A Writer's Life*, Murray, London, 1991

Eschenbach, W. von, *Parzival,* tr. A.T. Hatto, Penguin, Harmondsworth, 1980

Eskapa, S., *Woman versus Woman*, Bellew, London, 1998

Ettinger, E., *Hannah Arendt, Martin Heidegger*, Yale University Press, New Haven & London, 1995

Ferrante, J.M., *Woman as Image in Medieval Literature: From the Twelfth Century to Dante*, Columbia University Press, New York & London, 1975

Figes, E., *Patriarchal Attitudes: Women in Society*, Macmillan, London, 1986

Fisher, H.E., *Anatomy of Love: The Natural History of Monogamy, Adultery & Divorce,* Simon & Schuster, London, 1993

Flacelière, R., *Love in Ancient Greece*, tr. James Cleugh, Frederick Muller, London, 1962

Foot, M., *HG: The History of Mr Wells*, Black Swan, London, 1996

Fraser, A., *The Weaker Vessel: Woman's Lot in Seventeenth-Century England*, Weidenfeld & Nicolson, London, 1984

Freud, S., *Freud on Women: A Reader*, ed. Elisabeth Young-Bruehl, Hogarth Press, London, 1990

Fromm, E., *The Art of Loving*, Allen & Unwin, London, 1960

Garnett, A., *Deceived with Kindness: A Bloomsbury Childhood*, Chatto & Windus, London, 1984

Gerson, N.B., *Lillie Langtry*, Hale, London, 1972

Gerzina, G., *A Life of Dora Carrington 1893–1932*, Murray, London, 1989

Gilbert, S.M. & Gubar, S., *The Madwoman in the Attic: The Woman Writer & the Nineteenth-century Literary Imagination*, Yale University Press, New Haven & London, 1980

Gilson, E., *Héloise and Abélard*, Hollis & Carter, London, 1953

Gittings, R. & Manton, J., *Claire Clairmont & the Shelleys 1798–1879*, OUP, Oxford & New York, 1992

Glendinning, V., *Rebecca West: A Life*, Macmillan, London, 1987

Gonne MacBride, M., *A Servant of the Queen: Reminiscences*, Gollancz, London, 1974

Gordon, L., *Charlotte Brontë: A Passionate Life*, Chatto & Windus, London, 1994

Graves, R., *Greek Myths*, Cassell & Co., London, 1958

Greer, G., *Sex and Destiny: The Politics of Human Fertility*, Secker & Warburg, London, 1984

Greer, G., *The Female Eunuch*, MacGibbon & Kee, London, 1971

Grigson, G., *The Goddess of Love: the Birth, Triumph, Death & Return of Aphrodite*, Constable, London, 1976

Grunfeld, F.V., *Rodin: A Biography*, Hutchinson, London, 1988

Haight, G.S., *George Eliot: A Biography*, Clarendon Press, Oxford, 1968

Haight, G.S., *George Eliot & John Chapman, with Chapman's Diaries*, Yale University Press, New Haven, 1940

Haight, G.S. (ed.), *Selections From George Eliot's Letters*, Yale University Press, New Haven & London, 1985

Hamilton, E., *Heloise*, Hodder & Stoughton, London, 1966

Harding, M.E., *The Way of All Women: A Psychological Interpretation*, Longmans, Green & Co., London, New York, Toronto, 1933

Hardwick, E., *Seduction & Betrayal: Women & Literature*, Weidenfeld & Nicolson, London, 1974

Hardwick, J., *An Immodest Violet: The Life of Violet Hunt*, Deutsch, London, 1990

Harrison, J.E., *Myths of Greece & Rome*, London, 1927

Haskins, S., *Mary Magdalen: Myth & Metaphor*, HarperCollins, London, 1993

Hayman, R., *Brecht: A Biography*, Weidenfeld & Nicolson, London, 1983

Hays, H.R., *The Dangerous Sex: The Myth of Feminine Evil*, Methuen & Co., London, 1966

Hepburn, K., *Me: Stories of My Life*, Viking, London, 1991

Hillman, J., *Re-visioning Psychology*, Harper & Row, New York, 1977

Hillman, J., *The Myth of Analysis*, Harper & Row, New York, 1978

Hoey, B., *Mountbatten: The Private Story*, Sidgwick & Jackson, London, 1994

Holroyd, M., *Augustus John: The New Biography*, Vintage, London, 1997

Homer, *The Iliad*, tr. Robert Fagles, Viking, New York, 1990

Homer, *The Odyssey*, tr. Walter Shewring, OUP, Oxford, 1980

HRH Princess Michael of Kent, *Cupid and the King*, HarperCollins, London, 1991

Hughes-Hallett, L., *Cleopatra: Histories, Dreams & Distortions*, Bloomsbury, London, 1990

Hutchins, C. & Midgley, D., *Diana on the Edge: Inside the Mind of the Princess of Wales*, Smith Gryphon, London, 1996

Ibsen, H., *Rosmersholm* in *Plays: Three*, tr. Michael Meyer, Methuen, London, 1991, pp.31–110

Ibsen, H., *The Master Builder* in *Plays: One*, tr. Michael Meyer, Methuen, London, 1989, pp.245–319

Ivinskaya, O., *A Captive of Time: My Years with Pasternak*, tr. Max Hayward, Fontana/Collins, London, 1979

James, W. & Kedgley, S.J., *The mistress*, Abelard-Schuman, London, 1973

Jenkins, R., *Gallery of Twentieth Century Portraits*, David & Charles, London, 1988

Jones, M., *A Radical Life: The Biography of Megan Lloyd George, 1902–66,* Hutchinson, London, 1991

Jong, E., *Fear of Fifty*, Chatto & Windus, London, 1994

Judd, A., *Ford Madox Ford*, Collins, London, 1990

Jung, C.G., *Aspects of the Feminine*, tr. R.F.C. Hull, Ark Paperbacks, London, 1992

Jung, C.G., *Collected Works Vol. 5: Symbols of Transformation*, tr. R.F.C. Hull, Routledge, London, 1956

Jung, C.G., *Collected Works Vol. 9i: The Archetypes and the Collective Unconscious*, tr. R.F.C. Hull, Routledge, London, 1969

Jung, C.G., *Memories, Dreams, Reflections*, tr. Richard & Clara Winston, Fontana, London, 1983

Karl, F., *George Eliot: A Biography*, HarperCollins, London, 1995

Keays, S., *A Question of Judgement*, Quintessential, London, 1985

Kelso, R.K., *Doctrine for the Lady of the Renaissance*, University of Illinois Press, Urbana, 1956

Kerenyi, C., *The Gods of the Greeks*, Thames & Hudson, London, 1979

Kessler, R., *The Sins of the Father: Joseph P. Kennedy & the dynasty he founded*, Coronet, London, 1996

Keun, O., *I Discover the English*, John Lane, London, 1934

Kirk, G.S., *The Nature of Greek Myths*, Penguin, Hardmondsworth, 1974

Lawson, A., *Adultery: An Analysis of Love & Betrayal*, OUP, Oxford, 1990

Leaming, B., *Katharine Hepburn*, Weidenfeld & Nicolson, London, 1995

Lee, H., *Virginia Woolf*, Chatto & Windus, London, 1996

Levine, N.B., *Politics, Religion & Love: The Story of H.H. Asquith, Venetia Stanley & Edwin Montagu*, New York University Press, New York & London, 1991

Levy, M.J., *The Mistresses of King George IV*, Peter Owen, London & Chester Springs, 1996

Lilar, S., *Aspects of Love in Western Society*, tr. Jonathan Griffin, Panther, London, 1967

Lindsay, J., *Helen of Troy: Woman & Goddess*, Constable, London, 1974

Longford, R., *Frances, Countess Lloyd George: More than a mistress*, Gracewing, Leominster, 1996

Luscombe, D.E., Introduction to *Peter Abelard's Ethics*, Clarendon Press, Oxford, 1971

Macaulay, R., *Last Letters to a Friend, 1952–1958*, ed. Constance Babington Smith, Collins, London, 1962

Macaulay, R., *Letters to a Friend, 1950–1952*, ed. Constance Babington Smith, Collins, London, 1961

MacBride White, A. & Jeffares, A.N. (eds.), *The Gonne–Yeats Letters 1893–1938: Always Your Friend*, Pimlico, London, 1992

MacGregor-Hastie, R., *Picasso's Women*, Lennard, Luton, 1988

McLynn, F., *Carl Gustav Jung*, Bantam Press, London, 1996

Marcus, S., *The Other Victorians: A Study of Sexuality & Pornography in Mid-Nineteenth Century England*, Weidenfeld & Nicolson, London, 1966

Markale, J., *Women of the Celts*, tr. A. Mygind, C. Hauch & P. Henry, Gordon Gemonesi, London, 1975

Marler, R. (ed.), *Selected Letters of Vanessa Bell*, Bloomsbury, London, 1993

Meyer, M., *Ibsen*, Penguin, Hardmondsworth, 1985

Miles, R., *The Women's History of the World*, Paladin, London, 1989

Millington, B., *Wagner*, Dent, London & Melbourne, 1984

Mitford, N., *Madame de Pompadour*, Penguin, Harmondsworth, 1995

Montgomery Hyde, H., *A Tangled Web: Sex Scandals in British Politics & Society*, Constable, London, 1986

Moore, T., *Care of the Soul*, HarperPerennial, New York, 1994

Moore, T., *Soul Mates*, HarperPerennial, New York, 1994

Moore, T., *The Planets Within: The Astrological Psychology of Marsilio Ficino*, Bucknell University Press, Lewisburg, 1982

Morton, A., *Diana: Her New Life*, O'Mara, London, 1994

Morton, A., *Diana: Her True Story*, O'Mara, London, 1992

Neumann, E., *Amor & Psyche: The Psychic Development of the Feminine*, tr. Ralph Mannheim, Routledge & Kegan Paul, London, 1956

Orth, P., *An Enviable Position: The American Mistress from Slightly Kept to Practically Married*, D. McKay Co., New York, 1972

Otto, W.F., *The Homeric Gods: The Spiritual Significance of Greek Religion*, Thames & Hudson, London, 1955

Ovid, *Metamorphoses*, tr. A.D. Melville, OUP, Oxford & New York, 1986

Ovid, *The Art of Love*, tr. Rolfe Humphries, John Calder, London, 1958

Paglia, C., *Sexual Personae*, Penguin, Harmondsworth, 1992

Paglia, C., *Vamps & Tramps*, Penguin, Harmondsworth, 1995

Panofsky, D. & E., *Pandora's Box: The Changing Aspects of a Mythical Symbol*, Routledge & Kegan Paul, London, 1956

Paris, G., *Pagan Meditations: The Worlds of Aphrodite, Artemis, & Hestia,* Spring Publications, Woodstock CT, 1986

Paris, R–M., *Camille: The Life of Camille Claudel, Rodin's Muse & Mistress*, tr. Liliane Emery Tuck, Aurum Press, London, 1988

Partridge, F., *Memories*, Gollancz, London, 1981

Patmore, D. (ed.), *My Friends When Young: The Memoirs of Brigit Patmore*, Heinemann, London, 1968

Pearson, H., *Dickens: His Character, Comedy & Career*, Cassell, London, 1988

Perényi, E., *Liszt*, Weidenfeld & Nicolson, London, 1974

Pirani, A. (ed.), *The Absent Mother: Restoring the Goddess to Judaism & Christianity*, Mandala, London, 1991

Pomeroy, S.B., *Goddesses, Whores, Wives & Slaves: Women in Classical Antiquity*, Schocken, New York, 1976

Pope, A., 'Eloisa to Abelard', *Collected Poems*, ed. Bonamy Dobrée, M. Dent & Sons, London & New York, 1976

Porter, K.A., *Collected Essays & Occasional Writings*, Delacorte Press, New York, 1970

Radice, B. (ed.), *The Letters of Abelard and Heloise*, Penguin, Harmondsworth, 1974

Raine, K., *Autobiographies*, Skoob Books, London, 1991

Ranke-Heinemann, U., *Eunuchs for Heaven: The Catholic Church & Sexuality*, tr. John Brownjohn, Deutsch, London, 1990

Ray, G.N., *H.G. Wells & Rebecca West*, Macmillan, London, 1975

Réage, P., *Story of O*, Corgi, London, 1998

Réage, P., *Story of O Part Two*, Corgi, London, 1997

Redgrove, P., *The Black Goddess & the Sixth Sense*, Blooms-bury, London, 1987

Redinger, R.V., *George Eliot: The Emergent Self*, Bodley Head, London, Sydney, Toronto, 1976

Reibstein, J. & Richards, M., *Sexual Arrangements: Marriage, Monogamy & Affairs*, Mandarin, London, 1993

Rhys, J., *Letters, 1931–1966*, eds. F. Wyndham, & D. Melly, Deutsch, London, 1984

Roberts, N., *Whores in History: Prostitution in Western Society*, HarperCollins, London, 1992

Rollyson, C., *Rebecca West: A Saga of the Century*, Hodder & Stoughton, London, 1995

Rose, P., *Parallel Lives: Five Victorian Marriages*, Vintage Books, New York, 1984

Rosenbaum, S.P. (ed.), *The Bloomsbury Group: A Collection of Memoirs, Commentary & Criticism*, University of Toronto Press, Toronto & London, 1995

Rougemont, D. de, *Love in the Western World*, tr. Montgomery Belgion, Princeton University Press, Princeton NJ, 1983

Ruether, R.R. (ed.), *Religion & Sexism: Images of Woman in the Jewish & Christian Traditions*, Simon & Schuster, New York, 1974

Ruggiero, G., *The Boundaries of Eros: Sex Crime & Sexuality in Renaissance Venice*, OUP, New York & Oxford, 1985

Russell, B., *Marriage & Morals*, Allen & Unwin, London, 1930

Rutter, P., *Sex in the Forbidden Zone*, Aquarian, London, 1995

Shaw, G.B., *The Quintessence of Ibsenism*, Constable, London, 1929

Simons, J., *Rosamond Lehmann*, Macmillan, London, 1992

Slater, P.E., *The Glory of Hera: Greek Mythology & the Greek Family*, Princeton University Press, Princeton NJ, 1992

Smith, D.C., *H.G. Wells: Desperately Mortal*, Yale University Press, New Haven & London, 1986

Smith, J., *Different for Girls: How Culture Creates Women*, Chatto & Windus, London, 1997

Souhami, D., *Mrs Keppel & her Daughter*, HarperCollins, London, 1996

Spalding, F., *Vanessa Bell*, Weidenfeld & Nicolson, London, 1983

Stephen, L., *George Eliot*, London, 1902

Stone, L., *The Family, Sex & Marriage: In England 1500–1800*, Weidenfeld & Nicolson, London, 1977

Stone, L., *Uncertain Unions: Marriage in England 1660–1753*, OUP, Oxford, 1992

Symons, A. (ed.), *The Confessions of Saint Augustine*, tr. Pusey, London, 1898

Tannahill, R., *Sex in History*, Abacus, London, 1981

Taylor, A.J.P. (ed.), *Lloyd George: A Diary by Frances Stevenson*, Hutchinson, London, 1971

Tindall, G., *Rosamond Lehmann: An Appreciation*, Chatto & Windus, London, 1985

Tisdale, S., *Talk Dirty to Me: An Intimate Philosophy of Sex*, Pan, London, 1996

Todd, O., *Albert Camus: A Life*, tr. Benjamin Ivry, Chatto & Windus, London, 1997

Tomalin, C., *The Invisible Woman: The Story of Nelly Ternan & Charles Dickens*, Penguin, Harmondsworth, 1991

Troyes, C. de, *Arthurian Romances*, tr. William W. Kibler, Penguin, Harmondsworth, 1991

Trudgill, E., *Madonnas & Magdalens*, Heinemann, London, 1976

Van der Post, L., *Jung & the Story of Our Time*, Hogarth Press, London, 1976

Virgil, *The Aeneid*, tr. C. H. Sisson, Carcanet, Manchester, 1986

Wagner, R., *Parsifal*, tr. Andrew Porter, ENO, London & New York, 1986

Warner, M., *Alone of all her Sex: The Myth & Cult of the Virgin Mary*, Picador, London, 1990

Weldon, F., *Rebecca West*, Penguin, Harmondsworth, 1985

Wells, G.P. (ed.), *H.G. Wells in Love: Postscript to an Experiment in Autobiography*, Faber & Faber, London, 1984

West, A., *H.G. Wells: Aspects of a Life*, Hutchinson, London, 1984

West–Meads, Z., *To Love, Honour & Betray: Why affairs happen & how to survive them*, Coronet Books, London, 1997

Wilson, A.N., *The Rise & Fall of the House of Windsor*, Sinclair Stevenson, London, 1993

Wilson, H., *Memoirs of Herself & Others*, Peter Davies, London, 1929

Wise, T.J. & Symington, J.A. (eds.), *The Brontës: Their Lives, Friendships and Correspondence*, Vol. 1, Blackwell, Oxford, 1932

Yarnall, J., *Transformations of Circe: The History of an Enchantress*, University of Illinois Press, Urbana & Chicago, 1994

A NOTE ON THE AUTHOR

Victoria Griffin is a writer, poet and translator living in London. This is her first book.

A NOTE ON THE TYPE

This book is set using Bembo. The first of the Old Faces is a copy of a roman cut by Francesco Griffo for the Venetian printer Aldus Manutius. It was first used in Cardinal Bembo's *De Aetna*, 1495, hence the name of the contemporary version. Although a type cut in the fifteenth century for a Venetian printer, it is usually grouped with the Old Faces. Stanley Morison has shown that it was the model followed by Garamond and thus the forerunner of the standard European type of the next two centuries